Navigating Stakeholder Dynamics Surrounding Acquisitions

David R. King · Anjali Bansal
Editors

Navigating Stakeholder Dynamics Surrounding Acquisitions

Assessing Conflicting Interests and Impacts

palgrave
macmillan

Editors
David R. King
Florida State University
Tallahassee, FL, USA

Anjali Bansal
Indian Institute of Management
Lucknow
Lucknow, Uttar Pradesh, India

ISBN 978-3-032-03198-3 ISBN 978-3-032-03199-0 (eBook)
https://doi.org/10.1007/978-3-032-03199-0

This Palgrave Macmillan imprint is published by the registered company Springer Nature Switzerland AG
The registered company address is: Gewerbestrasse 11, 6330 Cham, Switzerland

Acknowledgements

Completing a book is a community effort that extends beyond scholars that contribute chapters. First, we express appreciation to Palgrave Macmillan for publishing the book, and the associated support they provided. Next, we would like to recognize additional scholars for serving as reviewers of submitted chapters, including Sina Amiri, Florian Bauer, Maria Goranova, Kalan Horton, Olimpia Meglio, Gonzalo Molina Sieiro, Christina Öberg, Svante Schriber, Carlo Mari, and Jennifer Sexton. Finally, scholars whose work we drew on indirectly supported the book, so any acknowledgement of those influencing this book is inherently incomplete.

King-Statement for New Book

Research has shown that while mergers and acquisitions have been a popular strategy to obtain new capabilities and/or access new markets, it is often challenging to make them successful. Finally, we have a book that explains the importance of stakeholders in M&As noting that successful M&As are only possible when stakeholders (e.g., investors, customers, suppliers, and employees, among others) of both acquiring and the acquired firms are carefully managed and integrated. I applaud King and Bansal for this excellent new book that describes how to manage stakeholders to achieve successful M&As.

Michael A. Hitt

Contents

Notes on Contributors

Ahmed Alsafwani is a Ph.D. student in the College of Business at Florida State University. His primary research interest is strategic sustainability in oil and gas sector, with an emphasis on advancing pathways toward cleaner and more sustainable operations.

Sina Amiri is an Associate Professor of Management at Georgia College & State University. He earned his Ph.D. in Management from Iowa State University. His research focuses primarily on strategic restructuring, corporate divestiture, and mergers and acquisitions (M&A).

Princess Anya is a Ph.D. student in the College of Business at Florida State University. Her primary research interests are neurodiversity in the workplace and dual leadership structures.

Anjali Bansal is an Assistant Professor of Management at the Indian Institute of Management Lucknow, India. Her primary research interests include change management, integration during M&A, diversity management and leadership.

Nicholas Beadles is a Full Professor of Management at Georgia College & State University. He earned his Ph.D. in Management from the University of Alabama. His research focuses primarily on issues associated with Human Resource Management.

Destiny Cole is a Ph.D. student in the College of Business at Florida State University. Her primary research interests are individual differences and justice in the workplace.

Katia M. Galdino received her Ph.D. from Florida State University. She is currently an associate professor of management at Georgia Southern University. Her primary research interests include foreign market entry strategies and mergers and acquisitions (M&As).

Silvia Gordano holds a Ph.D. from the University of Turin, where she is currently a Research Fellow. Her research focuses on strategic management and accounting of corporate sustainability, including in the context of acquisitions.

Janice M. Gordon received her Ph.D. from Florida State University and is an Assistant Professor of Management at Western Carolina University. Her research focuses on organizational learning and the role of formal and informal institutions, particularly in the context of acquisitions.

David R. King received his Ph.D. from Indiana University, and he is the Higdon Professor of Management at Florida State University. His primary research interest is acquisition activity and performance.

Christine Madonna Kirkland is an Assistant Professor at Western Carolina University. She received her Ph.D. from Florida State University, and her research explores strategic decision-making in response to institutional dynamism and uncertainty.

Olimpia Meglio is an Associate Professor at the University of Naples Federico II. Her research revolves around mergers and acquisitions, and family firms.

Gonzalo Molina-Sieiro is an Assistant Professor at the University of Nevada Las Vegas. He received his Ph.D. from Florida State University, and his research interests are international business strategy, including acquisitions.

Christina Öberg is professor/Chair in Marketing and International Business at Linnaeus University. She has been a visiting scholar at Harvard University, Stanford University, and the University of Exeter, among others. Her research interests include new ways to pursue business, including the sharing economy and effects of additive manufacturing.

Svante Schriber is a Professor of Organisation and Management at Stockholm Business School, Stockholm University, Sweden. His research centers on competitive strategy and specifically mergers and acquisitions (M&A).

Daniel Torchia is Assistant Professor of Business Administration at the University of Milan-Bicocca. He received his Ph.D. from Alliance Manchester Business School. His research focuses on the critical study of diverse organizational forms and the assessment of their social and environmental impacts.

List of Figures

List of Tables

Acquired Firm Employees: Strategies for Engagement and Retention

The Societal Impacts of Mergers and Acquisitions

Ecosystem Acquisitions: Integrating External Perspectives on Acquisition Environments

Stakeholder Performance

Relevance of Stakeholders to Acquisitions

David R. King and *Anjali Bansal*

Introduction

Acquisitions are recognized as a powerful tool for rapidly enhancing competitive advantage by enabling firms to access new technologies, expand customer bases, diversify product offerings, and enter new markets (De Man & Duysters, 2005; Shi et al., 2012). By combining resources and leveraging synergies, acquisitions can improve innovation capacity and operational efficiency, providing a clear advantage over competitors. Still, acquisitions do not occur in isolation and an acquisition's impacts go beyond an acquiring and target firm. What research exists on acquisition stakeholders largely looks at different stakeholder groups in isolation. We collect and summarize what is known about different stakeholders and their relationships with acquiring firms.

D. R. King (✉)
Florida State University, Tallahassee, FL, USA
e-mail: drking@fsu.edu

A. Bansal
Indian Institute of Management Lucknow, Lucknow, India
e-mail: anjali.bansal@iiml.ac.in

D. R. King and A. Bansal (eds.), *Navigating Stakeholder Dynamics Surrounding Acquisitions*,
https://doi.org/10.1007/978-3-032-03199-0_1

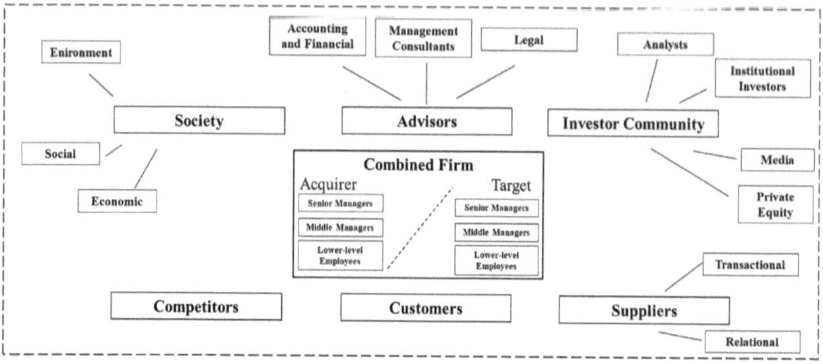

Fig. 1 Acquisition stakeholders

Covered stakeholders include advisors, investors, suppliers, customers, competitors, employees of both acquiring and acquired firms, society, and the broader ecosystem in which these entities operate, see Fig. 1. Please note that we have deliberately excluded the stakeholder role for government, as an acquisition will not complete without government support. Instead, we focus on actions and interests of stakeholders for acquisitions that complete. The role of stakeholders in shaping acquisition outcomes has been acknowledged in prior research (Bosse et al., 2022; Hitt et al., 2001; Martynova & Renneboog, 2008), yet the complex interplay of stakeholders during acquisitions requires further exploration. Before discussing implications of broader consideration of stakeholders in acquisitions, we summarize information on the primary stakeholders impacted by acquisitions and covered by research and their perspectives.

Acquisition Stakeholders

Acquisitions represent pivotal moments in corporate strategy, offering firms a powerful mechanism to enhance competitiveness, access new markets, acquire resources, and build organizational capabilities (Feldman & Hernandez, 2022; King et al., 2008; Lee & Lieberman, 2010). Despite their strategic importance, acquisition outcomes are often unpredictable, with many deals failing to meet expectations, highlighting the complexity, ambiguity, and multitemporal nature of acquisition phases and processes (Jemison & Sitkin, 1986; King et al., 2021).

While research traditionally focuses on internal organizational factors, such as strategic fit, financial returns, or employee integration (Bosse et al., 2022; Weber & Tarba, 2012), there is increasing recognition of the broader external environment. This includes suppliers (Kato & Schoenberg, 2014), customers (Rogan, 2014), competitors (King & Schriber, 2016), and other stakeholders who influence acquisition success or failure. However, stakeholder perspectives of acquisitions, such as their environmental impact (Battisti et al., 2024), remain relatively unexplored (Freeman et al., 2018).

Stakeholders are central to both internal and external acquisition dimensions, as the individuals and groups within and outside the acquiring and acquired organizations who are affected by and, in turn, influence an acquisition (cf. Clarkson, 1995; Freeman, 1984; Mason et al., 2007). Newman's (1979) stakeholder map identifies how corporate actions impact diverse groups such as employees, suppliers, customers, financiers, and the community. Stakeholders are not merely passive, and they react to actively shape organizational decisions (Frooman, 1999), making their recognition and engagement essential for acquisition success (King & Taylor, 2012).

A comprehensive stakeholder orientation involves understanding how corporate actions influence stakeholder welfare and cultivating strong intergroup relationships (e.g., Choi & Wang, 2009; Freeman et al., 2018) that can improve firm survival (Lehtinen et al., 2019). Although research often prioritizes shareholder interests (Meglio & Risberg, 2011), broader stakeholder engagement can create additional economic value (Bettinazzi & Zollo, 2017). For instance, it has been demonstrated that running several companies together creates more value for stakeholders than running them separately (Deng et al., 2013). Additionally, effective stakeholder management creates economies of scope by combining networks, resources, and expertise, which benefits all parties (Bosse et al., 2022).

We explore the issues, disagreements, opposition, and feelings that different stakeholder groups go through as it looks at the crucial role that stakeholder management plays during acquisitions. Navigating the intricate and cutthroat world of contemporary acquisitions requires an understanding of stakeholder dynamics (Gomes et al., 2013). By illuminating the many roles and influences of stakeholders, we seek to assist organizations in attaining more successful integration and long-term strategic advantage.

Primary Stakeholders for Acquiring Firms

Broadly defined a stakeholder is any individual or group that can affect or is affected by the actions, decisions, policies, practices, or goals of an organization (Freeman, 1984). Traditionally, managers focus on the interests of shareholders and groups that impact a business's operations directly, such as suppliers, customers, and employees. However, a stakeholder orientation considers the views of a wider set of groups, and the complexity of acquisitions drives the need to consider multiple stakeholders. To prioritize stakeholders to consider, research suggests focusing on powerful stakeholders interested in the implications of a firm's decision (e.g., Eden & Ackermann, 1998; Mitchell et al., 1997). In considering the primary stakeholders to an acquisition, we focus on advisors, investors, suppliers, customers, competitors, employees of both an acquiring and acquired firm, and society, as well as ecosystem effects and stakeholder performance. Next, we briefly describe each of these groups and topics that are more fully developed in individual chapters, see Appendix.

Advisors

Acquisitions represent high-stake transactions, are fraught with complexity and uncertainty, necessitating the involvement of specialized advisors (i.e., investment banks, consultants, and legal experts) to guide firms through the intricate process of acquisition completion. By delving into the multifaceted roles of advisors, we can explore advisors' influence on deal outcomes, ethical considerations that arise from their positions, and the strategies practitioners can effectively use advisors. Their contributions can enhance deal quality and increase the likelihood of synergy realization, especially when they possess sector-specific or cross-border expertise (Agrawal et al., 2013). Further, this chapter synthesizes research findings to illuminate the impact of advisor expertise on target selection, synergy realization, and post-acquisition integration. By identifying gaps in existing research, particularly concerning the strategic dimensions of advisor impact and the influence of emerging trends like AI and ESG, future research directions that promise are charted that can reshape our understanding of advisors' roles in acquisitions.

Investor Community

While often focused on shareholders, the investor community is more diverse and it comprises analysts, banks, institutional investors, media outlets, and private equity/venture capital firms. Each of these groups exert a profound and reciprocal influence on deals, shaping their trajectory and ultimate outcomes. Using a stakeholder-centric perspective enables exploring how the investor community impacts and is impacted by acquisition activity. Synthesizing research from finance, management, and economics, nuanced stakeholder roles are highlighted with their potential for both value creation and destruction. Ideas developed cover the inherent conflicts of interest that exist within and between these groups from both sides of organizations. Creating a framework to better navigate the complex dynamics associated with investors, offers to advance research and practice.

Suppliers

Recognizing the dual role of suppliers as short-term negotiation partners and long-term strategic partners, relationships of suppliers as major external stakeholders to an acquirer are reviewed (Kato & Schoenberg, 2014). Relationships with merging companies (e.g., complementarities or competition) shape the strategic significance of suppliers. For those closely aligned with the goals of combining firms, suppliers confront dangers, such as decreased demand, compromised negotiating strength, or contract exclusion. Further, there is also the possibility of anticompetitive behaviors that can damage suppliers and market competitiveness, as well as the growing buyer power often acquired by a merged firm, underlining the need for regulation. By developing a thorough awareness of suppliers' important position in the acquisition process, ideas for efficiently managing these complicated relationships can be improved.

Customers

Surprisingly, while other stakeholders are often valued for their financial and operational relevance during acquisitions, reactions from customers remain underexplored (Rogan, 2014). Addressing this gap requires positioning customers as pivotal stakeholders whose perceptions, reactions, and behaviors significantly influence the success or failure of initiatives. Recognizing that negative customer responses, including reduced satisfaction, decreased loyalty, and customer churn, can erode revenue streams and undermine intended benefits from an acquisition. Research on customer impacts pre- and post-acquisition is synthesized. While acquisitions have the potential to change product offerings and service qualities to customers, these repercussions may extend to changes at the price level and at brand management. For example, acquisitions have an impact on customer satisfaction and loyalty, driving a need to manage customer concerns more closely.

Competitors

Using research from management, economics, and finance, intricate dynamics of competitive behavior following acquisitions are explored to pinpoint the drivers of competitor behaviors and their consequences for performance. For example, by acquiring a target with new capabilities, firms aim to enhance their market presence, an acquirer impacts their competitive environment. In response, competitors with a spectrum of reactions whose impact is often underestimated (King & Schriber, 2016). Research increasingly acknowledges the importance of rivals as major stakeholders whose actions could significantly affect the outcome of a deal. Summarizing research on competitor reactions to acquisitions enables developing a framework to aid recognition of different competitor responses to acquisitions, including market changes from strategic adjustments in operations, innovation, and finance.

Acquiring Firm Employees

While previous research has extensively explored the perspectives and experiences of employees in acquired firms, the voices of those within the acquiring organization are often muted with their contributions and concerns largely overlooked. Nevertheless, acquiring firm responses and behaviors can significantly impact the success or failure of integration efforts and the realization of deal synergies. By focusing on acquiring firm employees at different hierarchal levels, we show that senior managers, middle managers, and frontline employees confront distinct challenges and opportunities. For example, senior leaders navigating strategic decisions and talent retention, middle managers balance conflicting expectations, and frontline employees grappling with job security concerns. Understanding the experiences and interactions of these often-overlooked stakeholders offers valuable insights for researchers, practitioners, and leaders seeking to foster employee adaptation, improve communication strategies, and enhance firm success.

Acquired Firm Employees

Acquisition failure is often attributed to the ineffective management and engagement of acquired firm employees (Graebner, 2004; Ranft & Lord, 2000). Target firm employees have unique skills, knowledge, and cultural insights, represent a valuable resource that can either fuel or hinder the realization of intended deal synergies. While the importance of acquired employees is widely recognized, we again break them out for different organizational levels (i.e., senior managers, middle managers, and lower-level employees). Adopting a more integrated approach to understanding and managing acquired employees acknowledges that their experiences are interconnected and it can improve acquisition success. For example, research offers how effective HR practices, cultural integration strategies, clear communication, and justice perceptions can enhance employee engagement, retention, and adaptation. This offers valuable insights for researchers, practitioners, and leaders seeking to navigate human aspects of acquisitions to foster a work environment where acquired employees feel valued, supported, and empowered in a combined organization.

Society

The effects of acquisitions extend beyond firms involved in corporate restructuring, as they are powerful economic and organizational forces that reshape society (Abramovitz, 1986). Acquisitions involve trillions of dollars in global assets annually, redefine the economics of production, consumption, financial resources, and employment, creating value and potential harm for communities worldwide. By moving beyond traditional financial metrics, we show how acquisitions influence economic equality, job creation, environmental sustainability and technological progress. For example, the impact of acquisitions on society has trade-offs. On one hand, acquisitions drive efficiency, innovation, and market development. On the other hand, they lead to job losses, increased market concentration, and wealth disparity.

The United Nations' Sustainable Development Goals (SDGs) can help to reconcile disparate acquisitions effects on society by aiding consideration of broader implications of acquisition activity. By mapping existing research onto the SDG framework, a comprehensive understanding of how acquisitions can either contribute to or hinder the achievement of a more sustainable and equitable society emerges. Acquisitions can serve as a catalyst for positive societal change, driving economic prosperity, social well-being, and environmental stewardship. As a result, there is a need to account for all stakeholders and to align firm strategy with the long-term interests of society.

Ecosystem

To aid looking at stakeholder groups in combination, an ecosystem perspective can be used to investigate the dynamics surrounding acquisitions (van Angeren et al., 2025). By integrating the stakeholder and competitive dynamics views, a more structured and comprehensive understanding of the wider environment and how its various relationships play out in acquisitions (Schriber & Meglio, 2024). Ecosystems consider firms as interconnected networks that create interdependence (Jacobides et al., 2018), allowing for the analysis of a range of actors with diverse interests, information, and perceptions. This also opens a broader interplay of cooperative and competitive actions from competitive dynamics to capture the complexity shaping acquisition outcomes. By exploring these effects, new insights for researchers, practitioners, and policymakers are developed for navigating the complexities of acquisitions and unlocking their full potential.

Stakeholder Performance

As the previous sections outline, acquisitions impact a variety of stakeholder groups other than shareholders, but research generally does not consider performance measures beyond stock or accounting performance (King et al., 2021). What research exists for stakeholders beyond shareholders is limited and suffers from a similar problem of only considering a single stakeholder perspective as research on shareholder impacts of acquisitions. Additional stakeholder-specific performance metrics, such as completion speed, employee turnover, price changes, and societal impacts, exist and can promote more comprehensive and multi-dimensional methods for evaluating acquisition outcomes. Additionally, different stakeholders sometimes have conflicting reactions to acquisitions that are shaped by stakeholder motivations, expected benefits, and perceived risks. Future research and managerial decision-making can take diverse stakeholder perspectives into account to understand when acquisitions value creation.

Discussion

Understanding the role of stakeholders in acquisitions reveals the multifaceted nature of value creation and risk management for these complex transactions. While individual stakeholder perspectives have been explored, the interconnectedness and potential conflicts among them remain largely underexamined. Our goal is to begin the process of synthesizing insights from research to highlight the strategic importance of engaging with multiple stakeholders throughout an acquisition's lifecycle. A more integrated stakeholder orientation can inform theory, shape managerial decision-making, and enhance acquisition outcomes. Addressing stakeholder tensions, trade-offs, and overlapping interests, can set the foundation for rethinking acquisition performance beyond traditional financial metrics and toward a more holistic, stakeholder-inclusive approach. Next, we cover implications for management research and practice.

Research Directions

While there is growing research attention on the primary stakeholders to acquisitions, associated research generally still looks at a given stakeholder group in isolation. However, acquisition success requires support of multiple stakeholders (Deng et al., 2013), and there is limited research on acquisition stakeholders in combination. Simply, research needs to examine and better understand engagement with internal and external stakeholders during acquisitions. The clearest solution is for research to use multiple measures of performance (King et al., 2021) that relate to the perspectives of different stakeholders.

There is also a need to develop theoretical relationships to be able to predict how acquisition decisions impact stakeholders and subsequent acquisition outcomes, as existing frameworks do not fully reflect stakeholder complexity (Lehtinen et al., 2019). For example, while the perspectives of primary stakeholders are developed, we do not integrate them across stakeholders. Simply, interconnectedness and potential conflicts across acquisition stakeholders remain largely unexplored. For instance, actions taken to satisfy investors may increase short-term returns but alienate customers or employees to undermine long-term value creation. Similarly, competitors can reduce planned benefits from acquisitions that are not captured by traditional models. Theoretical frameworks that better reflect the reciprocal, multilevel interactions among stakeholders are needed. This may require rethinking acquisition performance in terms of broader stakeholder value and long-term strategic impact.

Further, there is a need to consider contextual differences of acquisitions (King et al., 2021). For example, acquisitions also do not happen in isolation. For example, alliance partners are often targets of acquisitions (Porrini, 2004). This can also draw on alliance research (e.g., Cullen et al., 2000; Reuer & Ariño, 2007; Shijaku et al., 2022) that considers manager involvement with complex organizational dynamics. Other related areas of research, such as divestment (e.g., Amiri et al., 2022; Laamanen et al., 2014), can also aid understanding acquisition stakeholders. Additionally, cross-border acquisitions and differences between developed and developing economies may display differences in how acquisition stakeholders need to be engaged (e.g., Ramamurti, 2012; Reus & Lamont, 2009).

Practical Implications

Managers are the only group with a relationship with all stakeholders that also have direct control over firm resources and decisions (Hill & Jones, 1992). By recognizing primary stakeholders impacted by acquisitions and their perspectives, managers can make better decisions in making and integrating acquisitions. For example, achieving planned benefits from an acquisition requires maintaining legitimacy with internal and external firm stakeholders (Sinha et al., 2015).

To improve acquisition success, managers must adopt a more stakeholder-inclusive approach in several stages. First, early stakeholder mapping should be a core component of acquisition planning to identifying primary stakeholders to anticipate potential frictions, resource dependencies, and engagement needs. Recognizing that these groups are interrelated is essential, as neglecting one group may lead to cascading negative effects across others. Additionally, reactions by competitors designed to reduce the value from an acquisition need to be considered (King & Schriber, 2016). Second, increased communication with impacted stakeholders can increase value creation (Bansal & King, 2022). For example, employees require clarity on job security and career trajectories, while customers need reassurance about service continuity and value. Transparent, differentiated communication can build trust and mitigate uncertainty with stakeholders and increase acquisition success. Still, actions taken to positively influence one group may negatively impact another (Sinha et al., 2015). This relates to a third step to balance stakeholder interests to optimize collective value (Bunnell, 2000). For example, integration plans that ignore acquired firm culture or fail to retain key talent may undermine long-term performance, even if short-term cost reductions are achieved. Similarly, aggressively leveraging supplier power post-acquisition may reduce input costs but erode important relationships that support innovation and flexibility. Finally, traditional financial indicators like share price changes only tell part of the story. Managers, as well as researchers, should also consider employee turnover, customer retention, supplier continuity, and broader social or environmental impacts to better track and understand acquisition performance.

Limitations and Future Research

The primary limitation of our book is that we continue the practice of broader research in examining stakeholders separately. While an exception involves chapter "Ecosystem Acquisitions: Integrating External Perspectives on Acquisition Environments" on ecosystems, the summarized actors surrounding acquisitions are still largely examined separately. However, we know that they interact. For example, if competitors poach employees from a combined firm (Brown et al., 2003), then more than one stakeholder group is involved. While evidence suggests that employee turnover harms acquisition performance (e.g., Bilgili et al., 2017), we are not aware of research examining the impacts of employee gains on competitors. One related research finding is that personnel mobility is a primary mechanism for knowledge transfer (Ziegler, 1985). This reinforces the motivation for the book because what we know about acquisitions has largely focused on acquiring firms and their investors, and not the broader impacts of acquisitions. Additional research is needed to provide a more comprehensive view of acquisitions and their effects on impacted groups.

In closing, progress in acquisition research and practice hinges on recognizing multifaceted stakeholder dynamics that incorporate diverse performance metrics to account for the full spectrum of stakeholder interests. By moving past siloed perspectives and embracing integrated, stakeholder-centric approach, researchers and practitioners alike can better navigate the risks, trade-offs, and opportunities inherent in acquisitions. Further, an organizational capability to manage complex stakeholder interactions can offer acquiring firms a competitive advantage. A broader perspective of acquisitions and their outcomes offers the potential for them to better realize their potential to deliver sustainable, long-term value.

Appendix: Overview of Chapters

Chapter	*Stakeholder*	*Authors*	*Research gaps*	*Research focus*	*Foundation*	*Key findings*
The Role of Advisors in Acquisitions	Advisors	Gonzalo Molina-Sierra	• Limited understanding of advisors' long-term strategic impact	• Explore the multifaceted role of acquisition advisors • Clarify contributions, conflicts of interest, and shareholder value impact	• Financial restructuring • Conflict of interest • Dynamic capabilities literature	• Advisors can enhance deal execution and performance • Mixed evidence on long-term value creation • Roles in synergy realization and negotiation were noted, but firm performance impacts were inconclusive
Reciprocal Impacts Between M&A and the Investor Community	Investor community	Christine Kirkland	• Limited research on the impact of staged alliances pre-acquisition	• Explore acquisition capability formation • Review of investor roles in acquisitions	• Knowledge-based view • Organizational learning	• Staged alliances between related firms may facilitate acquisitions • Stakeholders positive and negative influence • Conflicts of interest affect value creation

(continued)

(continued)

Chapter	*Stakeholder*	*Authors*	*Research gaps*	*Research focus*	*Foundation*	*Key findings*
Suppliers in Mergers and Acquisitions	Suppliers	Christina Öberg	• Lack of empirical research on supplier integration	• Examine how embedded supplier relationships affect acquisition integration	• Network theory • Relationship-based literature	• Relationships with suppliers and partners strengthen acquisition capability • Highlights short- and long-term supplier roles (e.g., relational vs transactional)
Customers as Stakeholders to Mergers and Acquisitions	Customers	Sina Amiri	• Absence of research on customer reactions to acquisition success	• Study customer satisfaction, loyalty, and behavior during pre- and post-acquisition	• Customer value and behavior research	• Customer dissatisfaction and loss of loyalty can undermine acquisition goals • Transparent communication is critical • Emphasizes customer-centric approaches for value creation

(continued)

(continued)

Chapter	*Stakeholder*	*Authors*	*Research gaps*	*Research focus*	*Foundation*	*Key findings*
The Competitive Landscape Following M&A: A Review of Rivals' Responses	Competitors	Katia De Melo Galdino	• Limited research on competitor reactions to acquisitions	• Investigate strategic and financial responses of rival firms	• Competitive dynamics • Strategic group theory	• Two response types found: financial market and strategic • 56 studies analyzed • Managerial implications discussed for proactive rival response planning
Understanding and Addressing Acquiring Firm Employee Concerns	Acquiring firm employees	Anjali Bansal, David King, Ahmed Alsafwani	• Gaps in how different employee levels interact and affect integration outcomes	• Synthesize employee concerns during acquisition • Propose strategies for improving integration success	• Strategic management • Organizational Behavior & HRM Perspectives • Case-based	• Highlights concerns across employee levels (e.g., job security, role ambiguity) • Suggests tailored HR strategies and feedback mechanisms • Calls for research on specialized roles and cross-cultural integration

(continued)

(continued)

Chapter	*Stakeholder*	*Authors*	*Research gaps*	*Research focus*	*Foundation*	*Key findings*
Acquired Firm Employees: Strategies for Engagement and Retention	Acquired firm employees	Ahmed Alsafwani, Destiny Cole, Princess Anya	• Isolated view of acquired employees; limited study on middle managers' bridging role	• An integrated understanding acquired employees' experiences • Emphasize roles for communication and support	• Acquisition performance • Cultural and identity literature	• Identity conflicts emerge when legacy and acquiring cultures clash • Fair treatment and transparent communication enhance adjustment • Line manager support reduces uncertainty and boosts loyalty
The Societal Impacts of Mergers and Acquisitions	Community/ society	Silvia Gordano, Daniel Torchia	• Limited focus on societal outcomes especially from sustainable development goal perspectives	• Explore societal effects of acquisitions • Examine economic, social, and environmental consequences	• Practitioner focus • Human resources	• Acquisitions can support or hinder societal goals • Positive: innovation, green transformation • Negative: job loss, pollution displacement

(continued)

(continued)

Chapter	*Stakeholder*	*Authors*	*Research gaps*	*Research focus*	*Foundation*	*Key findings*
Ecosystem acquisitions: Integrating external perspectives on acquisition environments	Ecosystem	Olimpia Meglio, Svante Schriber	• Lack of analysis of broader ecosystem effects beyond direct stakeholders	• Propose an ecosystem framework integrating stakeholders and competitive perspectives • Analyze systemic industry-wide effects	• Organizational theory • Systems & network theory • Applied case examples	• Introduces "ecosystem acquisitions" concept • Acquisitions reshape industry norms, regulations, and geopolitics • Advocates for new metrics that account for relational ecosystem dynamics • A research agenda on governance orchestration and ecosystem typologies

(continued)

(continued)

Chapter	*Stakeholder*	*Authors*	*Research gaps*	*Research focus*	*Foundation*	*Key findings*
Stakeholder Performance	Stakeholder performance	David King, Anjali Bansal	Need for more diverse acquisition performance measures	• Stakeholder perspectives and acquisition performance	• Stakeholder	• Stakeholders view acquisitions vary • Limited research considers multiple performance measures reflecting different stakeholder viewpoints

References

Abramovitz, M. (1986). Catching up, forging ahead, and falling behind. *Journal of Economic History, 46*(2), 385–406.

Agrawal, A., Cooper, T., Lian, Q., & Wang, Q. (2013). Common advisers in mergers and acquisitions: Determinants and consequences. *Journal of Law and Economics, 56*(3), 691–740.

Amiri, S., King, D., DeMarie, S., & Brown, J. (2022). Predicting the divestment of prior acquisitions. *British Journal of Management, 33*(4), 1803–1819.

Bansal, A., & King, D. R. (2022). Communicating change following an acquisition.*The International Journal of Human Resource Management, 33*(9), 1886–1915.

Battisti, E., Nirino, N., Leonidou, E., Thrassou, A., & Vrontis, D. (2024). Mergers and acquisitions and environmental conditions: A systematic literature review to investigate their linkage. *Management Research Review, 47*(2), 226–244.

Bettinazzi, E., & Zollo, M. (2017). Stakeholder orientation and acquisition performance. *Strategic Management Journal, 38*(12), 2465–2485.

Bilgili, T., Calderon, C., Allen, D., & Kedia, B. (2017). Gone with the wind: A meta-analytic review of executive turnover, its antecedents, and postacquisition performance. *Journal of Management, 43*(6), 1966–1997.

Bosse, D., Harrison, J., & Hoskisson, R. (2022). Acquisitions, stakeholder economies of scope, and stakeholder orientation. *Strategic Management Review, 3*(1), 35–65.

Brown, C., Clancy, G., & Scholer, R. (2003). A post-merger IT integration success story: Sallie Mae. *MIS Quarterly Executive, 2*(1), 15–27.

Bunnell, D. (2000). *Making the Cisco connection: The story behind the real Internet superpower*. Wiley.

Choi, J., & Wang, H. (2009). Stakeholder relations and the persistence of corporate financial performance. *Strategic Management Journal, 30*(8), 895–907.

Clarkson, M. (1995). A stakeholder framework for analyzing and evaluating corporate social performance. *Academy of Management Review, 20*(1), 92–117.

Cullen, J., Johnson, J., & Sakano, T. (2000). Success through commitment and trust: The soft side of strategic alliance management. *Journal of World Business, 35*(3), 223–240.

De Man, A., & Duysters, G. (2005). Collaboration and innovation: A review of the effects of mergers, acquisitions and alliances on innovation. *Technovation, 25*(12), 1377–1387.

Deng, X., Kang, J., & Low, B. (2013). Corporate social responsibility and stakeholder value maximization: Evidence from mergers. *Journal of Financial Economics, 110*(1), 87–109.

Eden, C., & Ackermann, F. (1998*). Making strategy: The journey of strategic management*. Sage.

Feldman, E., & Hernandez, E. (2022). Synergy in mergers and acquisitions: Typology, life cycles, and value. *Academy of Management Review, 47*(4), 549–578.

Freeman, R. (1984). *Strategic management: A stakeholder approach*. Pitman.

Freeman, R., Harrison, J., & Zyglidopoulos, S. (2018). *Stakeholder theory: Concepts and strategies*. Cambridge University Press.

Frooman, J. (1999). Stakeholder influence strategies. *Academy of Management Review, 24*(2), 191–205.

Gomes, E., Angwin, D., Weber, Y., & Tarba, S. (2013). Critical success factors through the mergers and acquisitions process: Revealing pre-and post-M&A connections for improved performance. *Thunderbird International Business Review, 55*(1), 13–35.

Graebner, M. (2004). Momentum and serendipity: How acquired leaders create value in the integration of technology firms. *Strategic Management Journal, 25*(8–9), 751–777.

Hill, C. W., & Jones, T. M. (1992). Stakeholder-agency theory.*Journal of Management Studies, 29*(2), 131–154.

Hitt, M., Harrison, J., & Ireland, R. (2001). *Mergers & acquisitions: A guide to creating value for stakeholders*. Oxford University Press.

Jacobides, M., Cennamo, C., & Gawer, A. (2018). Towards a theory of ecosystems. *Strategic Management Journal, 39*(8), 2255–2276.

Jemison, D., & Sitkin, S. (1986). Corporate acquisitions: A process perspective. *Academy of Management Review, 11*(1), 145–163.

Kato, J., & Schoenberg, R. (2014). The impact of post-merger integration on the customer–supplier relationship. *Industrial Marketing Management, 43*(2), 335–345.

King, D., & Schriber, S. (2016). Addressing competitive responses to acquisitions. *California Management Review, 58*(3), 109–124.

King, D., Slotegraaf, R., & Kesner, I. (2008). Performance implications of firm resource interactions in the acquisition of R&D-intensive firms. *Organization Science, 19*(2), 327–340.

King, D., & Taylor, R. (2012). Beyond the numbers: seven stakeholders to consider in improving acquisition outcomes. *Graziadio Business Review*.

King, D., Wang, G., Samimi, M., & Cortes, A. (2021). A meta-analytic integration of acquisition performance prediction. *Journal of Management Studies, 58*(5), 1198–1236.

Laamanen, T., Brauer, M., & Junna, O. (2014). Performance of acquirers of divested assets: Evidence from the US. software industry. *Strategic Management Journal*, 35(6), 914–925.

Lee, G., & Lieberman, M. (2010). Acquisition vs. internal development as modes of market entry. *Strategic Management Journal, 31*(2), 140–158.

Lehtinen, J., Aaltonen, K., & Rajala, R. (2019). Stakeholder management in complex product systems: Practices and rationales for engagement and disengagement. *Industrial Marketing Management, 79*, 58–70.

Martynova, M., & Renneboog, L. (2008). A century of corporate takeovers: What have we learned and where do we stand. *Journal of Banking and Finance, 32*(10), 2148–2177.

Mason, C., Kirkbride, J., & Bryde, D. (2007). From stakeholders to institutions: The changing face of social enterprise governance theory. *Management Decision, 45*(2), 284–301.

Meglio, O., & Risberg, A. (2011). The (mis) measurement of M&A performance—A systematic narrative literature review. *Scandinavian Journal of Management, 27*(4), 418–433.

Mitchell, R., Agle, B., & Wood, D. (1997). Toward a theory of stakeholder identification and salience: Defining the principle of who and what really counts. *Academy of Management Review, 22*(4), 853–886.

Newman, M. (1979). Historical development of early accounting concepts and their relation to certain economic concepts. *Academy of Accounting Historians Working Paper Series, 1*, 157–186.

Porrini, P. (2004). Can a previous alliance between an acquirer and a target affect acquisition performance? *Journal of Management, 30*(4), 545–562.

Ramamurti, R. (2012). Competing with emerging market multinationals. *Business Horizons, 55*(3), 241–249.

Ranft, A., & Lord, M. (2000). Acquiring new knowledge: The role of retaining human capital in acquisitions of high-tech firms. *Journal of High Technology Management Research, 11*(2), 295–319.

Reuer, J., & Ariño, A. (2007). Strategic alliance contracts: Dimensions and determinants of contractual complexity. *Strategic Management Journal, 28*(3), 313–330.

Reus, T., & Lamont, B. (2009). The double-edged sword of cultural distance in international acquisitions. *Journal of International Business Studies, 40*, 1298–1316.

Rogan, M. (2014). Too close for comfort? The effect of embeddedness and competitive overlap on client relationship retention following an acquisition. *Organization Science, 25*(1), 185–203.

Shijaku, E., King, D., & Urtasun, A. (2022). Alliances as precursors to an acquisition. In *Acquisitions and corporate strategy* (pp. 13–25). Routledge.

Schriber, S., & Meglio, O. (2024). An ecosystem perspective of acquisition outcomes: A research agenda. In *A research agenda for mergers and acquisitions* (pp. 199–218).

Shi, W., Sun, J., & Prescott, J. (2012). A temporal perspective of merger and acquisition and strategic alliance initiatives: Review and future direction. *Journal of Management, 38*(1), 164–209.

Sinha, P., Daellenbach, U., & Bednarek, R. (2015). Legitimacy defense during post-merger integration: Between coupling and compartmentalization. *Strategic Organization, 13*(3), 169–199.

van Angeren, J., Miric, M., & Ozalp, H. (2025). Platform ecosystems, bottlenecks, and M&A activity: Implications for platform regulation. *Academy of Management Perspectives*. https://doi.org/10.5465/amp.2023.0447

Weber, Y., & Tarba, S. (2012). Mergers and acquisitions process: The use of corporate culture analysis. *Cross Cultural Management: An International Journal, 19*(3), 288–303.

Ziegler, C. (1985). Innovation and the imitative entrepreneur. *Journal of Economic Behavior & Organization, 6*(2), 103–121.

The Role of Advisors in Acquisitions

Gonzalo Molina-Sieiro

Introduction

Mergers and acquisitions (M&A) are among the most consequential strategic decisions firms undertake, often reshaping industries, altering competitive landscapes, and determining long-term corporate success. These transactions are complex and involve intricate financial structuring, negotiation complexities, and significant organizational change, requiring specialized expertise. Investment banks and legal advisors play a central role in this process, guiding firms through valuation, deal structuring, regulatory compliance, and post-merger integration. Their influence extends beyond financial engineering to shaping executive decision-making, mitigating risks, and unlocking potential synergies. However, despite their salient role in acquisitions, the precise value advisors bring to M&A transactions remains a topic of debate, with conflicting evidence on whether their involvement enhances shareholder wealth or merely facilitates deal completion (Golubov et al., 2012; Ismail, 2010; Kosnik &

G. Molina-Sieiro (✉)
University of Nevada, Las Vegas, USA
e-mail: gonzalo.molinasieiro@unlv.edu

Florida State University, Tallahassee, USA

D. R. King and A. Bansal (eds.), *Navigating Stakeholder Dynamics Surrounding Acquisitions*,
https://doi.org/10.1007/978-3-032-03199-0_2

Shapiro, 1997; Wang et al., 2020; Xing, 2016). Some scholars argue that close relationships between acquirers and advisors can lead to relational hazards—potential conflicts of interest arising from repeated exchanges—where advisors prioritize deal-making over shareholder value creation (Lee, 2013) while others find a good relationship with advisors increase acquisition performance (Sleptsov et al., 2013). This raises important questions about the long-term impact of advisor-client ties and whether such relationships enhance or diminish M&A performance.

Existing research highlights several key dimensions of M&A advisors' contributions. Studies emphasize their role in synergy realization, negotiation leverage, and industry expertise, demonstrating that advisors with sector-specific knowledge help acquirers avoid overpayment and structure deals for maximum efficiency (Chang et al., 2016; Wang et al., 2020). Advisors are particularly influential in cross-border M&As, where country-specific expertise is crucial for navigating regulatory environments and cultural integration challenges (Arena & Dewally, 2017; Koo, 2020). Financial advisors also influence target selection, valuation accuracy, and acquisition premiums, although evidence on their effectiveness remains mixed—some studies suggest that top-tier advisors generate superior returns, while others indicate that they drive excessive premiums or fail to protect shareholder interests (Golubov et al., 2012; Ismail, 2010; Porrini, 2006). Beyond financial structuring, advisors shape post-merger integration, particularly in governance adjustments and cultural alignment (Gordon et al., 2019; Schmitz & Sievers, 2020). However, the degree that strong relational ties between firms and advisors influence these outcomes remains unclear, as repeated interactions may lead to biased decision-making rather than objective guidance (Lee, 2013).

Despite these well-documented contributions, substantial gaps remain in understanding the true strategic impact of M&A advisors, particularly over the long term. One of the most critical unresolved questions concerns whether advisors contribute to sustained post-merger performance, synergy realization, or cultural integration success (Faias, 2017; Gordon et al., 2019; Guo et al., 2018; Wang et al., 2020). Additionally, the nature of firm-advisor relationships can shape acquisition outcomes, as information intermediation and advisory ties may impact deal structuring and post-merger performance (Sleptsov et al., 2013). Research suggests that firms with strong ties to investment banks may benefit from privileged access to information. While associated ties can improve acquisition performance under certain conditions, it may also introduce biases that reduce deal quality. This highlights the need for further investigation into whether advisor relationships create lasting competitive advantages beyond short-term increases in shareholder value or lead to overconfidence and suboptimal decision-making.

By reviewing existing research, I provide a roadmap for future research by clarifying how scholars can better assess the role of M&A advisors in corporate strategy. By synthesizing findings across strategic management, finance, and behavioral economics, I highlight areas where advisors demonstrably contribute to M&A success and where further empirical investigation is needed. This review integrates insights from agency theory, dynamic capabilities theory, and behavioral finance to propose new avenues for evaluating advisor influence. In doing so, it challenges researchers to move beyond transactional assessments and toward a longitudinal, multi-dimensional understanding of advisors' roles in value creation, executive decision-making, and post-merger integration.

Contributions of Advisors throughout the M&AMerger and acquisition

M&A have naturally a strong strategic imprint on organizations, requiring firms to, requiring firms to identify targets, evaluate synergies, structure deals, and navigate post-merger integration challenges. M&A advisors—primarily investment banks, strategy consultants, and legal professionals—are instrumental in these processes, influencing both the financial and operational dimensions of deal-making. Their contributions extend beyond valuation and due diligence to target selection, deal structuring, negotiation tactics, and post-merger value realization. However, while advisors are often credited with enhancing deal quality, their actual impact remains an area of debate, with studies revealing both value-adding and value-destroying dynamics (Chang et al., 2016; Golubov et al., 2012; Porrini, 2006; Wang et al., 2020). To guide the structure of this review, Table 1 outlines how major theoretical lenses align with different phases of the M&A advisory process, offering a foundation for the chapter's organization.

The selection of an investment bank as an advisor plays a crucial role in M&A outcomes, influencing both shareholder returns and the efficiency of deal execution. Prior research suggests that firms carefully choose advisors based on reputation, prior deal experience, and network centrality, as

Table 1 Theoretical lenses applied across key M&A advisory tasks

Acquisition phase	*Key advisory tasks*	*Theoretical lenses commonly applied*
Target selection	Target identification, synergy estimation	Agency theory, resource-based view
Deal structuring	Valuation, negotiation, compensation, governance terms	Agency theory, behavioral finance
Post-merger integration	Cultural alignment, operational restructuring	Dynamic capabilities, institutional theory
Advisor-client interaction	Influence, incentives, relational hazards	Agency theory, behavioral economics
Emerging trends (e.g., ESG, AI)	ESG screening, AI-enabled due diligence	Stakeholder theory, information economics, sociotechnical systems

these factors impact the quality of advisory services and access to proprietary market insights (Bowers & Miller, 1990; Servaes & Zenner, 1996). Additionally, investment banks with greater market share and expertise tend to provide more favorable deal terms, although their contingent fee structures may introduce conflicts of interest that bias their recommendations (Rau, 2000). The informational role of financial advisors is particularly critical, as their ability to facilitate transactions depends on their connectivity within financial and social networks (Chaudhry et al., 2022). Studies also indicate that advisory firms exert effort based on their incentives—advisors working on contingent fee structures may focus on deal closure rather than long-term value creation (Hunter & Jagtiani, 2003). However, some scholars argue that high-reputation advisors enhance shareholder wealth by reducing acquisition uncertainty and improving post-merger integration (Bao & Edmans, 2011; Kale et al., 2003). Given these mixed findings, future research should further explore how advisor selection criteria influence long-term acquisition performance.

Target Selection and Synergy Identification

One of the most fundamental roles of M&A advisors is to help acquiring firms identify optimal targets and evaluate potential synergies. By leveraging industry expertise, historical transaction data, and proprietary valuation models, advisors guide firms in selecting acquisition targets that align with their strategic goals. Research suggests that advisors with deep sector knowledge improve acquisition outcomes by facilitating more accurate valuations, enhancing synergy capture, and mitigating risks of overpayment (Arena & Dewally, 2017; Wang et al., 2020).

Advisors also play a critical role in cross-border M&As, where target selection involves complex considerations such as regulatory compliance, cultural integration, and geopolitical risk. Studies indicate that acquiring firms benefit from advisors with country-specific expertise, as they can navigate foreign investment regulations, tax structures, and political environments more effectively (Chang et al., 2016; Koo, 2020). However, not all advisory relationships yield positive results—some evidence suggests that advisors' recommendations may be influenced by proprietary interests, over-optimistic synergy projections, or deal momentum pressures, leading to suboptimal target selection (Aschbacher & Kroon, 2023; Golubov et al., 2012).

Despite the importance of target selection, a key research gap remains: To what extent do advisors improve long-term acquisition success beyond short-term financial metrics? While some studies associate top-tier advisors with higher initial bidder returns, their role in achieving sustained performance improvements post-merger remains underexplored (Schmitz & Sievers, 2020; Xing, 2016). Future research should adopt longitudinal approaches to assess whether advisory-driven target selection strategies contribute to sustained competitive advantage.

Deal Structuring and Negotiation Strategies

Advisors also shape the structuring and execution of M&A deals, influencing factors such as bidding strategies, acquisition premiums, financing mechanisms, and governance structures. Their ability to design optimal transaction structures—whether through cash deals, stock swaps, or earnout agreements—affects the financial and strategic viability of the acquisition (Porrini, 2006). Moreover, advisors play a key role in negotiation dynamics, leveraging their knowledge of precedent transactions and market conditions to secure favorable terms for their clients (Chang et al., 2016; Xing, 2016).

Evidence on the effectiveness of advisors in deal structuring is mixed. Some studies suggest that top-tier advisors enhance negotiation leverage, leading to more favorable acquisition terms and reduced information asymmetry (Golubov et al., 2012). Others caution that advisors may encourage higher acquisition premiums to justify their own fees, ultimately eroding shareholder value (Bakker & Veen, 2015; Ismail, 2010). For example, research on dual-role advisors—who both advise on and underwrite transactions—suggests they may push for higher deal values to maximize their compensation, creating potential conflicts of interest (Bakker &Veen, 2015; Kosnik & Shapiro, 1997).

Further, advisors' influence on governance structures and shareholder protections remains an area requiring deeper investigation. Some research suggests that financial advisors shape governance provisions such as poison pills, staggered boards, or earnout clauses, but the long-term impact of these mechanisms on acquisition success is not well understood (Demong et al., 2011; Porrini, 2006). Given these inconsistencies, future research should explore when and how advisors contribute to shareholder-friendly deal structuring versus self-serving financial engineering.

Post-Merger Integration and Organizational Alignment.

Beyond deal execution, M&A success depends significantly on post-merger integration (PMI), organizational restructuring, and cultural alignment. While traditionally viewed as financial engineers, advisors increasingly contribute to PMI strategies, helping firms navigate operational synergies, leadership transitions, and cultural integration challenges (Gordon et al., 2019; Schmitz & Sievers, 2020).

Recent research suggests that strategy consultants play a crucial role in PMI by facilitating cultural due diligence and process standardization, leading to smoother integrations (Schmitz & Sievers, 2020; Teeffelen, 2011). Additionally, legal advisors help redefine governance structures, align compliance frameworks, and mitigate post-deal legal risks (Demong et al., 2011). However, the extent of financial advisors' involvement in PMI remains debated—while some studies argue that they assist in operational execution, others indicate that their role largely ends at deal closure, leaving acquirers to navigate PMI challenges independently (Gordon et al., 2019; Haleblian et al., 2013).

An important research question is: Do advisors contribute to long-term post-merger success, or do their efforts primarily serve short-term deal completion? Given that most studies focus on pre-merger activities, future research should examine how advisors' recommendations translate into sustainable organizational integration and value creation.

The Unresolved Debate: Value Creation or Value Destruction?

While M&A advisors are often perceived as value-enhancing facilitators, their overall impact on acquisition outcomes remains contested. On one hand, advisors bring specialized expertise, market knowledge, and execution capabilities, leading to improved deal structuring and synergy realization (Golubov et al., 2012; Wang et al., 2020). On the other hand, concerns persist that their incentive structures, conflicts of interest, and deal-driven culture may contribute to overpayment, failed integrations, and wealth destruction (Bakker & Veen, 2015; Ismail, 2010; Kosnik & Shapiro, 1997). An important contextual factor may be the timing of performance effects of advisors. Yet, a key limitation in existing research is the lack of long-term performance assessments. Most studies evaluate advisors' impact based on short-term bidder returns, rather than analyzing whether advisor-led transactions generate sustained profitability, market share growth, or innovation synergies. Additionally, emerging trends such as AI-driven advisory tools and ESG-focused deal strategies introduce new complexities that require further exploration (Wang et al., 2020).

To resolve these debates, future research should do three things. First, research should adopt longitudinal methodologies to assess whether advisor-led deals lead to sustained financial and operational benefits. Second, research should examine alternative compensation models that align advisor incentives with long-term acquisition success. Third, research should investigate how emerging technologies (e.g., AI, big data) transform the advisory landscape and influencing strategic decision-making.

Conclusion

M&A advisors play a pivotal yet controversial role in shaping acquisition strategies, structuring deals, and influencing post-merger integration. While they provide critical expertise in target selection, negotiation, and synergy identification, concerns about misaligned incentives and inconsistent long-term value creation persist. Given the mixed evidence, future research must shift beyond short-term transactional metrics to evaluate the sustained strategic impact of advisors on corporate performance. Next, I examine the incentive structures and behavioral influences of M&A advisors, exploring conflicts of interest, cognitive biases, and deal momentum shape acquisition outcomes.

Incentives, Conflicts of Interest, and Behavioral Influences in M&A Advisory

While investment banks and advisors provide critical expertise in M&A transactions, their relationships with acquiring firms introduce incentive misalignments and decision biases that may distort deal-making outcomes (Lee, 2013). Strong pre-existing ties between firms and advisors can lead to relational hazards, where the trust and familiarity between parties reduce scrutiny and encourage overconfidence in deal recommendations. Research has shown that firms with long-standing advisory relationships may overlook alternative advisors with superior insights, leading to suboptimal acquisition decisions and inflated valuations (Sleptsov et al., 2013). These relational hazards create conditions where advisors may prioritize maintaining client relationships over delivering objective advice, reinforcing cognitive biases such as escalation of commitment and loss aversion.

One key issue in these relational dynamics is that investment banks have asymmetric access to deal information, allowing them to exert significant influence on acquisition strategy (Xing, 2016). Advisors may exploit information asymmetries by selectively presenting data that justifies higher acquisition premiums or accelerates deal closure, often at the expense of long-term value creation (Guo et al., 2018). Additionally, there is evidence that top-tier advisors charge premium fees based on reputation rather than demonstrated value-addition, which raises concerns about whether firms are overpaying for advisory services that do not necessarily enhance acquisition success (Wang et al., 2020). The financial incentives for advisors to complete deals—rather than ensure their quality—underscore the need for governance mechanisms that reduce conflicts of interest and improve decision accountability.

Further complicating the advisory landscape is the emergence of inter-firm advisor switching, where acquiring firms hire advisors previously engaged by target firms (Sleptsov et al., 2013). While such advisors may bring superior knowledge of the target firm, they may also introduce ethical dilemmas regarding information leakage, conflicts of interest, and biased recommendations (Arena & Dewally, 2017). Some studies suggest that these "advisor switches" create competitive advantages, enabling firms to negotiate more favorable terms (Chang et al., 2016). However, others argue that these practices may undermine deal integrity, particularly when advisors exploit privileged information in ways that compromise market fairness (Faias, 2017). The question of whether advisor switching benefits acquirers or distorts acquisition outcomes remains an open area for future research.

Given these complexities, firms must consider alternative compensation models and oversight mechanisms to align advisor incentives with shareholder interests. Some scholars advocate for performance-based advisory fees, where compensation is tied to post-merger performance rather than immediate transaction closure (Gordon et al., 2019). Others highlight the importance of independent deal committees that reduce the undue influence of advisors and introduce checks on valuation assumptions, negotiation tactics, and risk assessments (Schmitz & Sievers, 2020). Ultimately, addressing these incentive conflicts requires a multi-level approach, incorporating governance safeguards, regulatory oversight, and behavioral insights to enhance M&A decision-making quality.

Advisor Incentive Structures and Conflicts of Interest

The dominant compensation model for M&A advisors—success fees—creates inherent conflicts of interest. Since advisors typically earn a percentage of the transaction value upon deal completion, they are financially incentivized to push for deal closure, even when the transaction might not be in the long-term interests of shareholders (Bakker & Veen, 2015; Kosnik & Shapiro, 1997). This fee structure raises concerns about deal-driven motivations, where advisors may prioritize securing their payout over ensuring strategic alignment or post-merger feasibility.

Further, some financial advisors serve dual roles, simultaneously advising on a transaction while also underwriting its financing. This "stapled financing" arrangement creates additional conflicts, as advisors may encourage higher acquisition premiums or debt-heavy deal structures that maximize their own fees while increasing financial risk for the acquiring firm (Bakker & Veen, 2015; Xing, 2016). Studies suggest that such dual-role engagements inflate acquisition costs and may lead to value destruction, particularly when advisors are more focused on deal closure than long-term synergies (Bakker & Veen, 2015; Kosnik & Shapiro, 1997; McConnell & Sibilkov, 2016).

However, other research highlights the reputation effects of top-tier advisors, arguing that elite investment banks and advisory firms may act in clients' best interests to preserve their long-term credibility in the market (Golubov et al., 2012; Xing, 2016). While some studies indicate that high-reputation advisors reduce deal risks and improve terms, others suggest that they still contribute to overpayment and excessive premiums in high-stakes acquisitions (Ismail, 2010). This discrepancy raises an important question: Does advisor reputation mitigate conflicts of interest, or do even top-tier advisors prioritize deal volume over deal quality?

To resolve these concerns, future research should examine alternative compensation structures, such as milestone-based fees (where advisors are compensated based on post-merger performance rather than immediate deal completion), fixed-fee advisory models (which could reduce pressure to inflate valuations or rush transactions), and performance-linked incentives (where advisor compensation is partially tied to long-term deal success, such as post-merger integration effectiveness).

The Role of Behavioral Biases in Advisor-Executive Interactions

Beyond financial incentives, advisors also shape executive decision-making through cognitive and behavioral mechanisms. Research in behavioral finance and strategic management has identified several biases that advisors either introduce or reinforce, influencing acquisition outcomes in non-rational ways (Aschbacher & Kroon, 2023; Haleblian et al., 2013).

Studies suggest that advisors use framing techniques to influence how executives perceive acquisition opportunities, often highlighting potential synergies while downplaying risks (Aschbacher & Kroon, 2023). This can lead to overconfidence biases, where executives become overly optimistic about deal success, increasing the likelihood of overpayment, integration failures, and cultural mismatches (Aschbacher & Kroon, 2023; Haleblian et al., 2013). While some advisors are incentivized to see potential synergies realized (e.g., strategy consultants), most of the literature focuses on financial advisors which are incentivized for deal closure. In that vein, overstating potential synergies is purely positively incentivized as it makes deal closure more likely. On another vein, when synergy realization is incentivized, it may bias advisors to focus on cost synergies that are easier to realize.

Additionally, the deal-driven nature of M&A transactions creates an environment of urgency, where advisors may exploit time pressure to accelerate decision-making. Research shows that when executives perceive a need for speed, they are more likely to rely on advisors' guidance without critically evaluating alternative strategies (Drees, 2013). This behavior amplifies the power of advisors in shaping deal decisions, sometimes at the expense of rational analysis.

Once an M&A process is initiated, deal momentum can take on a life of its own—a phenomenon known as escalation of commitment. Advisors, particularly those with success-based fees, have a vested interest in sustaining deal momentum and discouraging reconsideration or abandonment, even in cases where red flags emerge (Aschbacher & Kroon, 2023; Drees, 2013). This pressure makes it increasingly difficult for executives to walk away from failing deals, leading to acquisitions that destroy value rather than create it.

One key gap in the literature is understanding how advisors' behavioral influence interacts with corporate governance mechanisms. Do firms with stronger board oversight or independent decision-making structures mitigate advisor-driven biases, or do they remain equally susceptible to deal momentum? Future studies should investigate governance safeguards that could counteract excessive advisor influence in acquisitions.

The Unresolved Debate: Are Advisors Independent Experts or Self-Interested Dealmakers?

Despite extensive research on advisor roles, there is no clear consensus on whether they ultimately enhance or undermine M&A outcomes. On one hand, advisors provide critical expertise in valuation, deal structuring, and post-merger planning, contributing to synergy realization and reduced transaction risks (Chang et al., 2016; Golubov et al., 2012; Wang et al., 2020). On the other hand, their conflicted incentives and behavioral influences may distort decision-making, leading to value-destroying acquisitions that prioritize transaction fees over long-term success (Bakker & Veen, 2015; Ismail, 2010; Kosnik & Shapiro, 1997).

Several areas require further empirical investigation to clarify this debate. First, longitudinal studies on advisor impact. Most research focuses on short-term deal metrics like bidder returns, but little is known about how advisor-led deals perform years after acquisition. Second, experimental studies on behavioral biases. Future research should test how advisors frame acquisition decisions and whether executives can be trained to resist framing effects and deal momentum pressures. Third, comparative analysis of compensation models. Studies should explore whether alternative incentive structures reduce conflicts of interest and lead to better acquisition decisions.

Conclusion

The incentive structures and behavioral influences of M&A advisors present a double-edged sword—while they offer expertise and market access, they also introduce conflicts of interest, cognitive biases, and deal-driven pressures that can distort acquisition strategy. Understanding these dynamics is crucial for firms seeking to maximize the value of M&A transactions while minimizing unnecessary risks.

Emerging Trends in M&A Advisory: ESG, AI, and the Future of Deal-Making

The landscape of M&A advisory is evolving, driven by technological advancements, shifting regulatory expectations, and changing stakeholder priorities. As firms navigate increasingly complex transactions, the traditional role of M&A advisors is being redefined. Two of the most significant developments in this transformation are the rise of environmental, social, and governance (ESG) considerations in deal-making and the integration of artificial intelligence (AI) and big data into M&A advisory processes. These trends are reshaping how advisors evaluate targets, structure deals, and mitigate risks. However, despite their growing importance, the academic literature has only begun to explore their implications for M&A strategy (Wang et al., 2020). This section examines how ESG and AI are influencing M&A advisory and highlights key research questions that remain unanswered.

Increased Role of ESG in M&A Strategy

Recently, ESG factors have emerged as critical components of corporate strategy, influencing investment decisions, risk assessments, and post-merger integration (Gordano et al., 2024). Acquiring firms increasingly recognize that sustainability, corporate governance, and social responsibility can affect long-term value creation, making ESG a core consideration in M&A transactions (Wang et al., 2020).

ESG considerations increasingly shape M&A strategy, influencing target selection, payment methods, and deal speed. Recent research shows that acquirers with stronger ESG performance relative to targets are more likely to acquire smaller firms, use cash payments, and complete deals faster (Gordano et al., 2024). Notably, ESG differences in acquisitions tend to enhance the combined entity's ESG performance post-merger, positioning M&A as a mechanism for ESG capability transfer. It is unclear how advisors shape this transfer or may aide ESG capability transfer.

Despite the growing focus on ESG, M&A advisors face challenges in quantifying its impact on deal performance. Unlike financial metrics such as EBITDA or revenue growth, ESG factors are often subjective, difficult to measure, and inconsistent across industries. Research suggests that firms with strong ESG profiles are more attractive acquisition targets because they exhibit lower regulatory risk, higher employee satisfaction, and better long-term financial stability (Wang et al., 2020). However, firms poorly performing on ESG factors may present attractive candidates for transferring acquirer capabilities (Gordano et al., 2024). ESG considerations are particularly relevant in cross-border acquisitions, where differences in regulatory standards, labor practices, and environmental policies can significantly impact deal success (Arena & Dewally, 2017).

As a result, advisors play a role in integrating ESG due diligence into the M&A process, helping acquirers assess potential liabilities and opportunities related to sustainability (Wang et al., 2020). For example, advisors can mitigate the risk of "greenwashing", or firms exaggerating their ESG credentials to attract investment—raising concerns about the reliability of ESG ratings and disclosures (Wang et al., 2020). The extent to which ESG due diligence influences post-merger success remains unclear, as few studies have examined whether ESG-focused acquisitions generate higher long-term returns or merely serve as reputational safeguards.

Research Gaps and Future Directions

The academic literature on ESG in M&A remains underdeveloped, with several key questions still unanswered. Three research questions come to mind. First, how does ESG performance influence acquisition premiums, valuation multiples, and shareholder responses? Second, do ESG-focused acquisitions outperform non-ESG transactions in long-term profitability and integration success? Third, what role should advisors play in standardizing ESG due diligence and mitigating greenwashing risks?

Artificial Intelligence and Big Data in M&A Advisory

As deal complexity increases, AI and big data analytics are transforming how M&A advisors evaluate targets, conduct due diligence, and optimize transaction structures. The ability to analyze massive datasets in real-time has the potential to enhance decision-making, reduce risks, and improve forecasting accuracy. However, these technological advancements also introduce new biases, ethical dilemmas, and regulatory concerns that must be addressed (Wang et al., 2020).

There are multiple ways that technology could influence acquisitions. For example, AI algorithms can identify acquisition targets based on predictive models, analyzing financial reports, market trends, and even non-traditional data sources such as news sentiment and social media activity (Wang et al., 2020). Additionally, machine learning models can enhance valuation accuracy by identifying patterns in historical transactions, allowing advisors to make more precise recommendations. For example, AI can reduce information asymmetry, helping firms avoid overpayment and post-merger surprises (Wang et al., 2020).

Despite its advantages, AI introduces several risks into the M&A advisory process. For example, there are three aspects which can raise the risk of AI in M&A advisory. First, the existence of algorithmic bias where AI models can reinforce existing biases in deal evaluation, leading to flawed decision-making if trained on incomplete or skewed datasets (Wang et al., 2020). Second, there can be over-reliance on automation that while AI can enhance efficiency, human judgment remains essential for evaluating qualitative factors such as corporate culture, leadership fit, and strategic alignment. Third, there are concerns over data privacy and regulatory concerns where the use of AI in M&A raises questions about data security, compliance with GDPR and SEC regulations, and the ethical implications of automated deal sourcing (Wang et al., 2020).

The role of AI in M&A advisory (both in practice and research) is still in its early stages, leaving several areas for future research. First, how do AI-driven valuations compare to traditional financial advisor assessments in terms of accuracy and deal outcomes? Second, what regulatory frameworks should be established to ensure responsible AI usage in M&A advisory? Third, can AI tools mitigate behavioral biases in M&A decisions, or do they introduce new cognitive distortions?

Conclusion

The future of M&A advisory is being shaped by two dominant forces: the growing emphasis on ESG in corporate strategy and the integration of AI and big data into deal evaluation and execution. While these trends offer new opportunities for enhancing target selection, valuation accuracy, and post-merger success, they also introduce challenges related to regulatory compliance, algorithmic biases, and the measurement of non-financial factors.

Given the scarcity of empirical research on these emerging trends, future studies should focus on quantifying ESG's impact on M&A outcomes, evaluating AI's reliability in financial forecasting, and developing best practices for integrating new technologies into advisory roles. A broad overview of frameworks for understanding research on advisors is shown in Table 2.

Conclusion and Future Research Directions

The role of M&A advisors remains one of the most contested topics in corporate strategy, with scholars and practitioners debating their value contribution, conflicts of interest, and evolving responsibilities in an era of technological and regulatory transformation. While investment banks, legal advisors, and strategy consultants undeniably facilitate deal-making, structure transactions, and provide industry expertise, their long-term impact on firm performance remains inconclusive. Existing research offers contradictory evidence—some studies highlight the ability of top-tier advisors to enhance synergies and improve shareholder returns, while others point to inflated acquisition premiums, deal momentum biases, and conflicts of interest that erode value (Golubov et al., 2012; Ismail, 2010; Kosnik & Shapiro, 1997; Wang et al., 2020).

The findings on advisor selection and incentive structures highlight the dual role of investment banks in M&A transactions—acting both as facilitators of value creation and as potential sources of conflicted decision-making. Firms often select advisors based on reputation, market share, and network position (Bowers & Miller, 1990; Servaes & Zenner, 1996), but long-standing relationships between acquirers and advisors can create relational hazards that reduce the objectivity of deal evaluations (Lee, 2013). Investment banks with strong prior ties to acquirers may exhibit less scrutiny in valuation assessments or encourage deals that

Table 2 Summary of key areas in M&A advisory research

Key area	*Established roles and findings*	*Open questions*	*Future research directions*
Strategic contributions	– Advisors shape acquisition strategies through target selection, deal structuring, and synergy identification	– Do advisors contribute to long-term competitive advantage beyond short-term financial gains?	– Conduct longitudinal studies to assess advisors' long-term impact on firm performance
	– Industry-specific expertise supports synergy capture and prevents overpayment	– How do advisors' decisions influence sustainability and post-merger success?	– Apply frameworks like dynamic capabilities theory to evaluate advisory influence on integration
Organizational behavior and culture	–Advisors facilitate cultural due diligence and integration planning	– How can advisors best support post-merger integration beyond operational synergies?	– Investigate advisors' roles in post-merger integration and leadership transitions
	– Advisors influence decision-making through framing effects and deal momentum	– How do advisors' cognitive biases influence executives' risk perception in M&A decisions?	– Use behavioral experiments to explore the impact of advisors on executive decision-making
Incentives and conflicts of interest	– Success-fee structures and dual roles create potential misaligned incentives	– How can new compensation models better align advisors' incentives with long-term shareholder value?	– Test new compensation structures like milestone-based or performance-linked fees
	– Top-tier advisors may reduce risk but also contribute to acquisition premium inflation	– Do reputational concerns meaningfully prevent advisors from prioritizing self-interest?	– Explore governance mechanisms that mitigate advisor-driven conflicts of interest

prioritize advisor fees over shareholder returns (Sleptsov et al., 2013). At the same time, research suggests that top-tier advisors can enhance acquisition outcomes by leveraging superior market knowledge, reducing transaction uncertainty, and improving post-merger integration (Bao & Edmans, 2011; Kale et al., 2003). However, the conflicting incentives embedded in contingent fee structures (Rau, 2000) and the influence of social networks on advisor effort levels (Chaudhry et al., 2022) raise important questions about whether advisory firms act in the best interests of acquiring shareholders. Future research should examine how firms can structure advisory relationships to balance the benefits of information access with the risks of overdependence, ensuring that advisor incentives align with long-term acquisition success.

As firms continue to engage in M&A as a critical strategic tool, understanding when and how advisors contribute to long-term value creation, rather than short-term deal execution, is essential. This paper has provided a comprehensive review of the literature, identifying key themes, research gaps, and emerging trends that shape the future of M&A advisory. Below, I outline five priority areas for future research to advance our understanding of advisors' roles in corporate acquisitions.

Rethinking Advisor Value: From Transactional Facilitation to Long-Term Strategic Impact

Most research on M&A advisors focuses on immediate financial outcomes, such as cumulative abnormal returns (CARs) and acquisition premiums, while neglecting post-merger performance, integration success, and sustained competitive advantage (Gordon et al., 2019; Guo et al., 2018; Schmitz & Sievers, 2020; Wang et al., 2020). Future studies should shift toward longitudinal research designs that address three issues. First, they should track advisor involvement beyond deal closure to assess their impact on post-merger operational performance, cultural integration, and synergy realization. Second, research should investigate whether firms advised by top-tier investment banks and strategy consultants consistently outperform those that do not employ advisors. Third, research should develop comprehensive performance metrics that extend beyond short-term stock price reactions to include operational effectiveness and governance improvements. This is an issue that has been consistently identified in other research where metrics of acquisition performance are inadequate (Molina-Sieiro et al., 2025) and may lead to inconclusive results (King et al., 2004, 2021).

Addressing Conflicts of Interest: New Compensation Models and Governance Mechanisms

Despite extensive research on success fees and dual-role advisors, the question of how to align advisor incentives with long-term shareholder value remains unresolved (Bakker & Veen, 2015; Kosnik & Shapiro, 1997; Mcconnell & Sibilkov, 2016). Future research should compare traditional success-fee structures with alternative compensation models, such as milestone-based, fixed-fee, or performance-linked advisory contracts. Research should also explore whether corporate governance mechanisms, such as independent deal committees and stricter regulatory oversight, can mitigate advisor-driven incentive misalignment. Further, research should conduct field experiments and case studies to analyze the decision-making dynamics between M&A advisors and executives, particularly in high-stakes transactions.

Behavioral Influences and Cognitive Biases in M&A Advisory

A growing body of literature suggests that advisors not only provide financial expertise but also shape executive decision-making through framing effects, deal momentum, and behavioral biases (Aschbacher & Kroon, 2023; Drees, 2013; Haleblian et al., 2013). However, research on these influences remains fragmented. Future studies should apply behavioral finance and organizational psychology frameworks to examine how advisors influence executives' perceptions of risk, deal urgency, and acquisition rationale. Future research should also investigate whether behavioral interventions, such as debiasing strategies or structured decision-making frameworks, can mitigate advisor-driven biases. Lastly, researchers could explore the interaction between advisor influence and corporate governance structures, assessing whether firms with stronger independent oversight are less susceptible to deal-driven escalation effects.

The Future Role of Advisors in Cross-Border and Industry-Specific M&A

M&A advisors play a particularly crucial role in cross-border deals, where regulatory complexity, cultural differences, and geopolitical risks require specialized expertise (Arena & Dewally, 2017; Chang et al., 2016; Dikova et al., 2010). Much research has been done on understanding research on how distance shapes acquisitions (Beugelsdijk et al., 2018). However, little is known about how advisors' effectiveness varies across industries and regions. Future studies should conduct comparative research on advisor effectiveness in different sectors, such as technology, countries, healthcare, and energy, to determine where their expertise is most valuable. Researchers could also examine how advisors facilitate (or hinder) knowledge transfer and cultural integration in cross-border acquisitions (Reus & Lamont, 2009). Lastly, research could try to apply dynamic capabilities theory to assess whether advisors enhance firms' adaptability in navigating global M&A challenges (Eisenhardt & Martin, 2000). While this chapter outlines empirical gaps in M&A advisory research, these opportunities are grounded in distinct theoretical traditions. Table 3 maps each research priority to relevant theoretical frameworks to guide future scholarly inquiry.

Final Thoughts: Toward a More Nuanced Understanding of M&A Advisors

This review highlights the complex, multifaceted nature of M&A advisors' contributions, challenging the notion that they are either purely value-enhancing facilitators or self-interested dealmakers. While investment banks, legal advisors, and consultants undoubtedly play a critical role in deal execution, their long-term impact remains an open question. Moving forward, researchers must adopt interdisciplinary approaches, combining insights from finance, strategic management, behavioral economics, and technology studies to develop a more holistic, evidence-based understanding of M&A advisory dynamics. By addressing identified gaps, future research can provide greater clarity on when, why, and how M&A advisors contribute to (or detract from) acquisition success, offering valuable insights for both academia and corporate practitioners navigating high-stakes transactions.

Table 3 Linking future research priorities to theoretical frameworks

Future research priority	*Core theoretical frameworks*	*Rationale for theoretical fit*
Rethinking advisor value: from transactional facilitation to long-term strategic impact	Dynamic capabilities theory, resource-based view	Helps assess whether advisors contribute to firms' long-term adaptability, synergy realization, and competitive advantage beyond short-term financial outcomes
Addressing conflicts of interest: new compensation models and governance mechanisms	Agency theory, stakeholder theory	Explains incentive misalignments and principal-agent problems between advisors and acquiring firms; stakeholder theory highlights broader governance and accountability mechanisms
Behavioral influences and cognitive biases in M&A advisory	Behavioral economics, bounded rationality, organizational psychology	Frames how advisors may shape or distort executive decision-making through framing effects, escalation of commitment, and overconfidence
Cross-border and industry-specific M&A	Institutional theory, cultural distance theory	Explains how institutional environments and national/regional differences shape advisor effectiveness across countries and sectors
Emerging trends: ESG and AI in M&A advisory	Stakeholder theory, sociotechnical systems theory, information economics	Helps understand the role of non-financial metrics (e.g., ESG), AI-driven decision tools, and their integration into traditional advisory and governance processes

References

Arena, M., & Dewally, M. (2017). Investment bank expertise in cross-border mergers and acquisitions. *Journal of Financial Research, 40*(1), 81–112.

Aschbacher, J., & Kroon, D. (2023). Falling prey to bias? The influence of advisors on the manifestation of cognitive biases in the pre-M&A phase of organizations. *Group & Organization Management, 50*(1), 41–81.

Bao, J., & Edmans, A. (2011). Do investment banks matter for M&A returns? *Review of Financial Studies, 24*(7), 2286–2315.

Bakker, M., & Veen, K. V. (2015). Dual role advisors in acquisitions: Examining the effect on shareholder value. *Lund University, Master's Thesis.*

Beugelsdijk, S., Kostova, T., Kunst, V., Spadafora, E., & Van Essen, M. (2018). Cultural distance and firm internationalization: A meta-analytical review and theoretical implications. *Journal of Management, 44*(1), 89–130.

Bowers, H., & Miller, R. (1990). Choice of investment banker and shareholders' wealth of firms involved in acquisitions. *Financial Management, 19*(4), 34–44.

Chang, X., Shekhar, C., Tam, L., & Yao, J. (2016). The information role of advisors in mergers and acquisitions: Evidence from acquirers hiring targets' ex-advisors. *Journal of Banking & Finance, 70*, 247–264.

Chaudhry, A. N., Kontonikas, A., & Vagenas-Nanos, E. (2022). Social networks and the informational role of financial advisory firms centrality in mergers and acquisitions. *British Journal of Management, 33*(2), 958–979.

Demong, R., Harris, I., & Williams, S. (2011). Financial and legal advisors in merger and acquisition transactions. *International Journal of Business, Humanities, and Technology, 1.*

Dikova, D., Sahib, P., & Van Witteloostuijn, A. (2010). Cross-border acquisition abandonment and completion: The effect of institutional differences and organizational learning in the international business service industry, 1981–2001. *Journal of International Business Studies, 41*, 223–245.

Drees, J. (2013). The polycentricity of expansion strategies: Beyond performance as a main driver. *Dissertation. University of Amsterdam.*

Eisenhardt, K., & Martin, J. A. (2000). Dynamic capabilities: What are they? *Strategic Management Journal, 21*(10–11), 1105–1121.

Faias, J. (2017). Merger waves and the importance of financial advisors reputation for acquirers. *Working Paper* https://doi.org/10.2139/ssrn.3055582

Golubov, A., Petmezas, D., & Travlos, N. (2012). When it pays to pay your investment banker: New evidence on the role of financial advisors in M&As. *Journal of Finance, 67*(1), 271–311.

Gordano, S., Bauer, F., & King, D. (2024). Environmental, social, and governance (ESG) acquisitions: Deal structure and outcome. *Business Strategy and the Environment, 33*(6), 6010–6028.

Gordon, J., Sieiro, G., Ellis, K., & Lamont, B. (2019). Chapter 3 M&A advisors: Padding their pockets or source of expertise?. *Advances in Mergers and Acquisitions, 18*, 27–49.

Guo, J., Li, Y., Wang, C., & Xing, X. (2018). The role of investment bankers in M&As: New evidence on acquirers' financial conditions. *Journal of Banking & Finance, 119*, Article 105298.

Haleblian, J., Steinbach, A., & McNamara, G. (2013). With experience comes wisdom? Difficulties learning from and using adviser acquisition experience. *Academy of Management Proceedings*. https://doi.org/10.5465/AMBPP.2013.13125ABSTRACT

Hunter, W., & Jagtiani, J. (2003). An analysis of advisor choice, fees, and effort in mergers and acquisitions. *Review of Financial Economics, 12*, 65–81.

Ismail, A. (2010). Are good financial advisors really good? The performance of investment banks in the M&A market. *Review of Quantitative Finance and Accounting, 35*, 411–429.

Kale, J., Kini, O., & Ryan, H. (2003). Financial advisors and shareholder wealth gains in corporate takeovers. *Journal of Financial and Quantitative Analysis, 38*(3), 475–501.

King, D., Dalton, D., Daily, C., & Covin, J. (2004). Meta-analyses of post-acquisition performance: Indications of unidentified moderators. *Strategic Management Journal, 25*(2), 187–200.

King, D., Wang, G., Samimi, M., & Cortes, A. (2021). A meta-analytic integration of acquisition performance prediction. *Journal of Management Studies, 58*(5), 1198–1236.

Koo, J. (2020). How do advisors influence mergers and acquisitions? An analysis of acquisitions in Japan. *Journal of Asian Finance, Economics and Business, 7*(7), 123–129.

Kosnik, R., & Shapiro, D. (1997). Agency conflicts between investment banks and corporate clients in merger and acquisition transactions: Causes and remedies. *Academy of Management Perspectives, 11*(1), 7–20.

Lee, J. J. (2013). Dancing with the enemy? Relational hazards and the contingent value of repeat exchanges in M & A markets. *Organization Science, 24*(4), 1237–1256.

Mcconnell, J., & Sibilkov, V. (2016). Do investment banks have incentives to help clients make value-creating acquisitions? *Journal of Applied Corporate Finance, 28*(3), 103–117.

Molina-Sieiro, G., Lim, S., King, D., & Hitt, M. (2025). Predicting acquisition specific goodwill write-downs. *Long Range Planning, 58*(2), Article 102512.

Porrini, P. (2006). Are investment bankers good for acquisition premiums? *Journal of Business Research, 59*(1), 90–99.

Rau, P. (2000). Investment bank market share, contingent fee payments, and the performance of acquiring firms. *Journal of Financial Economics, 56*(2), 293–324.

Reus, T., & Lamont, B. (2009). The double-edged sword of cultural distance in international acquisitions. *Journal of International Business Studies, 40*, 1298–1316.

Schmitz, A., & Sievers, S. (2020). What are the effects of strategy consultants, financial, and legal M&A advisors on M&A S=success? *Working Paper* https://doi.org/10.2139/ssrn.3874903

Servaes, H., & Zenner, M. (1996). The role of investment banks in acquisitions. *Review of Financial Studies, 9*, 787–815.

Sleptsov, A., Anand, J., & Vasudeva, G. (2013). Relational configurations with information intermediaries: The effect of firm-investment bank ties on expected acquisition performance. *Strategic Management Journal, 34*(8), 957–977.

Teeffelen, L. (2011). Are advisors an asset or redundant in SME mergers and acquisitions? Evidence from North-West Europe. *Working Paper* https://doi.org/10.2139/SSRN.1866200

Wang, C., Xie, F., & Zhang, K. (2020). Expert advice: Industry expertise of M&A advisors and acquirer shareholder returns. *Journal of Financial and Quantitative Analysis, 57*(2), 599–628.

Xing, X. (2016). Reputation-quality mechanism in the context of mergers and acquisitions: Financial advisors, financial analysts and acquirer performance. *Durham University, Doctoral Thesis.*

Reciprocal Impacts Between M&A and the Investor Community

Christine Madonna Kirkland and Janice M. Gordon

Introduction

The investor community centered around merger and acquisition (M&A) activity can be a source of competitive advantage for focal firms. In this chapter, we focus on five key stakeholders within this community: financial analysts, investment banks, institutional investors, the media, and private equity and venture capital firms. Evidence suggests that these stakeholders can positively and negatively affect M&A outcomes (Bodnaruk & Rossi, 2016; Goranova et al., 2017; Nary, 2024; Renneboog & Vansteenkiste, 2019). These stakeholders are central to M&A processes in that they each hold a vested interest and exert influence over M&A outcomes, collectively shape and reinforces norms and legitimacy surrounding dealmaking, and provide critical resources including capital, information, and reputational support, grounding these relationships in stakeholder, institutional, and resource dependence theories, respectively.

Beyond their immediate effects, investor community stakeholders have different goals, resulting in conflicting interests within and between

C. M. Kirkland (✉) · J. M. Gordon
Western Carolina University, Cullowhee, NC, USA
e-mail: ckirkland@email.wcu.edu

D. R. King and A. Bansal (eds.), *Navigating Stakeholder Dynamics Surrounding Acquisitions*,
https://doi.org/10.1007/978-3-032-03199-0_3

these groups. For example, Bodnaruk and Rossi (2016) find that when institutional investors hold equity and debt in the target firm, the acquiring firm pays a lower premium. Therefore, when acting as "dual holders," institutional investors have conflicting interests. They can gain an advantage by targeting firms they own for acquisition, decreasing their risk and increasing their holdings. As stakeholder impacts on firms increase, understudied conflicting interests within and between stakeholders must be made explicit. We identify stakeholders' impacts by reviewing existing finance, management, and economics research, as discussed in the methodology in Appendix A. We then discuss the stakeholders' reciprocal impacts with M&A deals to uncover their potential conflicting interests within and between each stakeholder. Finally, we discuss conflicts of interest in three categories (i.e., ownership stakes, access to insider information, and time horizons). Overall, our review and summary classify conflicting interests within the investor community.

We contribute to M&A research by highlighting the joint effects of investment community involvement to expose these conflicting interests. We present each listed stakeholder's effects on M&A outcomes, categorize the types of conflicts encountered, and advance a research agenda based on joint consideration of conflicting interests within the investor community. We provide research implications, including the need to further investigate the interaction of conflicting interests with the effectiveness of governance mechanisms. Finally, we provide managerial implications, allowing practitioners to implement actions based on our findings.

Stakeholders and M&A Performance

The investor community and M&A activity are interconnected as firms and stakeholders influence each other. Investors provide the capital for deals and apply pressure to increase performance. For example, investors and the media provide market sentiment that can aid or hinder acquisition activity. Further, market sentiment from the investor community, including voting on expected financial outcomes of specific M&A transactions, shapes managers' investment decisions and M&A activity. In the following paragraphs, we summarize the influences of major investor community stakeholders, shown in Table 1.

Table 1 Investor community impacts on M&A performance

Type	*Dependent variable*	*Positive relationship*	*Negative relationship*	*Nonlinear relationship*	*No effect*
Analysts	Announcement returns	Cortes and Marcet (2023)	Lee (2013)		
	Deal completion	Becher et al. (2015)	Cortes and Marcet (2023)		
	Post merger integration performance	Cortes and Marcet (2023)			
	Premia	Lee (2013)			
	Other	Kolasinski and Kothari (2008) and Tehranian et al. (2014)			
Banks	Announcement returns	Bao and Edmans (2011), Bharadwaj and Shivdasani (2003), Chemmanur et al. (2019), Golubov et al. (2012), Huang et al. (2022) and Yawson and Zhang (2021)	Rajamani et al. (2017)		
	Deal completion	Bodnaruk et al. (2009), Kisgen and Song (2009) and Rau (2000)			
	Post merger integration performance	Chemmanur et al. (2019)			

(continued)

Table 1 (continued)

Type	*Dependent variable*	*Positive relationship*	*Negative relationship*	*Nonlinear relationship*	*No effect*
	Premia	Bodnaruk et al. (2009)	Kisgen and Song (2009) and Yawson and Zhang (2021)		
	Other	Haushalter and Lowry (2011) and Rau (2000)			
Institutional Investors	Announcement returns	Agrawal and Mandelker (1990), Bodnaruk and Rossi (2016), Greenwood and Schor (2009) and Li et al. (2018)	Bruner (1999), Gaspar et al. (2005), Goranova et al. (2017), Lee (2013) and Steinbach et al. (2017)		Matvos and Ostrovsky (2008)
	Deal completion	Ferreira et al. (2010)	Iliev et al. (2015) and Ye (2014)		
	Post merger integration performance	Bu et al. (2024)			
	Premia	Ayers et al. (2003), Bargeron et al. (2008), Lee (2013), Moeller (2005) and Steinbach et al. (2017)	Bodnaruk and Rossi (2016) and Ye (2014)		
	Other		Johan et al. (2013)		

Type	*Dependent variable*	*Positive relationship*	*Negative relationship*	*Nonlinear relationship*	*No effect*
Media	Announcement returns	Ahern and Sosyura (2014), Buehlmaier and Zechner (2021) and Schmidt (2020)	Liu and McConnell (2013), and Sinha et al. (2012)		Ahern and Sosyura (2015)
	Deal completion	Yiu et al. (2024)	Liu and McConnell (2013)		
PE/VC	Announcement returns	Acharya et al. (2013), Arikan and Capron (2010), Cohn et al. (2022), Humphery-Jenner et al. (2017) and Masulis et al. (2011)	Benson and Ziedonis (2010) and Nary (2024)		
	Exit	Brander et al. (2015), Nahata (2008), Ozmel et al. (2013), Ragozzino and Blevins (2016), Wang et al. (2022) and Yao and O'Neill (2022)		Bellavitis et al. (2020)	Ball et al. (2011) and Ragozzino and Blevins (2016)
	Post merger integration performance	Acharya et al. (2013) and Humphery-Jenner et al. (2017)	Yang et al. (2009)	Benson and Ziedonis (2009)	
	Premia	Brau et al. (2010), Demiroglu and James (2010) and Reuer et al. (2012)			

Analysts

Analysts evaluate the financial condition and performance of organizations to provide investment recommendations to stakeholders. Their assessments guide investor decisions on whether to buy, hold, or sell stocks, thereby influencing market sentiment and corporate strategic direction (e.g., Becher et al., 2015; Cortes & Marcet, 2023; Tehranian et al., 2014). For example, analysts' favorable profit outlook of Salesforce protected the company against activist investors and helped boost its stock price (Seal, 2023). Analysts making favorable acquirer recommendations after a merger announcement are associated with an increased probability of deal completion. In contrast, favorable target recommendations are associated with a decreased likelihood of deal completion. Unfavorable recommendations have the opposite effect on acquirers and targets (Becher et al., 2015). Further, when the same analyst covers both the acquirer and the target in an acquisition, there is evidence of reduced completion (Cortes & Marcet, 2023).

While stock analysts have a more indirect role in M&A activity, they can impact completion and post-acquisition performance (Becher et al., 2015; Cortes & Marcet, 2023). Regarding post-acquisition performance, stock analysts covering target firms are likely to have more accurate earnings forecasts, optimistic stock recommendations, and growth forecasts than those covering acquiring firms (Tehranian et al., 2014). When one analyst covers both the acquiring and target companies, there are higher synergy gains, increased announcement returns, and improved post-acquisition performance due to information access (Cortes & Marcet, 2023).

In summary, analysts play a pivotal yet indirect role in shaping M&A outcomes. Their investment recommendations influence deal completion probabilities and investor sentiment. At the same time, their coverage, especially when overlapping between acquirer and target, can affect both the likelihood of deal success and post-acquisition performance. By shaping market expectations and enhancing transparency, analysts play a significant role in the strategic and financial trajectory of M&A transactions.

Banks

Investment banks offer expertise and financial services to firms seeking to be involved in M&As. Banks provide advisors to acquirers and targets regarding financial and legal aspects of potential acquisitions (e.g., Bao & Edmans, 2011; Bodnaruk et al., 2009; Chemmanur et al., 2019; Golubov et al., 2012; Kisgen & Song, 2009; Rajamani et al., 2017) and provide debt financing for firms seeking to complete M&As. Please see Chapter 2 for more detail on the advising role of banks.

Investment bankers can positively impact acquisitions. For example, fairness opinions that provide legal protections can help acquiring firms pay lower premia and increase the likelihood of deal completion (Kisgen & Song, 2009). Further, evidence suggests that a bank's reputation is positively associated with acquisition outcomes. The past performance of financial advisors is predictive of positive returns on acquisitions (Bao & Edmans, 2011), and the reputation of investment banks is associated with faster acquisition completion and higher bidder returns (Golubov et al., 2012). Individual investment bankers are also associated with improved acquisition returns and post-acquisition performance, and acquirers often follow experienced bankers when they switch firms (Chemmanur et al., 2019). Additionally,the network centrality of advisors can positively influence M&A activity (Yawson & Zhang, 2021).

However, banks tend to focus on deal completion over acquirer success (Rau, 2000). Acquirers who obtain whole-bank financing experience large and positive announcement returns, and even partial bank financing can produce positive outcomes (Bharadwaj & Shivdasani, 2003). These positive effects are even higher than cash M&A deals (Huang et al., 2022) and are attributed to banks providing a monitoring role.

Further, advisors can harm acquisition performance when they are vested in the acquisition's completion (Bodnaruk et al., 2009; Lee, 2013). Also, deals are less viable when financial conglomerates have a stake in a target firm (Bodnaruk et al., 2009). Similarly, when acquiring firms repeatedly use an investment bank, there is an increased likelihood that they will overpay for targets (Lee, 2013). For example, AOL relied heavily on investment banks for its advisory services for the Time Warner acquisition and fell victim to the "winner's curse" (Lee, 2013), where the winning bid overpriced the target firm. Overpayment may also occur when an investment bank has a broad reach, as with internationally diversified advisors, and can result in lower announcement returns for bidders (Rajamani et al., 2017). However, evidence suggests that the adverse effects can be mitigated through financial and market incentives for advisors (Rajamani et al., 2017).

Investment banks can enhance M&A outcomes by providing capital, reducing information asymmetries (Reuer et al., 2012), and offering strategic guidance. However, their dual roles as financiers and advisors introduce potential conflicting interests (Kesner et al., 1994). While their involvement can signal deal quality, careful oversight is needed to ensure alignment with long-term value creation.

Institutional Investors

Institutional investors are substantial shareholders who collectively manage capital for their clients, representing 70% of the overall market as of 2017, up from 30% in 1980 (Lewellen & Lewellen, 2022). Institutional investors often own shares in both acquiring and target firms (Matvos & Ostrovsky, 2008; Shi et al., 2021). On average, when institutional investors hold more (less) value in the acquiring firm than in the target firm, acquirers tend to pay lower (higher) acquisition premia (King et al., 2021), though paying a high premium may not destroy value for the acquirer when targets have strategic resources (Laamanen, 2007).

These outcomes have prompted institutional investors to take a more active role in monitoring management and influencing their firms (Agrawal & Mandelker, 1990; Renneboog & Vansteenkiste, 2019). While they can directly influence M&As through target selection (Johan et al., 2013; Ye, 2014) and strategic development (Greenwood & Schor, 2009), monitoring and governance are crucial factors in M&A performance (Bodnaruk et al., 2009; Bruner, 1999; Goranova et al., 2017; Greenwood & Schor, 2009).

The combination of high ownership and interest also offers institutional investors greater access to information (Shi et al., 2021), allowing them to intervene in poorly performing situations to mitigate or reverse the escalation of managers' commitment to bad M&A deals (Bruner, 1999; Sinha et al., 2012). Similarly, monitoring can mitigate extreme gains and losses by curbing executives' risky tendencies (Goranova et al., 2017). As demonstrated by the Volvo-Renault merger, executives' hubris can adversely affect the outcome of a deal. Self-interested CEOs are more likely to pursue riskier M&A transactions, resulting in favorable deals yielding exceedingly high abnormal returns and unfavorable deals causing significant shareholder losses (Goranova et al., 2017).

Beyond governance, institutional investors can directly influence deal structure and outcomes. For example, "dual holders" of both target equity and debt may push for lower acquisition premia (Bodnaruk & Rossi, 2016) with higher premia related to the presence of institutional investors (Moeller, 2005). However, the target ownership of institutional investors can ease the tax burden linked to certain corporate acquisitions (Ayers et al., 2003). Additionally, institutional investors may approve an acquisition at the acquirer's expense if their gain from the target firm offsets expected losses (Shi et al., 2021). Their voting power also plays a role: institutional votes increase the likelihood of deal completion (Iliev et al., 2015) and enhance announcement returns when voting is mandatory (Li et al., 2018). Additionally, they may propose antitakeover amendments to protect their interests (Agrawal & Mandelker, 1990).

Therefore, institutional investors comprise various types of large shareholders that differentially impact the likelihood and performance of M&As. These impacts are direct, indirect, and nuanced depending on culture (Ferreira et al., 2010; Johan et al., 2013), dual ownership of debt and equity (Bodnaruk & Rossi, 2016), investor time-horizon (Gaspar et al., 2005), and the TMT variables, including incentives (Steinbach et al., 2017).

Media

Media refers to various channels that disseminate information to the public, including traditional news outlets, financial press, and social media platforms. Media is ubiquitous, permeating many business areas (e.g., Graf-Vlachy et al., 2020). Acquisitions attract media attention due to their dollar value and often disruptive effects on employees and other stakeholders. Subsequent news coverage can impact M&A performance, with research mainly focusing on stock returns (e.g., Ahern & Sosyura, 2014, 2015; Buehlmaier & Zechner, 2021; Schmidt, 2020) and deal completion (e.g., Liu & McConnell, 2013; Sinha et al., 2012).

Research demonstrates varying effects on the relationship between media coverage and stock returns (e.g., Fang & Peress, 2009). A subsection of this literature considers the impact of media when there are rumors of upcoming M&As. For example, stock prices move in response to media-covered takeover rumors, with takeover rumors held by short-term investors considered more credible and having higher stock returns (Schmidt, 2020). Additionally, firms with broad audience appeal are more likely to receive media coverage of merger rumors, though the rumors are less likely to be true. However, the reduced accuracy of media speculations is not reflected in the stock returns (Ahern & Sosyura, 2015).

Firms may strategically manage media to influence deal dynamics. Positive media coverage can temporarily boost the bidder's stock price, potentially affecting the takeover price (Ahern & Sosyura, 2014). Yet, financial media coverage often leads to underreaction in stock prices, limiting the effectiveness of such strategies (Buehlmaier & Zechner, 2021). Media tone also plays a role in deal completion. Negative coverage following poor stock reactions can reduce the likelihood of a deal closing (Liu & McConnell, 2013). The Air New Zealand-Ansett Australia case illustrates how shifting media sentiment can erode public and stakeholder support, ultimately undermining a deal (Sinha et al., 2012).

The effect of media on M&A outcomes is multifaceted, impacting deals through the publicization of rumors of acquisitions (e.g., Schmidt, 2020), the manipulation of media by firms planning an acquisition (e.g., Ahern & Sosyura, 2014), the media's tone when discussing a potential acquisition (e.g., Liu & McConnell, 2013; Sinha et al., 2012), and the sentiment portrayed via social media (e.g., Yiu et al., 2024). While firms may attempt to leverage media strategically, the unpredictable nature of narratives and conflicting interests make their impact on M&A both powerful and complex.

Private Equity and Venture Capital Firms

Private equity (PE) refers to investment firms that acquire ownership stakes in companies to improve performance and sell via public offering or create value from acquisition activity. Venture capital (VC) firms are PE firms that specialize in funding younger firms, and their reputation similarly confers financial benefits. PE firms were involved in about 30%of all M&A activity in 2021 (Zhang, 2021) and generally increase the value of M&A activity (Acharya et al., 2013). PE firms acquire target firms at lower premia than public firms (Bargeron et al., 2008), and companies experience lower divestment returns when the acquirers are PE firms versus other corporate acquirers (Nary, 2024). However, combining private venture capital (VC) with government VC increases investment (Brander et al., 2015). Further, PE buyouts often create value by relieving financing constraints (Cohn et al., 2022). Additionally, PE-backed acquirers improve operating performance after cross-border acquisitions because their networks effectively mitigate poor information environments (Humphery-Jenner et al., 2017). An essential mechanism for PE firms in driving M&A performance is their reputation (Demiroglu & James, 2010; Nahata, 2008). The reputation of PE firms allows them to influence the financing structure of their acquisitions, particularly for leveraged buyouts, improving pricing and agency costs (Demiroglu & James, 2010).

VC firms serve as a sorting mechanism for quality firms and improve exits through initial public offerings (IPOs) and M&A (Nahata, 2008), particularly when the private firm seeks an acquirer while filing for an IPO in hopes of withdrawing it (Brau et al., 2010). The prominence of a VC firm does not increase a venture's acquisition likelihood, but it enhances the potential of a new venture's IPO (Ragozzino & Blevins, 2016), a choice unrelated to market timing (Ball et al., 2011).

Following the IPO, the reputation of VC firms enhances their performance when the newly public firm announces an acquisition (Arikan & Capron, 2010). This outcome is likely because the market views these VC firms as prestigious. However, when the VC firm is retained as an advisor, the market reacts negatively (Arikan & Capron, 2010). Beyond reputation, the network position of the VC firm also influences its ability to add value to acquired companies (Ozmel et al., 2013; Wang et al., 2022). For example, Gridiron Systems and Carbonite were VC-backed companies offering data storage services. However, Gridiron had increased collaboration with VC partners and was acquired in 2013, whereas Carbonite did not have those relationships with VCs and went public in 2011 (Wang et al., 2022).

Corporate venture capital (CVC), another PE variant, has a mixed impact. It can destroy shareholder wealth in the acquired firm, even as it successfully acquires other entrepreneurial firms (Benson & Ziedonis, 2010). However, CVC experience, through selection and valuation, can increase shareholder wealth (Benson & Ziedonis, 2009, 2010; Yang et al., 2009). The number of previous co-investments also affects the probability of a successful exit, whether through an IPO or acquisition (Bellavitis et al., 2020). Therefore, VC exit pressure can affect new ventures differently (Yao & O'Neill, 2022).

Therefore, private equity, particularly through its venture capital and corporate arms, plays a multifaceted role in M&A. Its influence extends to deal pricing, financing, post-acquisition performance, and exit strategies. While reputation and network strength can drive positive outcomes, the effects of PE involvement vary based on firm type, investment stage, strategic alignment with the target, and underlying conflicting interests. As such, PE continues to be a powerful but nuanced force in shaping M&A performance.

Summary: Conflicting Interests

A common theme in the articles about analysts, banks, institutional investors, the media, and PE firms highlights that each investment community stakeholder plays multiple roles in the effects of M&As on firm value creation. These multifaceted roles can create conflicts of interest within and between members due to ownership stakes, insider information access, and differing time horizons. As we will discuss, these three types of conflicts can benefit or harm M&A value creation.

Conflicts Due to Ownership Stakes

Institutional investors' role in ownership increasingly takes the form of governance (Bodnaruk et al., 2009; Bruner, 1999; Goranova et al., 2017; Greenwood & Schor, 2009) as their overall ownership stake increases. As mentioned, governance includes monitoring and suggesting targets for acquisition (Johan et al., 2013; Ye, 2014), which creates conflicts based on risk and the ownership structure, helping and harming M&A performance (Bu et al., 2024). The acceptable risk level for the TMT differs from that of owners because owners diversify their investments while the TMT members' finances and reputations are tied to the firms in which they work. Additionally, owners can refuse to recognize losses (Ye, 2014), which can negatively affect M&A performance while maintaining their personal financial performance.

Jardine Matheson's cross-shareholding strategy exemplifies how ownership structure can influence M&A performance. Their long-time antitakeover strategy as a holding company relies on cross-shareholding between the holding company and its subsidiaries. Cross-shareholding and maintaining similar board members lead to conflicting interests and erode shareholder value (Jacob & Lucas, 2000).

PE ownership can create conflicts in investment portfolios and compensation structures. Often, PE owners serve as board members of firms they've invested in, which can conflict with their primary obligations to the PE firm. Given their multiple investments, PE owners face conflicts regarding resource allocation, such as time, attention, and finances (Masulis & Nahata, 2011).

Analysts, advisors, and media face similar conflicts if they own shares of the companies they cover. Through biased reporting, they can increase stock prices or make a potential target firm less desirable (Ahern & Sosyura, 2014; Kolasinski & Kothari, 2008). They may also cover both the acquiring and target firms, otherwise influencing their advice.

While conflicts exist within individual investment communities, they can also exist between different stakeholders. These conflicts may stem from efforts to gain personal advantage. For example, Oracle's $9.3B bid to acquire NetSuite in 2016 was supposedly undervalued, according to T. Rowe Price. The concern centered on Larry Ellison, the Chairman of Oracle, who concurrently owned about 40% of NetSuite's shares. Given Ellison's position in both firms, T. Rowe Price argued the deal could not be managed fairly (Greene, 2016). Regardless, the $9.3B deal was completed (Etherington, 2016).

Conflicts Due to Insider Information Access

Institutional investors, banks, and PE firms can influence M&A performance by accessing insider information, which may be used to serve their own interests rather than those of the firm. Additionally, analysts and media members must maintain relationships with the firms they cover, leading them to report more favorably than they might otherwise. Finally, information from the deal may circulate within an investment bank, influencing investment decisions across different departments (Haushalter & Lowry, 2011; Lowry et al., 2019).

There is a similar conflict between each prominent investment community member, stemming from access to insider information. Each stakeholder's networks and network ties allow different access to insider information, with analysts, banks, and media outlets responsible for reporting certain information. Conflicts frequently arise due to the complexity of these network ties, the nature of these relationships, and the parties' respective responsibilities. Additionally, for PE firms, analysts, and media, maintaining one's reputation may come at the expense of the acquiring or target firm, decreasing overall M&A value creation (Demiroglu & James, 2010).

Conflicts Due to Differing Time Horizons

A third type of conflict arises from differing time horizons. While one party may prefer gains or losses in a specific period, that may not optimize M&A outcomes. For institutional investors, this may stem from their unwillingness to recognize losses (Ye, 2014), while for PE firms, it may be that they seek a firm's successful exit through high-value M&A or IPO. Analysts and media may time the release of information to maximize market impact. Further, CEOs with a short-term orientation may be reactive to negative media coverage, potentially influencing future M&A decisions (Gamache & McNamara, 2019). Thus, long-term performance can be sacrificed to bolster short-term performance.

As discussed, some firms or individuals may desire gains or losses in specific periods at the expense of long-term value creation in M&As. While there can be conflicts among institutional investors, there can also be conflicts between institutional investors and PE firms, analysts, banks, and media. It is more likely that the acquiring firm will have a longer time horizon than the target firm so that the conflict will depend on the interests of the acquirer and the target stakeholders.

Discussion

A review of the main investment community stakeholders for M&A reveals that each member plays multiple roles, affecting value creation differently. These various roles create conflicting interests within and between stakeholders. Research in this area has demonstrated the existence of these conflicts and, in some cases, provided quantitative evidence that they impact M&A performance (e.g., Masulis & Nahata, 2011). Below are additional implications for management research, practice, and limitations.

Research Implications

While conflicting interests in investor community stakeholders are recognized, most M&A research disregards them or merely mentions their existence. Much discussion of these conflicts occurs among individual stakeholders, but research has overlooked conflicts between stakeholder groups within the investor community. Yet, conflicts regularly occur and interact to both the success and detriment of acquisitions.

The institutional environment is essential and plays a crucial role in M&As, yet it remains understudied. For example, the government can exert more influence over the media in certain countries, such as China (Borochin & Cu, 2018). This research is vital, as the institutional environment is also likely to impact the conflicting interests within and between stakeholders.

While we acknowledge the ineffectiveness of governance mechanisms due to these conflicting interests, governance and conflicts are likely to interact. Conflicting interests may impede the effectiveness of governance, but they may also facilitate better or more informed governance. Therefore, conflicts may be a two-edged sword for some investor community stakeholders, and associated research questions represent an important line of inquiry.

Managerial Implications

A primary managerial implication from our review is the need for acquiring firms to engage with and manage investor community stakeholders (e.g., Bosse et al., 2022). As shown, each stakeholder contributes to M&A failure and success. While some stakeholders wield more influence, necessitating closer relationships, effective stakeholder management enables managers to navigate the complexity of acquisitions more efficiently. For example, managers must be aware of conflicting interests within and between stakeholders to communicate effectively. Communication can involve implementing governance and ethical guidelines to mitigate these conflicts. Proactively addressing these conflicts can build trust and potentially reduce their harm.

Finally, managers should prioritize long-term value creation. Although stakeholders can achieve personal gain through short-term goals, firms should ultimately focus on long-term value creation, leading to sustainable M&A performance outcomes. Therefore, managers must balance the stakeholders' interests, prioritizing decisions that contribute to the firm's long-term success.

Limitations and Future Research

The primary limitation of our review is that it is not exhaustive, as we focused on the main investor community stakeholders. For example, short sellers are also part of the investor community that impacts acquisitions and their performance (Goranova et al., 2010; Shi et al., 2021). However, limited research is available to summarize investor community stakeholders beyond those in our review. Additional research is needed on the different investor community stakeholders and their relationships with acquisition performance, specifically examining their joint effects.

Additionally, most acquisition research uses samples from the United States (Meglio & Risberg, 2011), and the impact of investor community stakeholders may vary in other institutional environments. For example, banks play a larger role in Germany's economy (Tuschke & Gerrard Sanders, 2003) and therefore may have varying effects on the M&A outcomes.

Future research focused on conflicting interests within and between stakeholders in M&A offers multiple opportunities. Research on ownership stakes and governance by institutional investors or PE firms can be extended to consider the extent to which these institutions are embedded in the acquiring and target firms. Further, what ownership roles are most significant when determining firms for acquisition and subsequent success?

Second, the relationship between access to insider information and stakeholder influence on acquisition performance is an area ripe for further investigation. Different stakeholders may have access to sensitive firm data, with likely disparities in how they use that access to influence the deal outcome and act in their interests. Network ties and business groups may provide an incentive for stakeholders with diverse individual interests to collaborate.

Third, the conflicting interests resulting from stakeholder attention to varying time horizons merit further study. Firms are incentivized to share positive returns in quarterly and annual reports, potentially motivating them to complete a deal to boost returns and report them in a particular report. At the same time, other stakeholders may be focused on a different time horizon. This potential future research agenda could include post-merger performance, a relatively understudied area of M&A performance.

Conclusion

A review of the leading members within the investment community regarding M&As reveals that each stakeholder plays multiple roles, each of which affects M&A value creation differently. Because of the nature of these various roles, conflicting interests are prevalent within and between these same stakeholders due to ownership stakes, access to insider information, and differing time horizons. Associated research indicates that these conflicts exist, and in some cases, it provides quantitative evidence that they impact M&A performance (e.g., Masulis & Nahata, 2011). However, M&A research often disregards these conflicting interests, and some researchers merely mention their existence. Much of the discussion on conflicting interests occurs among stakeholders, but none addresses the conflicts between community members. Our review highlights investor community roles in M&A by capturing existing knowledge and outlining a future research agenda.

Appendix: Literature Search Methodology

Our systematic literature review is on the impacts of five stakeholder groups (analysts, banks, institutional investors, the media, and private equity and venture capital firms) on M&A outcomes. Due to the study of acquisitions across multiple disciplines within business, we searched a cross-section of journals from the Financial Times 50 Journals focused on Management, Economics, and Finance.

The selection of articles for review began by conducting searches on Web of Science and EBSCO ProQuest. In addition to the journal selection, we focused the search using terms related to the topics of interest. Thus, we used the following search terms: *(merger* OR acquisition* OR M&A* OR corporate strateg*)* AND *(stakeholder* OR shareholder* OR institutional investor* OR analyst* OR media* OR venture capital OR private equity OR advisor* OR bank*)*. We did not restrict the publication date of the studies. This resulted in an initial 1956 articles, which both authors assessed to reduce potential bias regarding inclusion in the review. First, we reviewed the abstract of each article to determine whether it empirically studied one of the selected stakeholder groups and its relationship to an M&A performance outcome. We excluded duplicates, conceptual and review papers, papers that did not look at the selected stakeholder groups as moderators or independent variables, and papers that did not have M&A performance as a dependent variable. After a discussion to resolve differences in opinion by the coders, we identified 60 articles to include in the review.

References

*Acharya, V., Gottschalg, O., Hahn, M., & Kehoe, C. (2013). Corporate governance and value creation: Evidence from Private Equity. *Review of Financial Studies, 26*(2), 368–402

*Agrawal, A., & Mandelker, G. (1990). Large shareholders and the monitoring of managers: The case of antitakeover charter amendments. *Journal of Financial and Quantitative Analysis, 25*(2), 143.

*Ahern, K., & Sosyura, D. (2014). Who writes the news? Corporate press releases during merger negotiations. *Journal of Finance, 69*(1), 241–291.

*Ahern, K., & Sosyura, D. (2015). Rumor has it: Sensationalism in financial media. *Review of Financial Studies, 28*(7), 2050–2093.

*Arikan, A., & Capron, L. (2010). Do newly public acquirers benefit or suffer from their pre-IPO affiliations with underwriters and VCs? *Strategic Management Journal, 31*(12), 1257–1289.

*Ayers, B., Lefanowicz, C., & Robinson, J. (2003). Shareholder taxes in acquisition premiums: The effect of capital gains taxation. *Journal of Finance, 58*(6), 2783–2801.

*Ball, E., Chiu, H., & Smith, R. (2011). Can VCs time the market? An analysis of exit choice for venture-backed firms. *Review of Financial Studies, 24*(9), 3105–3138.

*Bao, J., & Edmans, A. (2011). Do investment banks matter for M&A returns? *Review of Financial Studies, 24*(7), 2286–2315

*Bargeron, L., Schlingemann, F., Stulz, R., & Zutter, C. (2008). Why do private acquirers pay so little compared to public acquirers? *Journal of Financial Economics, 89*(3), 375–390.

BBC News. (2016, June 1). *Dell $25bn buyout was underpriced, judge rules*. BBC News. https://www.bbc.com/news/business-36429124

*Becher, D., Cohn, J., & Juergens, J. (2015). Do stock analysts influence merger completion? An examination of postmerger announcement recommendations. *Management Science, 61*(10), 2430–2448.

*Bellavitis, C., Rietveld, J., & Filatotchev, I. (2020). The effects of prior co-investments on the performance of venture capitalist syndicates: A relational agency perspective. *Strategic Entrepreneurship Journal, 14*(2), 240–264.

*Benson, D., & Ziedonis, R. (2009). Corporate venture capital as a window on new technologies: Implications for the performance of corporate investors when acquiring startups. *Organization Science, 20*(2), 329–351.

*Benson, D., & Ziedonis, R. (2010). Corporate venture capital and the returns to acquiring portfolio companies. *Journal of Financial Economics, 98*(3), 478–499.

*Bharadwaj, A., & Shivdasani, A. (2003). Valuation effects of bank financing in acquisitions. *Journal of Financial Economics, 67*(1), 113–148.

*Bodnaruk, A., & Rossi, M. (2016). Dual ownership, returns, and voting in mergers. *Journal of Financial Economics, 120*(1), 58–80.
*Bodnaruk, A., Massa, M., & Simonov, A. (2009). Investment banks as insiders and the market for corporate control. *Review of Financial Studies, 22*(12), 4989–5026.
Borochin, P., & Cu, W. (2018). Alternative corporate governance: Domestic media coverage of mergers and acquisitions in China. *Journal of Banking & Finance, 87*, 1–25.
Bosse, D., Harrison, J., & Hoskisson, R. (2022). Acquisitions, stakeholder economies of scope, and stakeholder orientation. *Strategic Management Review, 3*(1), 35–65.
*Brander, J., Du, Q., & Hellmann, T. (2015). The effects of government-sponsored venture capital: International evidence. *Review of Finance, 19*(2), 571–618.
*Brau, J., Sutton, N., & Hatch, N. (2010). Dual-track versus single-track sell-outs: An empirical analysis of competing harvest strategies. *Journal of Business Venturing, 25*(4), 389–402.
*Bruner, R. (1999). An analysis of value destruction and recovery in the alliance and proposed merger of Volvo and Renault. *Journal of Financial Economics, 51*(1), 125–166.
*Bu, J., Shi, W., & Yin, C. (2024). Type Diversity of Institutional Investors and Opportunistic Acquisitions. *Journal of Management*, 01492063241244716.
*Buehlmaier, M., & Zechner, J. (2021). Financial media, price discovery, and merger arbitrage. *Review of Finance, 25*(4), 997–1046.
*Chemmanur, T., Ertugrul, M., & Krishnan, K. (2019). Is it the investment bank or the investment banker? A study of the role of investment banker human capital in acquisitions. *Journal of Financial and Quantitative Analysis, 54*(2), 587–627.
*Cohn, J., Hotchkiss, E., & Towery, E. (2022). Sources of value creation in private equity buyouts of private firms. *Review of Finance, 26*(2), 257–285.
*Cortes, F., & Marcet, F. (2023). Analysts' connections and M&A outcomes. *Management Science, 69*(7), 4108–4133.
Dell, Inc. v. Magnetar Global Event Driven Master Fund Ltd., 177 A.3d 1 (Del. 2017).
*Demiroglu, C., & James, C. (2010). The role of private equity group reputation in LBO financing. *Journal of Financial Economics, 96*(2), 306–330.
Etherington, D. (2016, July 28). Oracle buys enterprise cloud services company NetSuite for $9.3B. TechCrunch. https://techcrunch.com/2016/07/28/oracle-buys-enterprise-cloud-services-company-netsuite-for-9-3b/
Fang, L., & Peress, J. (2009). Media coverage and the cross-section of stock returns. *Journal of Finance, 64*(5), 2023–2052.

*Ferreira, M., Massa, M., & Matos, P. (2010). Shareholders at the gate? Institutional investors and cross-border mergers and acquisitions. *Review of Financial Studies, 23*(2), 601–644.

*Gaspar, J., Massa, M., & Matos, P. (2005). Shareholder investment horizons and the market for corporate control. *Journal of Financial Economics, 76*(1), 135–165.

Gamache, D. L., & McNamara, G. (2019). Responding to bad press: How CEO temporal focus influences the sensitivity to negative media coverage of acquisitions. *Academy of Management Journal, 62*(3), 918-943.

*Golubov, A., Petmezas, D., & Travlos, N. (2012). When it pays to pay your investment banker: New evidence on the role of financial advisors in M&As. *Journal of Finance, 67*(1), 271–311.

Goranova, M., Dharwadkar, R., & Brandes, P. (2010). Owners on both sides of the deal: Mergers and acquisitions and overlapping institutional ownership. *Strategic Management Journal, 31*(10), 1114–1135.

*Goranova, M., Priem, R., Ndofor, H., & Trahms, C. (2017). Is there a "Dark Side" to monitoring? Board and shareholder monitoring effects on M&A performance extremeness. *Strategic Management Journal, 38*(11), 2285–2297.

Graf-Vlachy, L., Oliver, A., Banfield, R., König, A., & Bundy, J. (2020). Media coverage of firms: Background, integration, and directions for future research. *Journal of Management, 46*(1), 36–69.

Greene, J. (2016). *T. Rowe price to oppose Oracle's deal to acquire NetSuite; investment firm sees conflict of interest in existing ties between companies.* Dow Jones & Company Inc. https://www.proquest.com/blogs-podcasts-websites/t-rowe-price-oppose-oracles-deal-acquire-netsuite/docview/1817200052/se-2

*Greenwood, R., & Schor, M. (2009). Investor activism and takeovers. *Journal of Financial Economics, 92*(3), 362-375.

*Haushalter, D., & Lowry, M. (2011). When do banks listen to their analysts? Evidence from mergers and acquisitions. *Review of Financial Studies, 24*(2), 321–357.

*Huang, S., Lu, R., & Srinivasan, A. (2022). Bank dependence and bank financing in corporate M&A. *Management Science, 68*(3), 2250–2283.

*Humphery-Jenner, M., Sautner, Z., & Suchard, J. (2017). Cross-border mergers and acquisitions: The role of private equity firms. *Strategic Management Journal, 38*(8), 1688–1700.

*Iliev, P., Lins, K., Miller, D., & Roth, L. (2015). Shareholder voting and corporate governance around the world. *Review of Financial Studies, 28*(8), 2167–2202.

Jacob, R., & Lucas, L. (2000, May 10). Investors plot to weaken fortress jardine walls: Fund managers say cross-holdings erode value: [London edition].

Financial Times. https://www.proquest.com/newspapers/investors-plot-weaken-fortress-jardine-walls-fund/docview/249028510/se-2
*Johan, S., Knill, A., & Mauck, N. (2013). Determinants of sovereign wealth fund investment in private equity vs public equity. *Journal of International Business Studies, 44*(2), 155–172.
Kesner, I., Shapiro, D., & Sharma, A. (1994). Brokering mergers: An agency theory perspective on the role of representatives. *Academy of Management Journal, 37*(3), 703–721.
King, D., Wang, G., Samimi, M., & Cortes, A. (2021). A meta-analytic integration of acquisition performance prediction. *Journal of Management Studies, 58*(5), 1198–1236.
*Kisgen, D., & Song, W. (2009). Are fairness opinions fair? The case of mergers and acquisitions. *Journal of Financial Economics, 91*(2), 179–207.
*Kolasinski, A., & Kothari, S. (2008). Investment banking and analyst objectivity: Evidence from analysts affiliated with mergers and acquisitions advisors. *Journal of Financial and Quantitative Analysis, 43*(4), 817–842.
Laamanen, T. (2007). On the role of acquisition premium in acquisition research. *Strategic Management Journal, 28*(13), 1359–1369.
*Lee, J. (2013). Dancing with the enemy? Relational hazards and the contingent value of repeat exchanges in M&A markets. *Organization Science, 24*(4), 1237–1256.
Lewellen, J., & Lewellen, K. (2022). Institutional investors and corporate governance: The incentive to be engaged. *Journal of Finance, 77*(1), 213–264.
*Li, K., Liu, T., & Wu, J. (Julie). (2018). Vote avoidance and shareholder voting in mergers and acquisitions. *Review of Financial Studies, 31*(8), 3176–3211.
Liu, B., & McConnell, J. (2013). The role of the media in corporate governance: Do the media influence managers' capital allocation decisions? *Journal of Financial Economics, 110*(1), 1–17.
Lowry, M., Rossi, M., & Zhu, Z. (2019). Informed trading by advisor banks: Evidence from options holdings. *Review of Financial Studies, 32*(2), 605–645.
*Masulis, R., & Nahata, R. (2011). Venture capital conflicts of interest: Evidence from acquisitions of venture-backed firms. *Journal of Financial and Quantitative Analysis, 46*(2), 395–430.
*Matvos, G., & Ostrovsky, M. (2008). Cross-ownership, returns, and voting in mergers. *Journal of Financial Economics, 89*(3), 391–403.
Meglio, O., & Risberg, A. (2011). The (mis) measurement of M&A performance—A systematic narrative literature review. *Scandinavian Journal of Management, 27*(4), 418–433.
*Moeller, T. (2005). Let's make a deal! How shareholder control impacts merger payoffs. *Journal of Financial Economics, 76*(1), 167–190.
*Nahata, R. (2008). Venture capital reputation and investment performance. *Journal of Financial Economics, 90*(2), 127–151.

*Nary, P. (2024). Do corporations benefit from divesting to private equity acquirers? An empirical investigation. *Strategic Management Journal*, *45*(10), 2122–2158.

*Ozmel, U., Robinson, D., & Stuart, T. (2013). Strategic alliances, venture capital, and exit decisions in early stage high-tech firms. *Journal of Financial Economics*, *107*(3), 655

*Ragozzino, R., & Blevins, D. (2016). Venture–backed firms: How does venture capital involvement affect their likelihood of going public or being acquired? *Entrepreneurship Theory and Practice*, *40*(5), 991–1016.

*Rajamani, A., Van Der Poel, M., De Jong, A., & Ongena, S. (2017). The international diversification of banks and the value of their cross-border M&A advice. *Management Science, 63*(7), 2211–2232.

*Rau, P. R. (2000). Investment bank market share, contingent fee payments, and the performance of acquiring firms. *Journal of Financial Economics, 56*, 293–324.

Renneboog, L., & Vansteenkiste, C. (2019). Failure and success in mergers and acquisitions. *Journal of Corporate Finance, 58*, 650–699.

*Reuer, J., Tong, T., & Wu, C. (2012). A signaling theory of acquisition premiums: Evidence from IPO targets. *Academy of Management Journal, 55*(3), 667–683.

*Schmidt, D. (2020). Stock market rumors and credibility. *Review of Financial Studies*, *33*(8), 3804–3853.

Seal, D. (2023). *Salesforce Profit Outlook Buoys Software Maker Against Activist Investors; The company's elimination of an M&A committee also helps propel a sharp rally in stock price*. Dow Jones & Company Inc.

Shi, W., King, D., & Connelly, B. (2021). Closing the deal: Managerial response to short sellers following M&A announcement. *Journal of Business Research, 130*, 188–199.

*Sinha, P., Inkson, K., & Barker, J. (2012). Committed to a failing strategy: Celebrity CEO, intermediaries, media and stakeholders in a co-created drama. *Organization Studies*, *33*(2), 223–245.

*Steinbach, A., Holcomb, T., Holmes, R., Devers, C., & Cannella, A. (2017). Top management team incentive heterogeneity, strategic investment behavior, and performance: A contingency theory of incentive alignment. *Strategic Management Journal*, *38*(8), 1701–1720.

*Tehranian, H., Zhao, M., & Zhu, J. (2014). Can analysts analyze mergers? *Management Science*, *60*(4), 959–979.

Tuschke, A., & Gerard Sanders, W. (2003). Antecedents and consequences of corporate governance reform: The case of Germany. *Strategic Management Journal*, *24*(7), 631–649.

*Wang, D., Pahnke, E., & McDonald, R. (2022). The past is prologue? Venture-Capital syndicates' collaborative experience and start-up exits. *Academy of Management Journal, 65*(2), 371–402.

*Yang, Y., Narayanan, V., & Zahra, S. (2009). Developing the selection and valuation capabilities through learning: The case of corporate venture capital. *Journal of Business Venturing, 24*(3), 261–273.

*Yao, T., & O'Neill, H. (2022). Venture capital exit pressure and venture exit: A board perspective. *Strategic Management Journal, 43*(13), 2829–2848.

*Yawson, A., & Zhang, H. (2021). Central hub M&A advisors. *Review of Finance, 25*(6), 1817–1857.

*Ye, P. (2014). Does the disposition effect matter in corporate takeovers? Evidence from Institutional Investors of target companies. *Journal of Financial and Quantitative Analysis, 49*(1), 221–248.

*Yiu, D., Wan, W., Chen, K., & Tian, X. (2024). A theory of host country sentiments: An illustration in cross-border acquisitions. *Academy of Management Journal, 67*(4), 1024–1054.

Zhang, H. (2021). Private equity now accounts for 30% of M&A activity. *Institutional Investor*. https://www.institutionalinvestor.com/article/b1v9ssw2f2tl0w/Private-Equity-Now-Accounts-for-30-of-M-amp-A-Activity

Suppliers in Mergers and Acquisitions

Christina Öberg

Suppliers in Mergers and Acquisitions

Synergies related to purchasing, cost-cutting, and supply coordination are described as important outcomes of many mergers and acquisitions (M&A; Bauer & Friesl, 2024; Chaturvedi & Weigelt, 2024; Larsson & Finkelstein, 1999; Zaheer et al., 2013). However, the opportunities for upstream improvements extend far beyond the transactional arrangement of purchasing more for less. Suppliers play a critical role in firms' sourcing strategies, knowledge-sharing, co-development efforts, and the processes through which supply chains evolve into value-creating offerings (e.g., Chen et al., 2024; Lambert & Enz, 2017; Scholten & Schilder, 2015; Wieland, 2020).

Despite this, research on the supplier-side dynamics of M&A remains surprisingly limited. M&A are often viewed as vehicles for achieving synergies, but their effects on other aspects of supplier side of operations are rarely examined in depth. This chapter intends to address this gap by exploring three key dimensions: (1) suppliers' position relative

C. Öberg (✉)
Linnaeus University, Kalmar, Sweden
e-mail: christina.oberg@lnu.se

D. R. King and A. Bansal (eds.), *Navigating Stakeholder Dynamics Surrounding Acquisitions*,
https://doi.org/10.1007/978-3-032-03199-0_4

to the M&A parties which addresses risks and opportunities related to suppliers, (2) their role, ranging from simple sources of supply in transactional exchanges to active co-creators and co-developers in relational interactions, and (3) the short- and long-term effects of M&A on their operations.

To shortly elaborate on these dimensions, *positions* relate to potential overlaps, complementarities, and whether suppliers become redundant as the acquirer's or acquired firm's businesses compete with them. Overlaps describe situations where the M&A parties indeed buy from the same supplier, complementarities when suppliers are not shared before the M&A, but procurement indeed could be integrated past it. *Roles* refer to suppliers' importance for the M&A parties, and whether they partake in co-creational activities or only appear as quite replaceable suppliers of standardized goods or services. *Short- and long-term effects* denote how initial synergies may have long-term consequences for development and offerings, and converse.

The purpose of this chapter is *to provide an overview of the effects of M&A on suppliers*, focusing on cases where suppliers remain external stakeholders—or potentially redundant stakeholders—after the M&A[1]. This perspective does not exclude the impacts of vertical M&A, as parallel suppliers to an acquired supplier may also be affected by such M&A (Laussel, 2008), as may upstream suppliers (i.e., suppliers' suppliers). The chapter addresses the following topics:

- Present research on suppliers in M&A. This is based on as *Web of Science* search for suppliers in M&A, resulting 100 journal articles. Of these, a lion part dealt with acquired suppliers, and were thereby excluded, with only 41 articles raising potential questions of interest when investigating suppliers in relation to M&A.
- *Supplier positions:* Various types of supplier changes and synergies related to acquirers' and acquired parties' upstream overlaps, complementarities and competition: This includes examining how

[1] While acquired suppliers are undoubtedly affected by M&A, their status as owned entities makes them controllable units. In such cases, cost reductions are achieved as efficiencies, rather than negotiated price reductions, and the long-term effects are related to integration and governance. These issues are well-covered in research on synergies and sourcing decisions, often framed by the recurring "make or buy" question (e.g., Lei & Hitt, 1995).

overlaps in business operations between the acquiring and acquired firms, along with their strategic intentions and procurement integration, affect suppliers. It includes whether the acquisition is upstream or downstream relative to such suppliers.

- *Supplier roles:* Effects on supplier connections, including interdependencies, negotiation powers, collaborative efforts, and supplier reactions. For suppliers, significant risks arise when a major customer (i.e., the acquiring or acquired firm) is involved in M&A. These risks include: (a) The possibility of being excluded if the acquiring party consolidates supply sources; (b) A reduction in negotiation power; and (c) The introduction of new strategies, such as preferred supplier agreements, which may bring in new competitors or reduce demand, even if the supplier had previously served one or both M&A firms. Conversely, some suppliers may benefit from becoming the chosen provider, increasing their supply across the acquiring and acquired firms. Each outcome has implications for ongoing collaborations, knowledge exchanges, and the quality of future deliveries.
- *Short- and long-term effects* highlighting specifically the missing perspective in past research on the long-term effects on co-developments and co-creation related to suppliers, integrations and their reactions. This includes how suppliers, as relational stakeholders, develop strategies to mitigate negative changes while contributing to the development of offerings. It emphasizes the dual role of suppliers as stakeholders who actively participate in co-development projects and co-creation initiatives, while also serving as negotiation counterparts for achieving short-term synergies through cost reductions and procurement integration, highlighting the inherent tension between short-term gains and the long-term contributions of suppliers.

The contributions of this chapter address the broader gap in M&A research regarding suppliers. By discussing suppliers who remain external to the acquirer and acquired firm post-M&A, the chapter not only highlights practical and strategic concerns but also introduces theoretical perspectives into the M&A field (cf. Angwin et al., 2023), through integrating M&A research with discussions from the marketing, supply chain, and innovation literature.

The chapter is structured as follows: After this introduction, an overview of previous research on suppliers in M&A is presented. This is followed by a discussion on the outlined dimensions of: suppliers' positions, roles, and long-term effects, integrating insights from prior M&A research with perspectives on transactional and relational exchanges, as well as ecosystem perspectives (Agarwal & Kapoor, 2023; Schriber & Meglio, 2024; Shipilov & Gawer, 2019). For additional discussion of acquisitions and ecosystems, please see Chapter 10. This chapter concludes with final remarks and suggestions for future research directions.

Research on Suppliers in M&A

As previously stated, research on suppliers in M&A is limited, a point underscored by the Web of Science search yielding only 41 relevant articles. Most studies focus on synergies related to improved deals, larger batch purchases, cost reductions, and negotiation efficiency—primarily addressing how the acquirer and acquired party integrate their procurement processes (Carlton & Israel, 2011; Mills, 2010; Olcay et al., 2019; Rahman & Lambkin, 2015) Additionally, research emphasizes the internalization of upstream sourcing parties through backward vertical integration in M&A (Chen et al., 2017; Öberg, 2012b; Shenoy, 2012), a perspective purposefully excluded from this chapter. These studies largely overlook the role of suppliers who remain external parties following M&A.

To provide a brief overview of past research on suppliers in M&A, with such suppliers remaining external to the M&A following it, Moatti et al. (2015) explore how horizontal M&A affect bargaining power with suppliers in the short term, comparing this to organic growth, which provides better long-term efficiency. Zhu and Westphal (2021) highlight how acquiring firms leverage bargaining power by selecting parties based on strategic positioning rather than simply creating a larger entity. Chae et al. (2022) argue for considering entire supply chains in M&A, showing how structural equivalence in supplier networks enhances M&A performance. Similarly, Pei and Song (2025) emphasize the importance of evaluating the value of parties across the acquired firm's supply chain to achieve post-M&A efficiencies. Lan et al. (2019) demonstrate supplier and retailer preferences in retail chains, showing that suppliers may perceive M&A among retailers as advantageous. Yang-Sun et al. (2024) examine how M&A reshape supply base structures, affecting performance.

Other studies provide nuanced perspectives on supplier dynamics. Hunold and Werner (2024) investigate firms' willingness to purchase from rivals partially owned by suppliers, while Kadner-Graziano (2024) examines whether suppliers face pre-M&A constraints or gain pricing leverage post-M&A. We can thus see how suppliers play a part related to M&A performance, and how the recent literature seems to suggest more of a holistic perspective on supply chains, rather than referring to direct suppliers only. Suppliers may at times benefit from an acquisition, but increased market power from M&A may not persist long term.

Anderson et al. (2001) problematize the consequences of M&A on business relationships, showing changes ranging from confined adjustments to complete disruptions. However, their study—and subsequent work by Anderson et al. (2012)—does not distinguish between suppliers and customers, despite the differing synergy objectives for each. For suppliers, the focus is often on cost reductions and coordinated supply, while for customers, the aim is generally to expand offerings, increase revenues, and strengthen branding (e.g., Chaturvedi & Weigelt, 2024; Wang et al., 2024). This creates an upstream asymmetry in business relationship dynamics that these studies do not acknowledge.

Chakkol et al. (2018) show, in line with Anderson et al. (2001), how business relationships cannot be taken for granted following M&A. More precisely, Chakkol et al. (2018) indicate how the social capital embedded in the business connections cannot be acquired. Continuing a relational view related to suppliers, Öberg and Holtström (2006) explore how horizontal M&A may prompt upstream supplier M&A (or vice versa) as firms respond to shifts in power dynamics or aim to secure preferred supplier status (cf. Öberg, 2012a). Relatedly, Zhu et al. (2016) highlight how power changes in supply chains trigger reactions from vertical parties. Li (2019) provides an example of collaborative purchasing as a response to supplier M&A, illustrating an alternative example of the M&A contagiousness described by Öberg and Holtström (2006), as business partners would react and respond to changes. Boehm and Sonntag (2023) show that relationship dissolution risks are higher following related vertical M&A (i.e., where the M&A parties are part of the same supply chain or engage in operations where they could have been so based on the businesses they pursue) than unrelated ones, while Kanter (2009) links supplier distress to M&A outcomes, drawing parallels to employee and customer reactions.

Wei and Clegg (2018) connect supplier-oriented resources to integration speed, and Chang and Yen (2017) emphasize the importance of repeated M&A in consolidating supply chain positions. From an ecosystem perspective, Laussel (2008) demonstrates how independent suppliers (i.e., firms not supplying to either of the M&A parties but effectively being competitors to their suppliers) benefit when M&A reduce supplier competition, leading to higher prices and profits. Domnenko and Sibley (2023) further explore pricing dynamics, showing how vertically integrated firms may lead or follow rivals in pricing games, depending on their M&A involvement.

Although fragmented, the literature underscores how acquirers strategize in relation to suppliers—whether through negotiations, supply chain integration, or changes brought about by M&A. The inclusion of supply-chain or supplier network analyses in due diligences become vital, as Pei and Song (2025) point out. The literature though also describes reactions and responses to M&A, which stretch beyond the suppliers of the acquirer and acquired firm, where such reactions would be connected to changed competition in vertical M&A and changed power-balances in horizontal M&A. There are the exclusion effects that follow from competitive situations or undermined power. There are also those where suppliers try to regain positions or negotiation powers through M&A.

Overall, the literature not only approaches suppliers from diverse perspectives and with different ontological underpinnings, but it also provides some varied glimpses of suppliers in M&A. The general impression is though that of M&A parties treating suppliers as negotiation parties to obtain short-term gains, where such suppliers would have direct competitors, and the M&A parties thereby can use its power or the fact that they now buy higher volumes and thereby can expect better prices. This leaves aspects of long-term and relational effects largely aside, as well as the problematization of suppliers relative the position of the acquirer and acquired firm.

Extending Perspectives on Suppliers in M&A—Position, Role, and Time

Based on the fragmentation in past research, while also then foremost focusing on synergy gains related to suppliers, this section adds perspective though discussing suppliers relative the M&A parties in terms of (1) their positions—affected by whether the M&A is horizontal or vertical, but also how the M&A parties' supply overlaps; (2) their roles where a supplier may provide a firm with highly customized, integrated solutions, or with standard goods at spot market prices; and 3) the long-term effects as the M&A may change co-creational balances or even interrupt supplier connections based on reactions or based on the hunt for short-term gains. Combined, this extends the discussion on suppliers related to M&A into notions on suppliers as depicted in research on marketing, supply chains and innovation, see Table 1.

Suppliers' Position Relative M&A Parties

The positioning of suppliers in M&A thus relates to potential overlaps, complementarities, and whether suppliers risk becoming redundant due to competition with the acquirer's or acquired firm's businesses. A supplier's relative position determines how the M&A parties can strategize toward it. When Boehm and Sonntag (2023) advocate that risks are higher for relationship dissolution following related vertical M&A, than when unrelated M&A are pursued, this is what they tackle: It reflects how supplier impacts are influenced by the degree of operational or supply overlap between the acquirer and acquired firm. If no overlap exists, the gains for M&A parties in relation to suppliers are minimal. Conversely, overlapping businesses may share a similar supplier base—or one that differs geographically—leading to varied opportunities or limitations for supplier integration and operational efficiencies.

Positioning also involves a power dimension. Before the M&A, the acquirer or acquired party may hold a favorable position as a customer in an asymmetric dependency with the supplier (cf. Casciaro & Piskorski, 2005). Imbalances in size or bargaining power (cf. Porter, 1980) may already exist or emerge following the M&A. Considering these dynamics, we can envision the following scenarios:

A. *Unrelated M&A with non-overlapping and non-complementary suppliers:* In these cases, supplier bases neither overlap nor complement one another. The primary impact for suppliers stems from the potential creation of a financially stronger combined entity. This new entity might decide to leverage its size to negotiate better terms for either firm, such as improved pricing or priority status. Suppliers face minimal risks compared to other types of M&A, though they may still face redundancies or worse contract conditions. It is

Table 1 Summary of suppliers in M&A

Dimension	*Type*	*Concerns*	*Strategies*
Position	Unrelated M&A with non-overlapping and non-complementary suppliers	Limited supplier risks Limited efficiency gains related to procurement	Use power of larger party Generic suppliers (general consultancy, for instance) possible to integrate
	Horizontal M&A with overlapping suppliers	Suppliers risk lowered margins, albeit potentially higher volumes	Coordinate procurement between acquirer and acquired firm for efficiency gains and bargaining power
	Horizontal M&A with complementary suppliers	Supplier redundancy or order expansion	Procurement coordination
	Upstream vertical integration with potentials of the acquired party being or becoming a supplier to the acquirer	Risks for acquired firm losing customers Risk for suppliers becoming redundant. Potential for larger orders for acquired firm's suppliers, but also stricter governance	Internalization of supply
	Downstream vertical integration, where the acquisition challenges the acquired firm's suppliers	Competing suppliers to acquired firm risk losing ground Extended supply from acquirer's suppliers	Acquirer becomes supplier to acquired firm
Role	Transactional suppliers	Direct supplier affected by price cuts, redundancy, replaceability	Push for price reductions, coordinated supply
	Relational suppliers	Risks of long-term, knowledge and critical resource losses if integrated Supplier reactions reversing expected effects	Retaining suppliers due to unique knowledge, products, and skills
Time	Short-term	Long-term consequences of suppliers' being affected overlooked	Efficiency and cost cuts
	Long-term	Loss of knowledge and unique capabilities	Suppliers' responding strategies

here important to distinguish between whether the operations of the acquirer and acquired firm are non-related or if their supplier bases are. Even an unrelated M&A may involve common suppliers, particularly for transactional goods or services of a more generic nature, such as auditing, consulting, and general equipment (see further below). A notable example of such an acquisition is when the Swedish car manufacturer Volvo acquired the pharmaceutical company Pharmacia in the 1980s, illustrating an extreme case of conglomerate M&A. In such cases, corporate level consultancies of the acquired firm would likely be replaced by those of the acquirer, while suppliers of raw material, equipment, and inventory would remain unaffected.

B. *Horizontal M&A with overlapping suppliers:* Horizontal M&A involving overlapping suppliers enables the acquirer and acquired firm to coordinate procurement processes. This can yield efficiency gains and provide stronger bargaining power for better prices (not least if the number of alternative customers is low, Porter, 1980), improved services, and preferential treatment from suppliers. Suppliers may benefit from increased order sizes and coordinated deliveries, improving efficiency. However, they risk reduced revenues if lower prices per unit erode margins. The net impact on suppliers depends on the tradeoff between price reductions and operational efficiency gains. Generally, domestic acquisitions among manufacturing firms within the same business niche—such as the announced merger between Nissan and Honda—tend to dominate this category, offering significant potential for supplier integration.

C. *Horizontal M&A with complementary suppliers:* When suppliers are complementary, existing suppliers face risks of redundancy or opportunities for expanded orders. Integration of supplier bases would likely involve procurement coordination, enhancing the combined firm's negotiating position. This would result in suppliers being evaluated against one another, with some winning larger contracts and others losing entirely. Even for successful suppliers, this evaluation process may involve inviting new competitors, as the focus on supplier assessment opens the door for alternatives. Consequently, the process may interrupt relationships even for seemingly successful suppliers. In cases such as the Nissan-Honda merger, suppliers that do not overlap but provide similar components may face comparison and subsequent redundancy, as the merging firms seek to identify the most reliable, efficient, or cost-effective supplier.

D. *Upstream vertical integration with potentials of the acquired party being or becoming a supplier to the acquirer:* Vertical integration introduces scenarios where the acquired firm becomes or already is a supplier to the acquirer. This reduces reliance on external suppliers, internalizing supply within the M&A. For external suppliers, this can result in lost market share, while the acquired supplier may lose external customers if the acquirer competes with them. Additionally, there are broader effects on the acquired supplier's upstream suppliers, as the acquirer might impose new preferences, sustainability practices, or supply-chain management policies (e.g., Fontana et al., 2021; Qiao et al., 2024). These changes may manifest as larger orders, supplier abandonments, or stricter governance requirements. Ford Motor Company's 1961 acquisition in 1961 of Autolite, a producer of batteries and spark plugs, is an example of an upstream acquisition that allowed the company to streamline its supply chain while reducing its reliance on external suppliers. Suppliers' suppliers would likely have benefitted from this internalization, while the acquirer's competing suppliers would have risked losing ground.

E. *Downstream vertical integration, where the acquisition challenges the acquired firm's suppliers:* This situation mirrors upstream vertical integration. In this case, though, the acquirer may begin supplying, increase its supply, or outperform the acquired firm's existing suppliers. If the acquirer controls the integration, the impact on competing suppliers may be more significant than in reverse vertical integration. As with upstream vertical integration, these effects can also extend to the acquirer's suppliers, who may benefit from increased demand.

Past research shows that a strong acquirer in vertical M&A can interrupt market pricing mechanisms, potentially impacting suppliers beyond direct suppliers and thereby their competitors (Laussel, 2008). Vertical M&A, therefore, has ripple effects across the supply chain, influencing upstream and downstream parties, as well as to competing suppliers, creating wider ecosystem impacts. Meanwhile, horizontal M&A would have greater potential to affect their supplier bases, with downstream advantages if cost cuts are pushed forward, while indirect, suppliers'

suppliers upstream may experience pressure for price reductions, thus pointing at a supply-chain orientation of ecosystem pressure and advantages.

In summary, the position of suppliers in M&A influences their treatment, risks, and opportunities. Supplier outcomes vary based on the degree of overlap, complementarity, and power dynamics, as well as whether the M&A involves horizontal or vertical integration. This dimension shapes how suppliers may be evaluated, integrated, or displaced in the post-M&A situation.

Supplier Roles Relative M&A Parties

The relational view on M&A emphasizes the interdependencies between firms and their business partners (Clegg et al., 2022; Dyer & Singh, 1998; Hallén et al., 1991). These interdependencies are characterized by mutual adjustments, customized offerings, co-creation, and the co-development of innovations—developments that often manifest over the long term (Ford & Håkansson, 2006), along with their associated consequences of M&A. In contrast, research focused on price cuts and negotiation power reflects a more transactional orientation to suppliers. This perspective highlights immediate effects, such as reduced supplier numbers and enhanced bargaining power.

Although the relational and transactional orientations toward suppliers can be interpreted as purely ontological concepts—which they fundamentally are—real-life supplier connections exist along a continuum. This continuum is shaped by factors such as what the supplier delivers, their strategic importance to the firm, their substitutability, and their capacity to influence customers (in this case, the M&A parties). For example, office supplies are typically transactional purchases, as are standardized raw materials bought at world-market prices. Further, digitalization has heightened transparency and reduced transaction costs, making services increasingly platform- coordinated rather than relationally negotiated (Geissinger et al., 2021; Xu et al., 2021). Even when relational arrangements exist, not all suppliers play an equally critical role in the buyer's (here: the M&A parties') operations.

Recognizing the diverse roles of suppliers in M&A allows for a nuanced understanding of how different suppliers are affected based on their positions and their roles in relation to the acquirer or acquired firm. Supplier reactions also vary in magnitude, depending on these roles.

A. *Transactional suppliers:* For suppliers of standardized goods or transactional services, M&A parties would assumably push for price reductions or consolidate orders to benefit from volume discounts. These suppliers are typically substitutable, meaning M&A parties can switch suppliers unless they dominate the market and manipulate prices. Coordinated procurement and larger batch orders enable efficiencies and cost reductions, with limited upstream or ecosystem effects beyond suppliers trying to push their suppliers for price cuts, in turn. Most consequences for transactional suppliers though occur directly between the supplier and the M&A parties, with minimal ripple effects on competitors or other suppliers.

   Upstream effects (suppliers' suppliers) may present themselves as the acquirer and acquired party would easily coordinate across if the goods and services are shared between the parties, and some suppliers are abandoned for shared ones, also leading to more or less need for supply upstream the supply chain.

B. *Relational suppliers:* At the other end of the continuum, interdependencies between M&A parties and suppliers create distinct consequences. Relational arrangements often involve co-creational activities and ongoing adjustments between the supplier and buyer (Chen et al., 2024; Ranjan & Read, 2016). These suppliers are not easily replaceable due to their unique knowledge, inventory, manufacturing capabilities, and tacit knowledge embedded in social connections (cf. Chakkol et al., 2018). This specificity makes them integral to their customers' operations, and the rationale for retaining such suppliers often lies in these embedded relational ties (Öberg, 2010).

   Even in such scenarios, acquirers may opt to integrate suppliers between the acquirer and the acquired firm. While this approach may yield efficiencies, it poses risks of knowledge loss and interruption of customized offerings, as both immediate and latent effects. Replacing specific products and services often requires re-adjustments, potentially forcing the acquirer and acquired firm to modify their operations. In vertical M&A, if the adjusting supplier is not the one acquired, the risk of losing critical knowledge and downstream advantages increases.

Relational suppliers face significant challenges when their customers undergo M&A. They may struggle to replace lost business partners, lose shared knowledge, and encounter difficulties finding new buyers for their customized solutions. For M&A parties, relational suppliers represent both value and vulnerability, requiring careful consideration during integration.

An intriguing contrast emerges between studies adopting a relational view and those emphasizing transactional dynamics in M&A. Studies that examine how M&A can prompt subsequent M&A or lead to coordinated supply to counterbalance increased power from horizontal M&A tend to adopt a more relational perspective (Li, 2019; Öberg & Holtström, 2006). These studies highlight the long-term interplay of interdependencies and strategic reactions across the supply chain, while the gains of negotiations would fundamentally relate to more transactional suppliers.

The Long-Term Perspective

While past literature on M&A often focuses on synergies such as lowered supply costs, quantity discounts, and increased negotiation power (Chaturvedi & Weigelt, 2024; Perkins & Shekhar, 2024), suppliers are typically treated indirectly, with an emphasis on short-term gains. However, a relational view on supplier relationships underscores the long-term consequences of M&A, which extend beyond immediate cost savings.

Cost reductions, discounts, and increased negotiation power may persist over time, but they are likely to influence and be influenced by changes in supplier operations. From a supplier's perspective, decreased revenues resulting from reduced per-unit payments could incentivize strategies aimed at regaining importance, establishing stronger relational ties, and bolstering their position of power. To adapt to such strategies, suppliers might: (1) Offer integrated solutions to deepen customer relationships and customer dependency (e.g., Chaudhary et al., 2022; Davies, 2003); (2) Focus on value-based offerings to justify higher prices and create differentiation (e.g., Vargo & Lusch, 2004); (3) Take on upstream responsibilities, such as sustainability compliance (Andersson et al., 2023; Gimenez & Tachizawa, 2012); or 4) Cost-cutting measures with their own suppliers or squeezing their own suppliers for compliance requirements (Fontana et al., 2021). These strategies reflect how suppliers may actively navigate the challenges posed by M&A, rather than passively absorbing its consequences.

Other types of effects relate to relational arrangements, where the M&A, emphasized by the integration of procurement and coordination of supply, would not only have short-term effects and create supplier reactions, but also have long-term consequences. This is not least related to the knowledge and adjustments enmeshed into the business relationships. As part of such adjustments and based on the related knowledge, co-development and co-creational aspects emerge. These may consist of attempts to improve the relationship between the parties, but also include new or improved offerings, innovation, and shared activities toward other parties. Hence, the lost knowledge if relational arrangements are interrupted due to cost-saving ambitions, may harm the capital built into the relational arrangements and decrease accumulated knowledge, and output in terms of new inventions. For instance, car manufacturers' reliance on suppliers for solutions is influenced by strategies such as replacing suppliers, which can impact their knowledge development. Moreover, downstream customers may experience changes to their offerings while these are not intended. Platform-based business models that rely on suppliers for service provision (e.g., in the sharing economy) or development (e.g., open-innovation platforms) may find that short-term efficiency gains achieved by pressuring suppliers can lead to reduced quality of supply, decreased innovation or a decline in overall innovativeness over time.

Is it all then negative? Like any type of change, it is often experienced as negative when not initiated or decided by a party. Changes are, namely, rarely desirable unless a party initiates them or is part of developing them, causing aspects beyond the supplier–buyer relationship. Meanwhile, for more radical ideas to emerge, new energy and input is generally needed (Story et al., 2014). Hence, changes to supplier connections may well make ground for developments that benefit the acquirer and acquired firm, as well as their downstream customers. However, looking only for reduced costs, if knowledge is enmeshed into the supplier relationships, is risky for the long-term development of the relationship and for ideas to emerge from it, regardless whether suppliers are changed or retained.

To capture the benefits of M&A, firms should carefully balance short-term goals of cost efficiency with long-term strategic considerations. This involves assessing not just the transactional benefits of cost reductions but also the relational value that suppliers bring. Maintaining a nuanced perspective can ensure that changes to supplier relationships drive innovation and long-term growth, rather than inadvertently harming the firm's ecosystem and downstream customers.

Discussion

By juxtaposing the dimensions outlined in Table 1 and comparing them to the limited past research on suppliers in M&A (see the section"Research on suppliers in M&A"), we can begin to recognize that the focus has primarily been on short-term effects, with the assumed integration of procurement often considered effective. More specifically, the asymmetry between customers and suppliers in terms of integration suggests a focus on integrating toward suppliers while keeping customer relationships separate (e.g., Chaturvedi & Weigelt, 2024; Wang et al., 2024), unless the acquisition involves highly valued brands (e.g., Homburg & Bucerius, 2005; Umashankar et al., 2022). Bargaining power is repeatedly emphasized in the literature (Domnenko & Sibley, 2023; Kadner-Graziano, 2024; Moatti et al., 2015; Zhu & Westphal, 2021), positioning suppliers in M&A as negotiation counterparts rather than as long-term stakeholders in co-creational activities. As a result, the dual role of suppliers as negotiation counterparts and co-creational stakeholders is largely overlooked, even though this duality can manifest simultaneously—linked to both short- and long-term perspectives and partially to the transactional or relational roles of suppliers. Meanwhile, there is also a complexity when discussing supplier relationships, as firms respond to M&A by leveraging their power (Li, 2019; Öberg & Holtström, 2006; Zhu et al., 2016), while also nurturing existing relationships.

By differentiating among positions, roles and short- and long-term effects, a multilayered understanding of suppliers in M&A emerges, based on firms' reliance on, negotiation power with, and co-creation alongside them. These perspectives, which are not well-covered in past research introduce an increased understanding of suppliers, but also complementary ontologies to past M&A research.

More specifically, the relational view serves both a framework to differentiate suppliers based on their substitutability versus interdependence—depending on the type and importance of the products or service they provide—and as a theoretical perspective that captures the interconnectedness within supply chains and supplier networks (cf. Chae et al.,

2022; Laussel, 2008; Pei & Song, 2025). Recognizing interdependencies and co-creational activities is crucial, as short-term benefits gained from pressuring suppliers may lead to long-term detrimental effects. Such actions can damage knowledge-sharing and co-creational processes, and provoke adverse supplier reactions (Chakkol et al., 2018), outweighing the initial advantages.

While outlined as three dimensions (position, role, and time), various combinations of these create the reality of suppliers in M&A, thereby envisioning three-dimensional aspects of suppliers, see Fig. 1. This means that for each M&A and each supplier, different combinations emerge: M&A parties would have both transactional and relational suppliers, some of which overlapping, others complementary or unrelated, where the horizontal or vertical nature of the M&A addressing different supplier effects.

Meanwhile, based on the chapter, we can envision a connection between relational suppliers and long-term consequences, and transactional suppliers and short-term gains. The replaceable, transactional supplier creates opportunities of squeezing the supplier for lower prices,

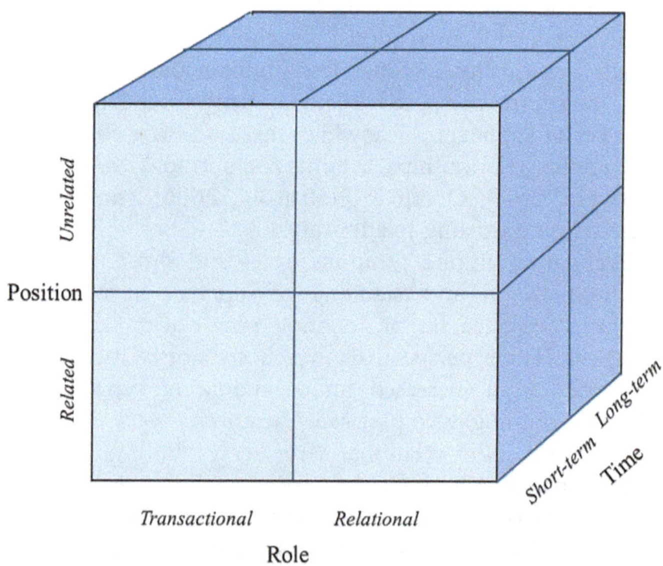

Fig. 1 Dimensions of suppliers in M&A

for instance, following from coordinated supply and increased negotiation power, with the supplier position (the extent of pre-M&A power and whether suppliers are unrelated, complementary, and overlapping in horizontal or vertical M&A) affecting action spaces. The transactional character of the supplier minimizes risks of knowledge losses and co-creational activities would per definition be non-existent. Meanwhile, the relational supplier comes with potential long-term effects—reactions, knowledge losses, etc.—not least if short-term gains are attempted. Here the position of complementary or overlapping suppliers creates the bigger opportunity for efficiency gains but at long-term costs. Playing with these connections, we can also start to consider the thought of long-term effects related to transactional suppliers and short-term ones related to relational suppliers, raising questions also along the line of time frame and ontology.

Research Implications

By addressing dimensions of relational suppliers, long-term consequences and customized offerings, co-creation, and the co-development of innovations between M&A parties and suppliers, and integrating them with existing M&A research, the chapter contributes to a literature base that has not extensively focused on suppliers. When supplier-related issues have been studied, they often present a fragmented view rooted in differing theoretical foundations and research foci. This chapter adds perspectives to this, while also structuring across dimensions of position, role, and time. Exploring these perspectives prompts reflections on the temporal aspects and ontological nature of suppliers, suggesting that the impact of M&A strategies on suppliers extends beyond immediate financial outcomes to encompass broader considerations of collaboration and innovation. An important outcome is the introduced tension between suppliers and co-creational stakeholders and negotiation counterparts, but also between the short-term gains and long-term consequences.

Practical Implications

As outlined, suppliers should be evaluated in light of how M&A affects competition (in vertical M&A) and whether the M&A involves overlapping supplier bases or complementary ones (in horizontal M&A). Additionally, suppliers should be assessed based on their roles in terms of: (1) Their *replaceability*: How easily can they be substituted?; (2) Their *value contribution*: How would integration affect knowledge, expertise, or other values that the acquirer or acquired firm derives from their offerings?; and (3) Their *specificity*: How tailored are their goods or services to the needs of the parties involved?

Suppliers with more relational ties to the acquirer or acquired firm also require consideration in terms of their role in future developments, such as innovation, co-creation, and potential risks if they are replaced. Existing research shows that unrelated M&A generally causes the least interruptions for suppliers (Boehm & Sonntag, 2023), and the dimensions discussed here help to clarify why this is the case.

Beyond direct suppliers, ecosystem considerations are important (Schriber & Meglio, 2024), where the shape of the ecosystem would be dependent on the positions of parties relative each other, as certain conditions would primarily include up- and downstream supply-chain implications, while others would be oriented to substitutes and competitors. The chapter emphasizes the interconnectedness of suppliers with the acquiring and acquired firms and highlights how different types of M&A—whether vertical, horizontal, or unrelated—impact the ecosystem. By providing a structured approach to evaluating supplier positions and roles, the chapter offers a tool for predicting and managing supplier-related risks and opportunities in M&A contexts.

Ideas for Further Research

This chapter highlights that past research on suppliers in relation to M&A parties is both limited and fragmented, opening several avenues for future investigation. The matrix of short- and long-term effects, combined with the spectrum of supplier relationships ranging from transactional or replaceable to strategic partnerships, provides multiple dimensions for further exploration. Future studies could compare across these dimensions or focus on specific conditions to gain more nuanced insights.

In today's context, trends such as reshoring and internalizing upstream supply chains to reduce risk are becoming increasingly prominent. Simultaneously, the ongoing digital and artificial intelligence revolution is reshaping business models, introducing hyper-connectivity, and, paradoxically, fostering disconnection in some areas. These developments significantly affect the nature of supplier connections in M&A and present timely opportunities for research with both theoretical and practical relevance.

Existing literature offers a variety of theoretical perspectives on suppliers, focusing on topics such as supply chains, supplier networks, bargaining power, co-creational innovation, and more. These perspectives reflect diverse ontological approaches and define distinct boundaries for studying suppliers. Integrating M&A research into these broader frameworks, while emphasizing interdisciplinarity and acknowledging the unique contributions of M&A literature, creates an exciting platform for addressing complex and pressing research questions.

This chapter aspires to spark interest in further research on the effects of M&A on suppliers, their roles, and their positions within the broader ecosystem. By exploring these dimensions and their intersection with contemporary trends, future studies can make meaningful contributions to both academic understanding and practical applications in the evolving landscape of M&A.

Conclusion

This chapter provides an overview of the effects of M&A on suppliers. It does so through discussing suppliers' positions and roles, and the short- and long-term effects of M&A. In doing so, the chapter shows the complexity of suppliers in M&A, indicates several gaps in present research, while providing sorting tools to better understand suppliers in M&A, ontologically as well as practically.

References

Agarwal, S., & Kapoor, R. (2023). Value creation tradeoff in business ecosystems: Leveraging complementarities while managing interdependencies. *Organizational Science, 34*(3), 1216–1242.

Anderson, H., Havila, V., & Salmi, A. (2001). Can you buy a business relationship? - On the importance of customer and supplier relationships in acquisitions. *Industrial Marketing Management, 30*(7), 575–586.

Anderson, H., Holtström, J., & Öberg, C. (2012). Do competition authorities consider business relationships? *Journal of Business to Business Marketing, 19*(1), 67–92.

Andersson, S., Svensson, G., Otero-Neira, C., Laurell, H., Lindgren, J., & Karlsson, N. (2023). Sustainable development considerations in supply chains: Firms' relationships with stakeholders in their business sustainability practices-A triangular comparison. *Business Strategy and the Environment, 32*(4), 1885–1899.

Angwin, D., Kroon, D., Mirc, N., Oliveira, N., Prashantham, S., Rouzies, A., & Tienari, J. (2023). Mergers and acquisitions research: Time for a theory rejuvenation of the field. *Long Range Planning, 56*(6), Article 102398.

Bauer, F., & Friesl, M. (2024). Synergy evaluation in mergers and acquisitions: An attention-based view. *Journal of Management Studies, 61*(1), 37–68.

Boehm, J., & Sonntag, J. (2023). Vertical integration and foreclosure: Evidence from production network data. *Management Science, 69*(1), 141–161.

Carlton, D., & Israel, M. (2011). Proper treatment of buyer power in merger review. *Review of Industrial Organization, 39*(1–2), 127–136.

Casciaro, T., & Piskorski, M. (2005). Power imbalance, mutual dependence, and constraint absorption: A closer look at resource dependence theory. *Administrative Science Quarterly, 50*(2), 167–199.

Chae, S., Son, B., Yan, T., & Yang, Y. (2022). Supply chains and the success of M&As: Investigating the effect of structural equivalence of merging firms' supplier and customer bases. *International Journal of Operations & Production Management, 42*(8), 1272–1293.

Chakkol, M., Finne, M., Raja, J., & Johnson, M. (2018). Social capital is not for sale: a supply network perspective on mergers and acquisitions. *Supply Chain Management-an International Journal*, *23*(5), 377–395.

Chang, H., & Yen, W. (2017). WPG holdings: Electronic integration of supply chain network. *Asian Case Research Journal, 21*(1), 207–230.

Chaturvedi, T., & Weigelt, C. (2024). Operating synergy and post-acquisition integration in corporate acquisitions: A resource reconfiguration perspective. *Long Range Planning, 57*(3), Article 102428.

Chaudhary, S., Dhir, A., Gligor, D., Khan, S., & Ferraris, A. (2022). Paradoxes and coping mechanisms in the servitisation journey. *Industrial Marketing Management, 106*, 323–337.

Chen, P., Xu, H., & Zou, X. (2017). The effects and incentive of vertical mergers: An analysis from the view of OM. *European Journal of Operational Research, 263*(1), 158–172.

Chen, Y., Chan, H., & Cai, Z. (2024). Towards a theoretical framework of co-development in supply chains: Role of platform affordances and supply chain relationship capital. *Journal of Business & Industrial Marketing, 39*(5), 1029–1045.

Clegg, S., da Cunha, J. V., & Cunha, M. (2022). Management paradoxes: A relational view. *Human Relations*, *55*(5), 483–503.

Davies, A. (2003). Integrated solutions, the changing business of systems integration. In A. Prencipe, A. Davies & M. Hobday (Eds.), *The business of systems integration*. Oxford University Press.

Domnenko, G., & Sibley, D. (2023). Simulating vertical mergers. *Review of Industrial Organization, 62*(2), 99–118.

Dyer, J., & Singh, H. (1998). The relational view: Cooperative strategy and sources of interorganizational competitive advantage. *Academy of Management Review, 23*(4), 660–679.

Fontana, E., Öberg, C., & Poblete, L. (2021). Nominated procurement and the indirect control of nominated sub-suppliers: Evidence from the Sri Lankan apparel supply chain. *Journal of Business Research, 127*, 179–192.

Ford, D., & Håkansson, H. (2006). The idea of interaction. *The IMP Journal, 1*(1), 4–27.

Geissinger, A., Laurell, C., & Öberg, C. (2021). Copycats among underdogs - Echoing the sharing economy business model. *Industrial Marketing Management, 96*, 287–299.

Gimenez, C., & Tachizawa, E. (2012). Extending sustainability to suppliers: A systematic literature review. *Supply Chain Management, 17*(5), 531–543.

Hallén, L., Johanson, J., & Seyed-Mohamed, N. (1991). Interfirm adaptation in business relationships. *Journal of Marketing, 55*, 29–37.

Homburg, C., & Bucerius, M. (2005). A marketing perspective on mergers and acquisitions: How marketing integration affects postmerger performance. *Journal of Marketing, 69*(1), 95–113.

Hunold, M., & Werner, V. (2024). Foreclosure and profit shifting with partial vertical ownership. *Journal of Economics & Management Strategy*. https://doi.org/10.1111/jems.12621

Kadner-Graziano, A. (2024). Vertical mergers without foreclosure. *Journal of Economics & Management Strategy, 34*(2), 593–611.

Kanter, R. (2009). Mergers that stick. *Harvard Business Review, 87*(10), 121-+.

Lambert, D., & Enz, M. (2017). Issues in supply chain management: Progress and potential. *Industrial Marketing Management, 62*, 1–16.

Lan, Y., Yan, H., Ren, D., & Guo, R. (2019). Merger strategies in a supply chain with asymmetric capital-constrained retailers upon market power dependent trade credit. *Omega-International Journal of Management Science, 83*, 299–318.

Larsson, R., & Finkelstein, S. (1999). Integrating strategic, organizational, and human resource perspectives on mergers and acquisitions: A case survey of synergy realization. *Organizational Science, 10*(1), 1–26.

Laussel, D. (2008). Buying back subcontractors: The strategic limits of backward integration. *Journal of Economics & Management Strategy, 17*(4), 895–911.

Lei, D., & Hitt, M. (1995). Strategic restructuring and outsourcing - The effect of mergers and acquisitions and LBOs on buiilding firm skills and capabilities. *Journal of Management, 21*(5), 835–859.

Li, L. (2019). Cooperative purchasing and preactive inventory sharing - Channel balancing and performance improvement. *European Journal of Operational Research, 278*(3), 738–751.

Mills, D. (2010). Buyer power and industry structure. *Review of Industrial Organization, 36*(3), 213–225.
Moatti, V., Ren, C., Anand, J., & Dussauge, P. (2015). Disentagling the performance effects of efficiency and bargaining power in horizontal growth strategies: An empirical investigation in the global retail industry. *Strategic Management Journal, 36*(5), 745–757.
Öberg, C. (2010). What happened with the grandiose plans? Strategic plans and network realities in B2B interaction. *Industrial Marketing Management, 39*, 963–974.
Öberg, C. (2012a). Mergers and acquisitions as embedded network activities. *European Journal of International Management, 6*(4), 421–441.
Öberg, C. (2012b). Network effects of upstream acquisitions of innovative firms. *The IMP Journal, 6*(1), 52–68.
Öberg, C., & Holtström, J. (2006). Are mergers and acquisitions contagious? *Journal of Business Research, 59*(12), 1267–1275.
Olcay, G., Öner, M., & Olcay, A. (2019). A conceptual view of exergy destruction in mergers and acquisitions. *Technological Forecasting and Social Change, 143*, 336–352.
Pei, X., & Song, J. (2025). Directors with supply chain experience as heterogeneous network pipes: How does it affect M&A efficiency. *Asia-Pacific Journal of Business Administration, 17*(1), 1–22.
Perkins, J., & Shekhar, S. (2024). Horizontal mergers and supplier power. *Review of Industrial Organization, 64*(4), 533–548.
Porter, M. (1980). *Competitive strategy: Techniques for analyzing industries and competitors*. Free Press.
Qiao, J., Li, S., & Capaldo, A. (2024). Why and how do suppliers develop environmental management capabilities in response to buyer-led development initiatives? *Supply Chain Management: An International Journal, 29*(7), 112–134.
Rahman, M., & Lambkin, M. (2015). Creating or destroying value through mergers and acquisitions: A marketing perspective. *Industrial Marketing Management, 46*, 24–35.
Ranjan, K., & Read, S. (2016). Value co-creation: Concept and measurement. *Journal of Academy of Marketing Science, 44*(3), 290–315.
Scholten, K., & Schilder, S. (2015). The role of collaboration in supply chain resilience. *Supply Chain Management, 20*(4), 471–484.
Schriber, S., & Meglio, O. (2024). An ecosystem perspective of acquisition outcomes: a research agenda. In *A research agenda for mergers and acquisitions* (pp. 199–218). Edward Elgar Publishing.
Shenoy, J. (2012). An examination of the efficiency, foreclosure, and collusion rationales for vertical takeovers. *Management Science, 58*(8), 1482–1501.

Shipilov, A., & Gawer, A. (2019). Integrating research on inter-organizational networks and ecosystems. *Academy of Management Annals, 14*(1), 92–121.

Story, V., Daniels, K., Zolkiewski, J., & Dainty, A. (2014). The barriers and consequences of radical innovations: Introduction to the issue. *Industrial Marketing Management, 43*(8), 1271–1277.

Umashankar, N., Bahadir, S. C., & Bharadwaj, S. (2022). Despite efficiencies, mergers and acquisitions reduce firm value by hurting customer satisfaction. *Journal of Marketing, 86*(2), 66–86.

Vargo, S., & Lusch, R. (2004). Evolving to a new dominant logic for marketing. *Journal of Marketing, 68*, 1–17.

Wang, Y., Rajagopalan, N., Yue, L., & Wu, B. (2024). The entry-deterring effects of synergies in complementor acquisitions: Evidence from Apple's digital platform market, the iOS app store. *Strategic Management Journal, 45*(13), 2791–2817.

Wei, T., & Clegg, J. (2018). Strategic resources: A missing role in understanding integration speed in international acquisition. *Thunderbird International Business Review, 60*(3), 411–426.

Wieland, A. (2020). Dancing the supply chain: Toward transformative supply chain management. *Journal of Supply Chain Management, 57*(1), 58–73.

Xu, Y., Hazee, S., So, K., Li, K., & Malthouse, E. (2021). An evolutionary perspective on the dynamics of service platform ecosystems for the sharing economy. *Journal of Business Research, 135*, 127–136.

Yang-Sun, Y., Chae, S., Yan, T., & Linderman, K. (2024). Consolidate? Diversify? Post-M&A supply base structural changes and operational performance. *Decision Sciences, 56*(2), 171–192.

Zaheer, A., Castañer, X., & Souder, D. (2013). Synergy sources, target autonomy, and integration in acquisitions. *Journal of Management, 39*(3), 604–632.

Zhu, D., & Westphal, J. (2021). Structural power, corporate strategy, and performance. *Strategic Management Journal, 42*(3), 624–651.

Zhu, J., Boyaci, T., & Ray, S. (2016). Effects of upstream and downstream mergers on supply chain profitability. *European Journal of Operational Research, 249*(1), 131–143.

Customers as Stakeholders to Mergers and Acquisitions

Sina Amiri and Nicholas Beadles

Introduction

Mergers and acquisitions (M&As) are strategic tools companies use to achieve various objectives, including growth, increased market share, diversification, and enhanced competitiveness (Cartwright & Schoenberg, 2006). M&A research has predominantly focused on financial and operational aspects, such as shareholder value creation, cost synergies, financial performance, and integration challenges; however, the impact of M&As on customers, who are vital for long-term business sustainability and profitability, has often been overlooked (Das & Kapil, 2012; Haleblian et al., 2009; Meglio & Risberg, 2011; Umashankar et al., 2022). Customers are pivotal to acquisitions as research has shown that reaching a larger market base through entering new product or geographic markets, and maintaining customer loyalty are significant acquisition motives (Mandl et al., 2000). Customers are key stakeholders whose perceptions and

S. Amiri (✉) · N. Beadles
Georgia College & State University, Milledgeville, Georgia
e-mail: sina.amiri@gcsu.edu

N. Beadles
e-mail: nick.beadles@gcsu.edu

D. R. King and A. Bansal (eds.), *Navigating Stakeholder Dynamics Surrounding Acquisitions*,
https://doi.org/10.1007/978-3-032-03199-0_5

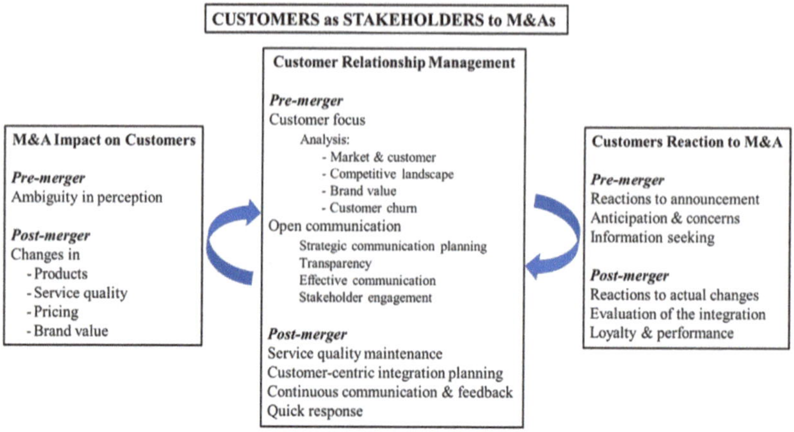

Fig. 1 Customers as stakeholders to M&A

behaviors can significantly influence the success or failure of an M&A (Öberg, 2014a). Negative customer reactions, such as decreased satisfaction, reduced loyalty, and customer churn, can erode revenue streams and undermine the intended benefits of the transaction. We address this gap by synthesizing the existing research on the role of customers. It examines how M&As affect customer satisfaction, loyalty, and behavior across the pre-merger and post-merger phases, it discusses effective management strategies, and identifies directions for future research. As Fig. 1 demonstrates, viewing customers as an integral stakeholder, this study discusses the impact of M&As on customers, customers reactions, and appropriate stakeholder relationship management strategies over the pre-merger and post-merger phases.

The Impact of M&As on Customers

This section explores the impact of M&As on customers across the pre-merger, defined as the period spanning through the deal is finalized, including due diligence, announcement, and everything happened in between, and post-merger integration (PMI) phases. Understanding these potential impacts is crucial for developing effective customer management strategies.

Pre-merger Phase

The pre-merger phase, encompassing due diligence and public announcement, sets the stage for customer perceptions and reactions. While direct operational changes affecting customers are typically minimal during this time, the anticipation of change can have significant effects. Poor implementation of the pre-merger process could delay deal settlement and extend the post-acquisition integration phase, leading to raised uncertainty among customers, and eventually losing them, which in turn can result in acquisition failure (Teerikangas et al., 2011). The elevated uncertainty around the acquisition announcement could turn disruptive to customer relationship, and thus, harmful to the market share (Rogan & Greve, 2015), while customer retention is essential to the thriving of the combined firms following a merger (Homburg & Bucerius, 2005). Thorbjornsen and Dahlen (2011) posit acquisition announcement can form negative perceptions among customers regarding undesirable changes in brand's identity, products, or marketing, that can result in customers' devaluation of the brand, or increased switching intentions.

Conversely customer focus during the pre-acquisition phase can elevate customers' perceptions and satisfaction. For instance, choosing the right acquisition target enables companies to obtain complementary resources needed to improve customer focus. Firms, through establishing effective interactions, can find about their customers' needs, and accordingly, pick appropriate acquisition targets. For example, Cisco acquired Crescendo in 1993 to meet the interests of Boeing and Ford, two of its major customers, in an attempt to continue winning their businesses (Brueller et al., 2014).

Moreover, M&As can significantly alter the competitive dynamics of the market, leading to changes in market concentration and competitive rivalry with implications for antitrust regulations, regulatory scrutiny, prices, and reactions of competitors (Schriber et al., 2022). Kato and Schoenberg (2012) argue that M&As can disrupt established relationships, create uncertainty, and lead to changes in service quality, pricing, and other factors that influence customer loyalty. Will the M&A reduce competition, potentially leading to price increases or reduced product variety? This anticipation can create customer anxiety, impact customers' perception of the merged entity's market power, and prompt customers to consider alternative providers.

Finally, the retention of customers and employees are interrelated as employees establish relations with customers during their tenure, and long-tenured employees' turnover can have a negative impact on customer retention (Sandhya & Kumar, 2011). Thus, there is a potential spillover effect of pre-merger mismanagement of the relationships of distinct stakeholders, customers, and employees.

Therefore, there is ambiguity in the pre-acquisition phase, and customers are mainly concerned about possible negative impacts of changes in product offerings, service quality, pricing, branding, and overall customer experience (Alvarez-Gonzalez & Otero-Neira, 2020; Mari & Meglio, 2021; Öberg et al., 2011; Öberg, 2022). Customer orientation, or the extent to which the merged entity maintains a strong customer focus is crucial to address customers' concerns in the pre-merger stage, and can help to avoid customer attrition. Major strategies to improve customer focus will be discussed later in this study.

Post-merger Integration (PMI) Phase

The PMI phase is where the impact on customers becomes tangible. Even though acquisitions conventionally pursue synergies and cost reductions, they often reduce customer satisfaction (Umashankar et al., 2022). For example, due to the ambiguity in customer ownership in the aftermath of the acquisition, customers may receive inconsistent information from different sources, leading to their confusion and frustration (Öberg, 2009). The changes inherent to the integration process can become disruptive to customer loyalty (Alvarez-González & Otero-Neira, 2023). Therefore, careful integration planning and execution are essential to minimize disruption, maximize customer value, and realize the strategic objectives of the M&A.

Changes in product offerings. PMI often leads to product rationalization, integration, or discontinuation. This can cause significant dissatisfaction if valued products are removed or if integration is poorly executed (Capron & Shen, 2007; Mitchell & Singh, 1993). Communicating these changes clearly, providing suitable alternatives, and managing the transition process effectively can mitigate negative reactions. Conversely, successful integration can lead to enhanced product offerings through the combination of complementary products or technologies, offering customers a wider range of choices, improved functionality, and potentially leading to innovation (Teece, 2010). This requires careful product portfolio management and a focus on customer needs and market trends.

Service quality integration. Integrating customer service operations is a significant post-merger challenge. Maintaining or improving service quality is crucial for customer retention (Bitner et al., 2008; Payne & Frow, 2005; Schweiger & Denisi, 1991). This requires careful integration of customer relationship management (CRM) systems, service processes, customer service staff training, and service delivery channels. Potential issues include inconsistent service standards, longer wait times, difficulties in resolving customer issues due to fragmented systems or processes, and cultural clashes between service teams. Service blueprinting and process mapping can be valuable tools for identifying and addressing potential integration challenges. Managing employee integration and its impact on service delivery is also a key consideration (Stahl & Voigt, 2008).

Pricing strategies post-merger. Pricing strategies need careful consideration post-merger. Harmonizing prices while considering market dynamics, cost structures, customer perceptions, and competitive pressures is important (Nagle et al., 2023; Shapiro, 1989). Simply averaging prices or adopting the higher price can lead to customer dissatisfaction and potentially trigger regulatory scrutiny. A more strategic approach involves analyzing price elasticity, customer value perceptions, cost synergies, and competitive pricing strategies to determine optimal pricing strategies that maximize profitability while minimizing customer churn. Dynamic pricing strategies may also be considered in certain contexts (Elmaghraby & Keskinocak, 2003).

Brand management and integration. Post-merger brand management decisions, such as brand consolidation, rebranding, or co-branding, directly impact customer perceptions and loyalty (Keller, 2016). These decisions should be based on a thorough understanding of brand equity, customer preferences, and the strategic objectives of the M&A. A poorly executed rebranding can alienate loyal customers, damage brand value, and create confusion in the market. Managing stakeholder expectations, including those of customers, is a key challenge during this process (Mitchell et al., 1997).

In summary, the impacts of M&As on customers can be distinguished between the pre-merger (due diligence/announcement) and PMI phases. During the pre-merger phase, key considerations revolve around understanding the combined customer base, assessing the altered competitive landscape, evaluating brand equity, and anticipating potential customer churn. These analyses inform strategic decisions regarding market positioning, pricing, brand management, and customer retention strategies post-merger. The post-merger phase brings these considerations to fruition, with tangible changes in product offerings, service quality, pricing strategies, and brand management influencing customer perceptions and behaviors directly. Effective management of these elements during both phases is crucial for minimizing disruption and maximizing customer value, ultimately contributing to the success of the M&A. Failing to adequately address these customer-related aspects can lead to negative consequences such as customer dissatisfaction, churn, and damage to brand reputation.

Customer Reactions to M&As

Customer reactions to mergers and acquisitions are complex and multifaceted, ranging from indifference to strong positive or negative responses (Öberg, 2014a). These reactions are crucial because they directly impact customer retention, loyalty, and ultimately, the success of the M&A (Thorbjornsen & Dahlen, 2011). This section examines how customer reactions evolve during the pre-merger and post-merger phases.

Pre-merger (Due Diligence/Announcement) Phase

As discussed earlier, the announcement of a merger or acquisition often creates uncertainty and anticipation among customers, driving customer reactions, and affecting acquisitions (Meglio & Park, 2019). For example, research indicates that customers can influence the acquisition decision, i.e., whether or not to acquire, or the method of payment (Cheng et al., 2022). In this phase, initial perceptions shape among customers, setting the stage for the post-merger relationships.

Initial reactions to the announcement. The initial announcement of M&A can trigger immediate customer reactions, often driven by uncertainty and speculation (Dutton & Dukerich, 1991; Gioia & Thomas, 1996). Media coverage, analyst reports, social media discussions, and public discourse can significantly influence these initial perceptions. Customers may react based on their prior experiences with M&As in general, or with the specific companies involved (Meyer & Schwager, 2007). Companies need to be prepared to address immediate concerns and provide accurate, consistent information in order to manage the narrative. The speed and method of communication are crucial here; a well-crafted initial message can help to frame the M&A in a positive light (Argenti, 2009).

Anticipation and concerns. Customers may anticipate changes in product offerings, service, and pricing, leading to concerns about potential negative impacts. These concerns may be based on past experiences with similar M&As, industry trends, or general anxieties about change (Ashforth & Mael, 1989). For example, customers might worry about price increases due to reduced competition, a decline in service quality due to integration challenges, or the discontinuation of favorite products (Öberg, 2022). This influences customers' value perception, i.e., their assessment of the trade-off between perceived benefits and costs (Zeithaml, 1988).

Information seeking. Customers may actively seek information about the M&A and its potential implications for them (Schenkel & Teigland, 2008). This information-seeking behavior can be driven by a need to reduce uncertainty, assess potential risks, and make informed decisions about their future relationship with the merged entity. This can involve visiting company websites, searching online news sources, engaging in social media discussions, contacting customer service, or relying on word-of-mouth (Mangold & Faulds, 2009). Proactive information management can help to shape customer perceptions and mitigate negative rumors (Heath, 2006).

Post-merger Integration (PMI) Phase

The post-merger phase is when customer reactions become more concrete, based on their direct experiences with the integrated entity. This is the critical period for managing customer relationships and ensuring long-term loyalty, a time wherein customer focus can facilitate an effective integration process that enhances responsiveness to market needs (Riviezzo, 2013).

Reactions to actual changes. Customers react to the actual changes implemented during the PMI. These reactions are based on their experiences with the integrated products, services, and brand. If the changes are perceived as positive, such as improved product features, enhanced service offerings, or more competitive pricing, customers may react favorably, leading to increased satisfaction and loyalty. However, if the changes are perceived as negative, such as reduced product quality, declining service standards, or higher prices, customers may become dissatisfied and consider switching to competitors (Reichheld, 1996; Thorbjornsen & Dahlen, 2011). Customers with greater bargaining power, e.g., customers on which the revenue of the firm is more dependent, are more likely to exercise their right of switching to competitors (Cheng et al., 2022). For example, the Warner Bros. Discovery merger of its HBO MAX and Discovery + in 2023 that restructured both services by dropping several less profitable films and shows without sufficient explanations, and rebranding as MAX, resulted in frustration and confusion among customers, driving strong negative reactions widely reflected in the press (Murphy, 2025).

Evaluation of the integration process. Customers are active participants in the integration process whose actions, assumptions, and arguments shape integration decisions and outcomes (Öberg, 2018). Meglio et al. (2017) provide evidence that customer interests and expectations can influence integration speed; while faster integration benefits quicker realization of synergies, it can be harmful to customer relationship. Customers evaluate the smoothness and effectiveness of the integration process (Marks & Mirvis, 2011). Disruptions in service, communication breakdowns, poorly integrated systems, or inconsistent customer experiences can lead to negative reactions, even if the ultimate changes are perceived as beneficial. If customers experience difficulties navigating a newly merged website or encounter inconsistencies in customer service interactions, they are likely to become frustrated and dissatisfied. For example, Elon Musk's acquisition of Twitter and rebranding it to X in 2022, led to a chaotic integration involving series of controversial policy changes, inconsistent enforcements, layoffs, and insufficient communication, resulting frustration and loss of trust among users (Davis, 2023).

Long-term impact on loyalty and performance. The long-term impact on customer loyalty and behavior depends on how well the M&A is managed from a customer perspective. If communication is consistent and transparent and customer concerns are addressed effectively, the M&A can strengthen customer relationships, increase loyalty, and even attract new customers. Research finds customer loyalty and customer retention are key post-merger value drivers, associated with increased financial performance and market valuation to the merged entity in long-term (Degbey, 2015; Gupta & Lehmann, 2003; Swaminathan et al., 2014). In addition, loyal customers are more willing to cooperate with the new entity and share their knowledge about critical issues, such as market trends, or competitive landscapes, a significant source of value creation (Degbey & Pelto, 2021). On the contrary, ignoring customer concerns, poor communication, or poor execution of the integration can lead to customer churn, damage long-term profitability, and negatively impact brand reputation. This has negative effects on employee morale and retention (Schweiger & DeNisi, 1991). For example, had the JetBlue and Spirit Airlines merger been not blocked due to the antitrust regulations, it could have triggered backlash among customers who were concerned with hiking air ticket prices, drawing long-term negative consequences for JetBlue (Raymond et al., 2024).

In summary, this section has explored the dynamic nature of customer reactions to M&As across the pre-merger and post-merger phases. In the pre-merger phase, customer reactions are primarily driven by anticipation and uncertainty surrounding the impending changes. Initial reactions to the announcement, anticipated concerns about potential negative impacts on products, services, and pricing, and active information-seeking behaviors characterize this period. Effectively managing communication and addressing customer concerns during this phase is crucial for shaping initial perceptions. The post-merger phase sees customer reactions shift from anticipation to direct experience. Customers react to the actual changes implemented during integration, evaluating the smoothness of the process and its effect on their relationship with the merged entity. The long-term impact on customer loyalty and behavior hinges on how well companies manage this transition, addressing concerns, maintaining service quality, and delivering on promised value. Ignoring customer reactions during either phase can have detrimental consequences for customer retention and the overall success of the M&A.

Managing Customer Concerns in M&As

Managing customer concerns is paramount to a successful M&A. A proactive and strategic approach, spanning both the pre-merger and post-merger phases, is essential for mitigating negative reactions and maintaining customer loyalty. This section outlines key strategies for managing customer concerns during these critical periods.

Pre-merger (Due Diligence/Announcement) Phase

Effective customer relationship management begins well before the official closing of the acquisition, and this study recognizes two major strategies emerging from the existing research: (1) customer focus, and (2) open communication. The customer focus strategies are as follows:

Market and customer analysis. A thorough market and customer analysis is crucial (Barney & Hesterly, 2020; Hitt et al., 2017). This extends beyond simply combining existing customer databases. It involves a deep dive into customer demographics, psychographics, purchasing behavior, loyalty patterns, customer lifetime value (CLV), and profitability, enabling firms to develop appropriate post-merger strategies (Porter, 1985) and proactively manage customer expectations throughout the process (Alvarez-Gonzalez & Otero-Neira, 2020). This analysis should consider the use of advanced analytics and CRM data to gain a more granular understanding of customer behavior (Reinartz et al., 2005). Competitive analysis should also be conducted to understand the impact of the merger on market structure, competitive intensity, and potential antitrust concerns (Porter, 1985). This analysis should identify potential vulnerabilities and opportunities related to customer relationships and inform decisions about market positioning post-merger (Ailawadi et al., 2001).

Competitive landscape. Assessing the competitive landscape post-merger is vital (Ghemawat, 2005; Porter, 1985). Acquisitions can alter the competitive dynamics of the market, leading to changes in market concentration and competitive rivalry, instigating competitor's reaction, and affecting customer loyalty (Kato & Schoenberg, 2012; Newmark, 1996; Schriber et al., 2022). Due diligence should include an analysis of potential antitrust implications, regulatory scrutiny, and the likely reactions of competitors, to enable corporates to address the anxiety arisen among customers from the anticipated change. Network analysis is essential to map and analyze the interactions of each party involved in the acquisition (Öberg, 2012). This analysis should also consider customers' perception of changes driven by acquisition in the target and acquirer network identity, market power and behavior (Öberg et al., 2011).

Brand evaluation. Evaluating the brand equity of both merging firms is vital (Keller, 2016). Understanding customer perceptions of each brand, including brand image, brand awareness, brand loyalty, brand associations, and brand resonance, helps inform post-merger brand strategy. This evaluation should consider the strength of each brand in different customer segments, as well as the potential for brand dilution or enhancement post-merger. Brand architecture decisions (e.g., brand consolidation, co-branding, new brand creation) are crucial and should be based on customer insights and market analysis. This process should also consider the emotional connection customers have with the brands (Thomson et al., 2005).

Potential customer churn assessment. Due diligence should include an assessment of potential customer churn based on anticipated changes in product offerings, service, or pricing (Gupta et al., 2004; Kumar et al., 2010; Mari & Meglio, 2021; Öberg, 2008). This involves estimating the number of customers who might switch to competitors due to dissatisfaction with the M&A. This assessment should consider factors such as switching costs, the availability of substitutes, the strength of customer relationships, and the perceived value proposition of competitors. This assessment can help to quantify the potential financial impact of customer churn and inform retention strategies. This should also consider the use of predictive analytics to identify customers at high risk of churn (Verbeke et al., 2011, 2012).

Effective communication throughout the M&A process is crucial to effective customer relationship management and acquisition success (Mari & Meglio, 2021). In the following section, the open communication strategies during the pre-merger period are briefly discussed.

Strategic communication planning. Developing a proactive communication plan to address customer concerns before and after the announcement is crucial (Argenti, 2009). This plan should be based on a thorough stakeholder analysis (Mitchell et al., 1997), identifying key customer segments and their respective levels of influence and interest in the M&A. This allows for tailored messaging and communication strategies.

The plan should also consider the timing and channels of communication, using a mix of traditional and digital channels to reach different customer groups. For example, direct mail might be used for established business-to-business (B2B) clients, while social media could be used for reaching younger demographics. The communication plan should also align with the overall change management strategy for the M&A.

Transparency and open communication. Communicating openly and transparently about the rationale for the M&A and its potential benefits for customers can help manage initial reactions (Dutton & Dukerich, 1991). This includes explaining the strategic rationale for the M&A in clear and accessible language, addressing potential concerns about changes in product offerings or service directly, and emphasizing the long-term benefits for customers, such as increased innovation, improved service offerings, or expanded geographic reach. Inconsistent communication or conflicting information will result in confusion and frustration among customers. This communication should be consistent with the firm's overall communication strategy (Argenti, 2009).

Stakeholder engagement. Engaging with key customer segments during the due diligence process, where legally permissible and strategically advisable, can provide valuable insights and build early support (Öberg, 2022). This aligns with the principles of stakeholder management (Donaldson & Preston, 1995) and emphasizes the importance of considering the interests of all affected parties. This can involve conducting customer surveys, or interviewing focus groups to gather feedback and understand their perspectives on the potential M&A. This feedback can then be used to refine communication strategies and integration plans. However, confidentiality concerns must be carefully managed during this phase. This engagement should be conducted ethically and transparently, respecting customer privacy and data protection regulations.

Post-merger Integration (PMI) Phase

The post-merger phase is the period where promises made during the pre-merger phase are put to the test. Keeping promises to customers can build trust and strengthen customer relationships, motivating customer knowledge transfer (Degbey & Pelto, 2021), which is extremely critical to the success of the post-merger integration (Öberg & Tarba, 2013). Keeping promises requires ongoing communication, careful integration of customer-facing operations, and a strong focus on assuring customer satisfaction, which in turn can lead to improved performance (Swaminathan et al., 2014). The appropriate strategies are discussed briefly as follows:

Maintaining service quality: Prioritizing service quality during integration is essential (Marks & Mirvis, 2011; Rust & Oliver, 2000). This requires careful attention to the integration of operational processes, CRM systems, and customer service staff. Companies should establish clear service standards and provide adequate training to ensure consistent service delivery across all customer touchpoints. This might involve cross-training employees from both merging companies on each other's products and services. Clear service agreements should be established and communicated to customers.

Customer-centric integration planning. Integrating customer-facing operations with a focus on minimizing disruption and maximizing value is important (Hitt et al., 2017). This includes aligning product offerings, service processes, and brand identities in a way that enhances the customer experience (Swaminathan et al., 2014). Companies should avoid making changes with possible negative impact on customers, even if they are intended to reduce costs or improve efficiency. Customer-relationship mapping can help to better understand the customer experience and identifying potential issues during integration. A well-coordinated team of integration managers overseeing the overall change process can contribute to acquisition success and synergy realization through facilitating communication, resource allocation (Teerikangas et al., 2011), and transfer of tacit knowledge from customers (Öberg & Tarba, 2013). For example, an integration team can effectively address the possible disruptions in customer-relationship management arising from the ambiguity around post-merger customer ownership by clearly defining the customer relationship roles and responsibilities, integrating CRM systems, and arranging training programs (Öberg, 2009).

Continuous communication and feedback mechanisms. Maintaining open communication channels and actively soliciting customer feedback throughout the integration process is necessary to communicate the benefits of the acquisition to customers and to maintaining existing ties with them (DiGeorgio, 2002a; Mari & Meglio, 2021; Teerikangas et al., 2011) with the intent to minimize customer attrition (Öberg, 2014b). Implementing feedback loops and actively monitoring customer sentiment are essential for identifying and addressing emerging issues. This continuous communication is a key aspect of managing stakeholder relationships during change.

Addressing customer issues promptly. Establishing effective mechanisms for addressing customer issues and resolving complaints promptly is essential for maintaining customer satisfaction. This includes empowering customer service staff to resolve issues quickly and efficiently, providing clear escalation paths for complex issues, and implementing systems for tracking and analyzing customer complaints. Speed and efficiency in addressing customer concerns can significantly mitigate negative word-of-mouth and improve customer retention (Alvarez-Gonzalez & Otero-Neira, 2020; Degbey, 2015; Mari & Meglio, 2021; Öberg, 2022).

In summary, key strategies for effectively managing customer concerns can be divided into pre-merger and post-merger phases. During the pre-merger phase, the focus is on proactive planning and communication. This includes developing a strategic communication plan tailored to different customer segments, prioritizing transparency and open communication about the rationale and expected M&A outcomes, and engaging with key customers to gather feedback and build early buy-in. In the post-merger phase, the emphasis shifts to execution and ongoing relationship management. Strategies include maintaining consistent service quality during the integration process, implementing customer-centric integration planning to minimize disruptions, establishing continuous communication and feedback mechanisms to monitor customer sentiment and address emerging issues promptly, and empowering customer-facing staff to resolve customer concerns effectively. By implementing these strategies, organizations can mitigate negative reactions from customers, maintain strong customer relationships, and maximize the likelihood of a successful M&A integration.

Discussions

This review synthesizes existing literature to underscore the critical role of customers as acquisition stakeholders. By examining the impact of these transactions on the customer experience across both pre- and post-merger phases, it highlights the importance of a customer-centric approach to M&A management. For example, research emphasizes the need for thorough pre-merger due diligence, including in-depth customer and market analysis, to anticipate potential impacts and inform subsequent integration strategies. This proactive approach allows organizations to identify potential customer concerns related to changes in product offerings, service quality, pricing, and brand identity. Yet, the post-merger integration phase presents the most direct impact on customers. Effective management of this phase is crucial for maintaining customer satisfaction and loyalty by including integration of customer-facing operations, consistent service delivery, and clear communication about changes and their rationale. Disruptions in service, poorly managed transitions, and inadequate communication can lead to negative customer reactions and erode the value created by the M&A.

A core finding is the critical role of communication throughout the M&A process. Transparent and consistent communication with customers, beginning before the transaction is finalized and continuing throughout the integration, is essential for managing expectations, mitigating anxieties, and building trust. This communication should be tailored to specific customer segments and address their unique concerns.

Overall, adopting a holistic stakeholder perspective in M&As is important. While shareholder value remains a key driver, neglecting customer needs and concerns can have significant negative consequences for long-term performance. A customer-centric approach, integrated into both strategic planning and execution, is essential for value creation. Failing to prioritize the customer experience can lead to customer churn, damage brand reputation, and ultimately jeopardize M&A success.

Research Implications

To further advance our understanding of customer dynamics in acquisitions, future research should prioritize several key areas. First, a more nuanced understanding of customer segmentation is critical. Investigating the differential impacts of M&As on diverse customer groups, such as loyal versus new customers or B2B versus B2C clients, will enable the development of more targeted and effective customer management strategies. Second, empirical studies are needed to determine the optimal communication strategies for managing customer reactions during M&As. This includes exploring the effectiveness of various communication channels, including digital and social media platforms, and assessing the impact of different message framing and delivery.

Further, longitudinal studies are essential to understand the long-term effects of M&As on customer relationships. Such research can shed light on changes in customer lifetime value, loyalty, and overall customer equity. Additionally, a comparative analysis of different M&A types, such as horizontal, vertical, and cross-border transactions, will illuminate how varying deal structures influence customer reactions and behaviors. Research should also investigate the mediating role of employee attitudes and behaviors, as employee morale and engagement can significantly impact customer perceptions. Finally, the application of digital technologies and data analytics in customer management during M&As warrants further exploration. This includes examining the use of social media analytics, sentiment analysis, and predictive modeling to anticipate and address customer concerns. Developing and testing Customer Experience Management (CEM) frameworks tailored to M&A contexts would also provide valuable practical insights.

Practice Implications

For organizations navigating acquisitions, a proactive and customer-centric approach is paramount. First, thorough customer due diligence during the pre-merger phase is essential. This involves conducting in-depth analyses to anticipate potential customer concerns and inform the development of robust integration strategies. Second, organizations should prioritize the creation of comprehensive communication plans, tailored to specific customer segments. These plans should emphasize transparency and open dialogue, ensuring customers are informed about the rationale and implications of the M&A.

During the integration phase, organizations should strive to minimize disruptions to customer-facing operations and ensure consistent service delivery. Investing in training for customer-facing employees is also vital, equipping them to effectively handle customer inquiries and concerns. Further, the implementation of robust feedback mechanisms allows organizations to monitor customer sentiment and address emerging issues promptly. To ensure the long-term success of M&As, organizations should integrate customer-centric metrics into the evaluation of the transaction's performance. This includes tracking key indicators such as customer satisfaction and churn rates.

Finally, a holistic stakeholder approach is necessary. Managers must recognize customers as key stakeholders and incorporate their needs into all phases of the M&A process, from initial planning to post-merger integration. By prioritizing the customer experience, organizations can mitigate potential negative reactions, maintain customer loyalty, and ultimately enhance the value created by the M&A.

Future Research Directions

While existing literature provides valuable insights into the impact of M&As on customers, there are avenues for future research. Future research directions can be categorized into areas related to customer segmentation, communication strategies, long-term relationship dynamics, M&A types, the role of employees, and the impact of digital technologies.

Impact on different customer segments. Future research should explore how M&As affect different customer segments, such as loyal customers, new customers acquired through the M&A, business-to-business (B2B) customers, and customers in different geographic regions or demographic groups. Investigating the unique needs, expectations, and reactions of these diverse segments can provide valuable insights for customer management strategies. For example, research could examine how different communication strategies impact the retention of high-value customers versus price-sensitive customers.

The role of communication in managing customer reactions. Further research is needed to examine the effectiveness of different communication strategies in mitigating negative customer reactions and building support for M&A integrations. This includes investigating the optimal timing, frequency, and channels of communication, as well as the content and tone of messages. The role of social media and other digital platforms in managing customer communication during M&As is a particularly relevant area for future research (Mangold & Faulds, 2009). Research could also explore the impact of two-way communication and active listening on customer perceptions of the integration process.

Long-term impact on customer relationships. Research should investigate the long-term impact of M&As on customer relationships, including customer lifetime value (CLV), customer loyalty, and customer equity

(Blattberg & Deighton, 1996; Gupta & Lehmann, 2003). Longitudinal studies tracking customer behavior and attitudes over time can provide valuable insights into the lasting effects of M&As on customer relationships.

Impact of different M&A types. Future research should examine whether different types of M&As (e.g., horizontal, vertical, conglomerate, cross-border) have distinct effects on customer reactions. For example, horizontal mergers, which involve direct competitors, might lead to greater customer concerns about reduced competition and price increases compared to vertical mergers. Cross-border M&As are more complex due to cultural differences and varying expectations.

The role of employee attitudes and behaviors. Research should explore the mediating/moderating effect of employee attitudes and behaviors on the relationship between M&As and customer reactions. How do employee morale, job satisfaction, and commitment to the merged entity influence customer perceptions and behaviors? Investigating the link between internal integration processes and customer-facing interactions could provide valuable insights.

Impact of digital technologies and data analytics. Future research should explore how digital technologies and data analytics can be leveraged to better understand and manage customer reactions during M&As. This includes investigating the use of social media analytics, customer sentiment analysis, and predictive modeling to identify potential customer churn and tailor communication and retention strategies. The use of CRM systems and data integration to create a unified view of the customer across the merged entities is also an important area for investigation (Reinartz et al., 2004).

Customer experience management (CEM) in M&A contexts. Customer Experience Management (CEM) frameworks could be another promising area. Research could investigate how mapping customer journeys and measuring customer satisfaction and loyalty at each stage can contribute to a smoother integration process and improved customer outcomes.

Conclusion

We synthesize research to underscore the critical importance of customers as acquisition stakeholders. By examining the impact of M&A on customers and vice versa, across pre-merger and post-merger phases, we show how these transactions can significantly influence customer perceptions, behaviors, and long-term relationships. The review emphasizes the need for a strategic, customer-centric approach to M&A management, encompassing thorough pre-merger due diligence, proactive communication, consistent service delivery, and careful integration of customer-facing operations. Addressing customer concerns effectively, maintaining service quality, and delivering on promised value are crucial for mitigating negative reactions, minimizing churn, and maximizing the potential for long-term value creation. By recognizing customers as integral to M&A success and integrating their needs into the strategic planning and execution of these complex transactions, firms can improve their chances of achieving desired outcomes and building sustainable competitive advantage in the post-merger landscape. Ignoring the customer perspective, conversely, can lead to significant financial and reputational damage, jeopardizing the entire M&A endeavor.

Appendix: Articles' Findings Summary

Article	*Impact customer*		*CRM*		*Customer reaction*		*Findings*
	Pre-M&A	Post-M&A	Pre-M&A	Post-M&A	Pre-M&A	Post-M&A	
Alvarez-González and Otero-Neira (2020)	✓		✓	✓			CRM strategies can mitigate negative customer reactions. Effective communication can help maintaining customer trust and loyalty throughout the process

(continued)

(continued)

Article	*Impact customer*		*CRM*		*Customer reaction*		*Findings*
	Pre-M&A	Post-M&A	Pre-M&A	Post-M&A	Pre-M&A	Post-M&A	
Alvarez-González and Otero-Neira (2023)		✓					Proactive CRM strategies can minimize customer churn and maintain loyalty during and after M&A. M&A outcomes are not solely dependent on financial synergies but also on the ability to retain and enhance customer relationships
Cartwright and Schoenberg (2006)			✓				Cultural fit facilitates smoother integration, leading to better employee morale, and by extension, more consistent and high-quality service delivery to customers

(continued)

(continued)

Article	*Impact customer*		*CRM*		*Customer reaction*		*Findings*
	Pre-M&A	Post-M&A	Pre-M&A	Post-M&A	Pre-M&A	Post-M&A	
Cheng et al. (2022)	✓				✓	✓	Target's high customer concentration could lead to substantial revenue loss if major customers are dissatisfied with changes post-merger. Managing relationships with concentrated customers pre-merger and understanding their reactions post-merger are critical for success
Degbey (2015)				✓		✓	Maintaining existing customer relationships post-merger is crucial for realizing the full value of an acquisition. Effective CRM strategies to preserve trust and minimize disruption, are vital to preventing customer churn and ensuring sustained revenue streams from acquired businesses

(continued)

(continued)

Article	*Impact customer*		*CRM*		*Customer reaction*		*Findings*
	Pre-M&A	Post-M&A	Pre-M&A	Post-M&A	Pre-M&A	Post-M&A	
Degbey and Pelto (2021)				✓		✓	Effective communication and expectation management can ensure customer retention and satisfaction after cross-border M&As. Involving customers in knowledge-sharing process mitigates negative reactions and fosters loyalty
DiGeorgio (2002a, 2002b)				✓			Poor integration can lead to post-merger customer dissatisfaction and churn. Strategic planning and effective integration can ensure the combined entity delivers consistent value
Gupta and Lehmann (2003)						✓	Viewing customers as long-term assets, emphasizes the importance of measuring and managing customer lifetime value in an M&A context. Acquirers need to carefully assess and retain target's customer base

(continued)

(continued)

Article	*Impact customer*		*CRM*		*Customer reaction*		*Findings*
	Pre-M&A	Post-M&A	Pre-M&A	Post-M&A	Pre-M&A	Post-M&A	
Gupta et al. (2004)			✓				Focusing on the value of a target company's customer base in an acquisition, reinforces the necessity of robust CRM strategies to exploit customer relationships in firm's overall valuation and future profitability
Kato and Schoenberg (2012)	✓		✓				Competitors may leverage customer dissatisfaction during M&A to gain market share; thus, it is important to mitigate negative customer reactions and prevent churn through proactive communication and effective CRM
Mari and Meglio (2021)	✓		✓	✓			Customers are key stakeholders whose perceptions and behaviors influence M&A outcomes. Potential risks and opportunities arise from changes in brand management, product offerings, service quality, and pricing

(continued)

(continued)

Article	*Impact customer*		*CRM*		*Customer reaction*		*Findings*
	Pre-M&A	Post-M&A	Pre-M&A	Post-M&A	Pre-M&A	Post-M&A	
Meglio et al. (2017)				✓		✓	Faster integration is not always better, but optimal speed depends on various factors. A carefully managed pace of integration can minimize disruption to customer-facing operations, indirectly supporting customer retention
Meglio and Park (2019)	✓				✓		Advances an institutionally embedded stakeholder view of mergers and acquisitions, broadening the focus beyond financial aspects to include various stakeholders, particularly customers
Newmark (1996)			✓				Effective CRM through proactive communication, clear strategies for integrating customer accounts, and consistent service quality, ensures a smooth transition that can prevent customer attrition

(continued)

(continued)

Article	*Impact customer*		*CRM*		*Customer reaction*		*Findings*
	Pre-M&A	Post-M&A	Pre-M&A	Post-M&A	Pre-M&A	Post-M&A	
Öberg (2008)			✓				Managing customers' behaviors and perceptions of change in service, product offerings, and branding, throughout the M&A process is critical to ensure successful integration and maintain customer loyalty
Öberg (2009)		✓	✓	✓			When the acquiring and target firms have different CRM systems, clarity in ownership and a seamless transition of customer interactions are vital to preventing customer confusion and churn
Öberg (2012)			✓				Applies network pictures to understand complex customer relationships, providing insights into potential disruptions and opportunities for CRM, and mitigating negative customer reactions during an M&A

(continued)

(continued)

Article	*Impact customer*		*CRM*		*Customer reaction*		*Findings*
	Pre-M&A	Post-M&A	Pre-M&A	Post-M&A	Pre-M&A	Post-M&A	
Öberg (2014a)					✓		Identifies customers' role in facilitating or hindering integration, influencing deal outcomes, and behavioral responding (e.g., switching, increased loyalty)
Öberg (2014b)				✓			Cultural differences, communication barriers, and differing customer expectations, are challenges in managing customer relationships following international acquisitions that can be overcome using tailored CRM strategies and effective customer-facing operations integration

(continued)

(continued)

Article	Impact customer		CRM		Customer reaction		Findings
	Pre-M&A	Post-M&A	Pre-M&A	Post-M&A	Pre-M&A	Post-M&A	
Öberg (2018)						✓	Customers' behaviors and expectations post-merger, such as willingness to adapt to new offerings, or resistance to changes, affect integration. Effective CRM strategies are important to ensure customer retention and positive reactions to the new entity
Öberg (2022)	✓		✓	✓	✓		Impact the customers on M&A outcomes, beyond financial or strategic synergies. Customer reactions to changes following acquistions can either facilitate or derail the integration process and overall success
Öberg and Tarba (2013)				✓			Effective CRM is pivotal to ensure customer retention and satisfaction post-merger, given the complexities introduced by international differences

(continued)

(continued)

Article	Impact customer		CRM		Customer reaction		Findings
	Pre-M&A	Post-M&A	Pre-M&A	Post-M&A	Pre-M&A	Post-M&A	
Öberg et al. (2011)	✓		✓				Changes in network identity can influence how customers perceive the merged entity and their willingness to continue engaging with it. Managing the perception of merged entity's identity among its customer network is crucial for maintaining relationships and preventing negative reactions
Schriber et al. (2022)	✓		✓				If an acquisition leads to market retaliation by competitors, customers might be impacted by changes in market dynamics, offerings, or pricing. Addressing customer experience, is part of a successful M&A strategy

(continued)

(continued)

Article	*Impact customer*		*CRM*		*Customer reaction*		*Findings*
	Pre-M&A	Post-M&A	Pre-M&A	Post-M&A	Pre-M&A	Post-M&A	
Swaminathan et al. (2014)				✓		✓	While efficiency gains are a primary driver for mergers, neglecting customer satisfaction can undermine long-term value creation. A balanced approach, prioritizing both operational efficiencies and maintenance or enhancement of customer relationships, is crucial for financial success post-merger
Teerikangas et al. (2011)	✓			✓			Effective integration process, facilitated by integration managers, can ensure continuity of service quality and customer relationship management, thereby indirectly impacting customer satisfaction and retention post-merger

(continued)

(continued)

Article	*Impact customer*		*CRM*		*Customer reaction*		*Findings*
	Pre-M&A	Post-M&A	Pre-M&A	Post-M&A	Pre-M&A	Post-M&A	
Thomson et al. (2005)			✓		✓		Strong emotional bonds between consumers and brands can lead to increased loyalty, positive word-of-mouth, and resistance to competitive offerings
Thorbjornsen and Dahlén (2011)	✓				✓	✓	Acquirer dominance can lead to negative reactions driven by psychological reactance
Umashankar et al. (2022)	✓	✓					Customer satisfaction often declines post-M&A, negatively impacting performance. Companies need to prioritize customer well-being and implement robust CRM strategies throughout the M&A process to prevent value erosion and maintain customer loyalty

(continued)

(continued)

Article	*Impact customer*		*CRM*		*Customer reaction*		*Findings*
	Pre-M&A	Post-M&A	Pre-M&A	Post-M&A	Pre-M&A	Post-M&A	
Verbeke et al. (2012)			✓				Develops a framework that integrates profit considerations into churn modeling, demonstrating how a profit-driven approach can lead to more economically beneficial customer retention strategies
Verbeke et al. (2011)			✓				Contemporary salespeople increasingly act as facilitators of information exchange between customers and their organizations, leveraging their knowledge to create value and solve customer problems
Zeithaml (1988)					✓		Consumers evaluate value based on a trade-off between perceived benefit (quality) and perceived sacrifice (price). Proposes a framework on how consumers form perceptions of value, which is crucial for pricing strategies and marketing communications

References

Ailawadi, K., Neslin, S., & Gedenk, K. (2001). Pursuing the value-conscious consumer: Store brands versus national brand promotions. *Journal of Marketing, 65*(1), 71–89.

Alvarez-González, P., & Otero-Neira, C. (2023). Mergers and acquisitions success: Examining customer loyalty. *Marketing Intelligence & Planning, 41*(1), 48–61.

Alvarez-González, P., & Otero-Neira, C. (2020). The effect of mergers and acquisitions on customer–company relationships: Exploring employees' perceptions in the Spanish banking sector. *International Journal of Bank Marketing, 38*(2), 406–424.

Argenti, P. (2009). *Corporate communication*. McGraw-Hill.

Ashforth, B., & Mael, F. (1989). Social identity theory and the organization. *Academy of Management Review, 14*(1), 20–39.

Barney, J., & Hesterly, W. (2020). *Strategic management and competitive advantage: Concepts and cases*. Pearson Education Limited.

Bitner, M., Ostrom, A., & Morgan, F. (2008). Service blueprinting: A practical technique for service innovation. *California Management Review, 50*(3), 66–94.

Blattberg, R., & Deighton, J. (1996). Manage marketing by the customer equity test. *Harvard Business Review, 74*(4), 136–144.

Brueller, N., Carmeli, A., & Drori, I. (2014). How do different types of mergers and acquisitions facilitate strategic agility? *California Management Review, 56*(3), 39–57.

Capron, L., & Shen, J. (2007). Acquisitions of innovation: A review and future research directions. *Academy of Management Journal, 50*(4), 755–789.

Cartwright, S., & Schoenberg, R. (2006). Thirty years of mergers and acquisitions research: Recent advances and future opportunities. *British Journal of Management, 17*(S1), S1–S5.

Cheng, M., Jaggi, J., & Young, S. (2022). Customer concentration of targets in mergers and acquisitions. *Journal of Business Finance & Accounting, 49*(7–8), 1314–1355.

Das, A., & Kapil, S. (2012). Explaining M&A performance: A review of empirical research. *Journal of Strategy and Management, 5*(3), 284–330.

Davis, W. (2023). *Twitter is being rebranded as X*. https://www.theverge.com/2023/7/23/23804629/twitters-rebrand-to-x-may-actually-be-happening-soon

Degbey, W. (2015). Customer retention: A source of value for serial acquirers. *Industrial Marketing Management, 46*, 11–23.

Degbey, W., & Pelto, E. (2021). Customer knowledge sharing in cross-border mergers and acquisitions: The role of customer motivation and promise management. *Journal of International Management, 27*(4), Article 100858.

DiGeorgio, R. (2002a). Making mergers and acquisitions work: What we know and don't know–Part I. *Journal of Change Management, 3*(2), 134–148.

DiGeorgio, R. (2002b). Making mergers and acquisitions work: What we know and don't know–Part II. *Journal of Change Management, 3*(3), 259–274.

Donaldson, T., & Preston, L. (1995). The stakeholder theory of the corporation: Concepts, evidence, and implications. *Academy of Management Review, 20*(1), 65–91.

Dutton, J. E., & Dukerich, J. M. (1991). Keeping an eye on the mirror: Image and identity in organizational adaptation. *Academy of Management Journal, 34*(3), 517–554.

Elmaghraby, W., & Keskinocak, P. (2003). Dynamic pricing in the presence of inventory considerations: Research overview, current practice, and future directions. *Production and Operations Management, 12*(4), 487–514.

Ghemawat, P. (2005). *Redefining global strategy: Crossing borders in a world where differences still matter*. Harvard Business Press.

Gioia, D., & Thomas, J. (1996). Identity, image, and reputation in organizations. *Academy of Management Review, 21*(1), 144–174.

Gupta, S., & Lehmann, D. (2003). Customers as assets. *Journal of Interactive Marketing, 17*(1), 9–24.

Gupta, S., Lehmann, D., & Stuart, J. (2004). Valuing customers. *Journal of Marketing Research, 41*(1), 7–18.

Haleblian, J., Devers, C., McNamara, G., Carpenter, M., & Davison, R. (2009). Taking stock of what we know about mergers and acquisitions: A review and research agenda. *Journal of Management, 35*(3), 469–502.

Heath, R. (2006). *Strategic issues management: Organizations and public policy challenges*. Sage Publications.

Hitt, M., Ireland, R., & Hoskisson, R. (2017). *Strategic management: Concepts and cases: Competitiveness and globalization*. Cengage learning.

Homburg, C., & Bucerius, M. (2005). A marketing perspective on mergers and acquisitions: How marketing integration affects post-merger performance. *Journal of Marketing, 69*, 95–113.

Kato, J., & Schoenberg, R. (2012). Customer and competitor responses to mergers and acquisitions: An empirical investigation in the logistics industry. *Advances in Mergers and Acquisitions, 11*, 155–180.

Keller, K. (2016). Reflections on customer-based brand equity: Perspectives, progress, and priorities. *Journal of Marketing, 80*(6), 108–123.

Kumar, V., Aksoy, L., Donkers, B., Venkatesan, R., Wiesel, T., & Tillmanns, S. (2010). Undervalued or overvalued customers: Capturing total customer engagement value. *Journal of Service Research, 13*(3), 297–310.

Mandl, A., Bohnett, D., Liddy, E., Komansky, D., Kozlowski, D.,... & Krekel, T. (2000). A CEO roundtable on making mergers succeed. *Harvard Business Review, 78*(3), 145-154.

Mangold, W., & Faulds, D. (2009). Social media: The new hybrid element of the promotion mix. *Business Horizons, 52*(4), 357–365.

Mari, C., & Meglio, O. (2021). A customer-based perspective in mergers and acquisitions. *Advances in Mergers and Acquisitions, 20*, 67–80.

Marks, M., & Mirvis, P. (2011). *Joining forces: Making one plus one equal three in mergers, acquisitions, and alliances*. John Wiley & Sons.

Meglio, O., King, D., & Risberg, A. (2017). Speed in acquisitions: A managerial framework. *Business Horizons, 60*(3), 415–425.

Meglio, O., Park, K. (2019). Mergers and acquisitions: Advancing an institutionally embedded stakeholder view. In *Strategic Decisions and Sustainability Choices: Mergers, Acquisitions and Corporate Social Responsibility from a Global Perspective*, (pp. 3–24).

Meglio, O., & Risberg, A. (2011). The (mis) measurement of M&A performance—A systematic narrative literature review. *Scandinavian Journal of Management, 27*(4), 418–433.

Meyer, C., & Schwager, A. (2007). Understanding customer experience. *Harvard Business Review, 85*(2), 116–126.

Mitchell, R., Agle, B., & Wood, D. (1997). Toward a theory of stakeholder identification and salience: Defining the principle of who and what really counts. *Academy of Management Review, 22*(4), 853–886.

Mitchell, W., & Singh, K. (1993). When do rivals cooperate? Toward a theory of cross-firm agreements. *Strategic Management Journal, 14*(3), 203–217.

Murphy, K. (2025). *Max, formerly known as HBO Max, launches new black-and-white logo and color palette, evoking HBO branding*. https://variety.com/2025/digital/news/max-changes-logo-black-and-white-hbo-1236352161/

Nagle, T., Müller, G., & Gruyaert, E. (2023). *The strategy and tactics of pricing: A guide to growing more profitably*. Routledge.

Newmark, N. (1996). Customer mergers and acquisitions: A topical round-up for concerned banks. *Banking Law Journal, 113*(3), 241–270.

Öberg, C. (2008). *The importance of customers in mergers and acquisitions*. Doctoral dissertation, Linkopings Universitet.

Öberg, C. (2009). Who owns a customer relationship following a merger or acquisition? *Corporate Ownership and Control, 6*(2), 212–221.

Öberg, C. (2012). Using network pictures to study inter-organisational encounters. *Scandinavian Journal of Management, 28*(2), 136–148.

Öberg, C. (2014a). Customer roles in mergers and acquisitions: A systematic literature review. *Advances in Mergers and Acquisitions, 12*, 59–74.

Öberg, C. (2014b). Customer relationship challenges following international acquisitions. *International Marketing Review, 31*(3), 259–282.

Öberg, C. (2018). Customer roles in M&A integration. *International Studies of Management & Organization, 48*(1), 43–70.

Öberg, C. (2022). Two becoming one: How customers can impact the outcomes of mergers and acquisitions. *Strategic Direction, 38*(11), 23–24.

Öberg, C., Grundström, C., & Jönsson, P. (2011). Acquisitions and network identity change. *European Journal of Marketing, 45*(9/10), 1470–1500.

Öberg, C., & Tarba, S. (2013). What do we know about post-merger integration following international acquisitions? In *Philosophy of Science and Meta-knowledge in International Business and Management* (pp. 469–492). Emerald Group Publishing Limited.

Payne, A., & Frow, P. (2005). A strategic framework for customer relationship management. *Journal of Marketing, 69*(4), 167–176.

Porter, M. (1985). *Competitive advantage: Creating and sustaining superior performance*. Free Press.

Raymond, N., Shepardson, D., & Singh, R. (2024). *US judge blocks JetBlue from acquiring spirit airlines*. https://www.reuters.com/markets/deals/us-judge-blocks-jetblue-acquiring-spirit-airlines-2024-01-16/

Reinartz, W., Krafft, M., & Hoyer, W. (2004). The customer relationship management process: Its measurement and impact on performance. *Journal of Marketing Research, 41*(3), 293–305.

Reinartz, W., Thomas, J., & Kumar, V. (2005). Balancing acquisition and retention resources to maximize customer profitability. *Journal of Marketing, 69*(1), 63–79.

Reichheld, F. (1996). *The loyalty effect: The hidden force behind growth, profits, and lasting value*. Harvard Business Press.

Riviezzo, A. (2013). Acquisitions in knowledge-intensive industries: Exploring the distinctive characteristics of the effective acquirer. *Management Research Review, 36*(2), 183–212.

Rogan, M., & Greve, H. (2015). Resource dependence dynamics: Partner reactions to mergers. *Organization Science, 26*(1), 239–255.

Rust, R., & Oliver, R. (2000). Should we delight the customer? *Journal of the Academy of Marketing Science, 28*(1), 86–94.

Sandhya, K., & Kumar, D. P. (2011). Employee retention by motivation. *Indian Journal of Science and Technology, 4*(12), 1778–1782.

Schenkel, A., & Teigland, R. (2008). Improved organizational performance through communities of practice. *Journal of Knowledge Management, 12*(1), 106–118.

Schriber, S., King, D., & Bauer, F. (2022). Retaliation effectiveness and acquisition performance: The influence of managerial decisions and industry context. *British Journal of Management, 33*(2), 939–957.

Schweiger, D., & Denisi, A. (1991). Communication with employees following a merger: A longitudinal field experiment. *Academy of Management Journal, 34*(1), 110–135.

Shapiro, C. (1989). Theories of oligopoly behavior. *Handbook of Industrial Organization, 1*, 329–414.

Stahl, G., & Voigt, A. (2008). Do cultural differences matter in mergers and acquisitions? A tentative model and examination. *Organization Science, 19*(1), 160–176.

Swaminathan, V., Groening, C., Mittal, V., & Thomaz, F. (2014). How achieving the dual goal of customer satisfaction and efficiency in mergers affects a firm's long-term financial performance. *Journal of Service Research, 17*(2), 182–194.

Teece, J. (2010). Business models, business strategy and innovation. *Long Range Planning, 43*(2–3), 172–194.

Teerikangas, S., Véry, P., & Pisano, V. (2011). Integration managers' value-capturing roles and acquisition performance. *Human Resource Management, 50*(5), 651–683.

Thomson, M., MacInnis, D., & Whan Park, C. (2005). The ties that bind: Measuring the strength of consumers' emotional attachments to brands. *Journal of Consumer Psychology, 15*(1), 77–91.

Thorbjornsen, H., & Dahlén, M. (2011). Customer reactions to acquirer-dominant mergers and acquisitions. *International Journal of Research in Marketing, 28*(4), 332–341.

Umashankar, N., Bahadir, S., & Bharadwaj, S. (2022). Despite efficiencies, mergers and acquisitions reduce firm value by hurting customer satisfaction. *Journal of Marketing, 86*(2), 66–86.

Verbeke, W., Dejaeger, K., Martens, D., Hur, J., & Baesens, B. (2012). New insights into churn prediction in the telecommunication sector: A profit driven data mining approach. *European Journal of Operational Research, 218*(1), 211–229.

Verbeke, W., Dietz, B., & Verwaal, E. (2011). Drivers of sales performance: A contemporary meta-analysis. Have salespeople become knowledge brokers? *Journal of the Academy of Marketing Science, 39*, 407–428.
Zeithaml, V. (1988). Consumer perceptions of price, quality, and value: A means-end model and synthesis of evidence. *Journal of Marketing, 52*(3), 2–22.

The Competitive Landscape Following M&A: A Review of Rivals' Responses

Katia M. Galdino

Introduction

Mergers and acquisitions (M&As) are a widely adopted strategy for firm growth, enabling the acquiring firm to rapidly expand its market presence and capabilities (Gomes et al., 2020). However, acquisitions affect not only the acquiring firms but also the competitive landscape, altering rival firms' short- and long-term performance, as well as their strategic decisions. For example, rivals (i.e., firms in the same industry as the acquiring firm) might respond to an M&A by adjusting their innovation strategy, to maintain or enhance their competitive position (Valentini, 2016). This response can include increasing research and development (R&D) investments and accelerating product development cycles (Fani et al., 2023; Uhlenbruck et al., 2017). Further, rivals may undertake defensive measures such as cost-cutting initiatives and market repositioning to mitigate the competitive pressure induced by the M&A or even engage in strategic alliances or joint ventures to increase their capability to compete in a changed competitive environment (Yin & Shanley, 2008).

K. M. Galdino (✉)
Georgia Southern University, Statesboro, GA, USA
e-mail: kdemelogaldino@georgiasouthern.edu

D. R. King and A. Bansal (eds.), *Navigating Stakeholder Dynamics Surrounding Acquisitions*,
https://doi.org/10.1007/978-3-032-03199-0_6

In sum, such responses may reduce the effectiveness of M&As as a growth strategy.

Rivals are, thus, an important stakeholder of M&As. Yet, the literature on rivals' responses to M&A announcements and the performance implications of such responses is still incipient. Research interest on the topic started in the 1980s (Eckbo, 1983) and most studies are published in finance and economics journals, focusing on financial market reactions (i.e., abnormal returns the days following the M&A announcement). Empirical analyses of rivals' strategic responses (e.g., corporate and operational actions) and their implications to firms' long-term performance are more recent and the number of studies is still limited (King & Schriber, 2016), although this research stream has been increasing consistently in the past couple of years. The results, nonetheless, are still inconclusive, as M&A activity in general, and rivals' responses in particular, are contingent on various firm-, deal-, industry-, and country-level aspects.

Hence, the purpose of this study is to systematically review the literature on rivals' responses to M&As published until the end of 2024, tacking stock of the general findings and providing a framework that can help scholars better understand the types of responses and the variables affecting them. A total of 56 studies were included in this review, and studies are aggregated into the two broad types of responses, namely financial market reactions and strategic responses. The latter are classified into: (1) corporate, operational, and competitive responses, (2) innovation and sustainability, and (3) finance, accounting, and disclosure practices.

Research on rivals' responses to M&As has recently gained momentum, as 46 percent of the articles included in the sample (i.e., 26 articles) were published in the past three years, see Fig. 1. Moreover, the topic is dominated by finance and economics scholars, as 30 papers (i.e., 54 percent) were published in finance and economics journals. While the foundations of management research on rivals' responses to M&As trace back to the late 1980s, particularly with Chatterjee's (1986) article on the value creation of merging firms and its impact on their rivals, rivals' responses to M&As mostly started to be empirically analyzed by management scholars in the 2010s. Nonetheless, this research stream has been growing substantially since then, following the use of M&As as a growth strategy in an increasingly globalized world (Gomes et al., 2020).

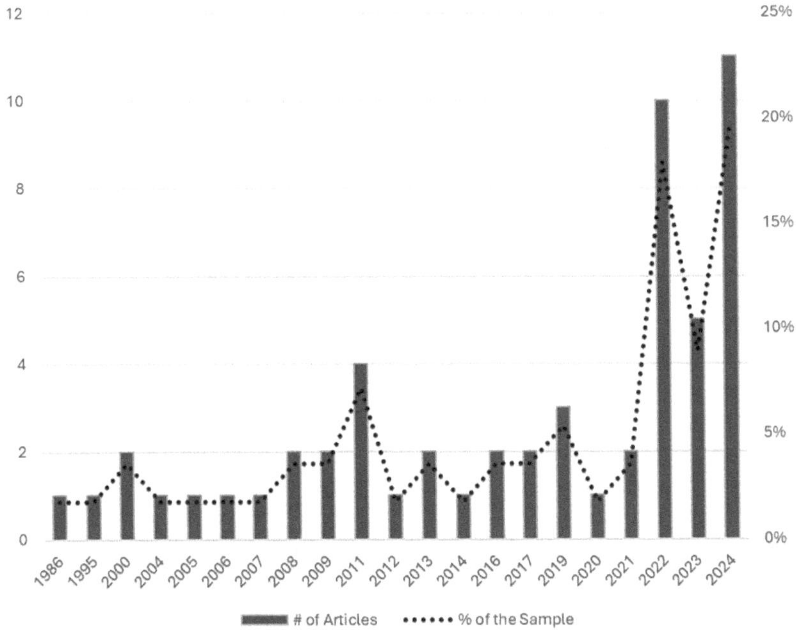

Fig. 1 Evolution of research on rivals' responses to M&As

Summary of Rival Actions

In organizing this review, I first summarize the information from the included articles, focusing on the type of response—either financial market reactions or strategic responses. The former is the prevalent concern of this research stream, as 71 percent of the sample (i.e., 40 articles) discussed the stock market reactions of rivals to M&A announcements. Research on the latter is more recent and limited. Only 16 articles discussed strategic or operational moves taken by rivals to either retaliate or protect themselves from the changes in the competitive landscape brought by a focal firm's merger or acquisition, including the threat of a subsequent acquisition (King & Schriber, 2016). Then, I provide a framework that helps scholars navigate the findings and identify opportunities for future research.

Financial Market Reactions

Studies analyzing financial market reactions of rival firms to M&A announcements focus on short-term stock price reactions, namely cumulative abnormal returns (CAR) the day(s) following a focal firm's acquisition announcement, which are generally measured using event study methodology. This means that such studies evaluate whether the market value of the rivals increases, decreases, or remains unchanged after a focal firm's acquisition. Early research on this topic emphasized competitive theory—the efficiency versus collusion (i.e., market power) debate—arguing that mergers might either positively or negatively affect rivals, depending on how the focal firm plans to act after the deal (Mullin et al., 1995).

On the one hand, positive returns tended to be more prevalent and were also explained by the signaling effect of a merger or acquisition, which signaled productivity increases or the possibility that rivals might become targets (Chatterjee, 1986; Eckbo, 1983; Song & Walkling, 2000). This means that M&As lead rivals to cut costs and improve efficiency, to compete against the newly merged firm and a changed market (Eckbo, 1983). On the other hand, negative returns were most often explained by the possibility of rivals' being shut out from the market (Kedia et al., 2011). Hence, despite the prevalence of positive returns, early studies sometimes led to inconclusive, mixed, or insignificant results (Chehab, 2002), often due to small sample sizes or the empirical analysis of a single deal (Wårell, 2007).

Moreover, these early studies mostly focused on large firms in traditional industries in the United States, such as banking (Hankir et al., 2011) and the airline industry, noting that the competitive landscape, including relative market shares and market positions, influenced the magnitude of the rivals' stock price reaction. This means that rivals' reactions vary depending on their size and position relative to the focal firm, in terms of how much market share they hold and whether the merger creates a monopoly (Gong & Firth, 2006). For example, Campa and Hernando (2008) found that the positive returns of rivals following M&A announcements of financial firms in Europe were higher for domestic rivals than for international rivals, which the authors attributed to increased market power in the focal country, given the decrease in competition immediately following the deal. Likewise, the positive returns found by Akhigbe et al. (2000) were contingent on the extent of M&A

activity in the industry, as well as the relative size of the rivals and having competing bidders.

Hence, the financial market reactions of larger and smaller rivals might differ, as the main determinant is their size relative to the focal firm. (Akhigbe et al., 2000; Gong & Firth, 2006). While larger rivals might have more resources to retaliate or adjust their strategy following an acquisition, including engaging in subsequent acquisitions (King & Schriber, 2016), smaller rivals might face a higher probability of becoming a target, as acquiring a smaller firm requires less resources (Song & Walkling, 2000). Such a probability not only leads to a negative relationship between market returns and rivals' relative size (Akhigbe et al., 2000) but also to strategic reactions by smaller firms that could increase their chance of being acquired, such as changes in their accounting choices and economic activities (Du et al., 2024).

Another important contingency affecting rivals' stock prices involved deal type (Fee & Thomas, 2004; Shahrur, 2005). Horizontal acquisitions involve deals where the acquiring and target firms operate in the same industry, usually as competitors. Although such deals might be perceived to hurt rivals, as the merging firms' increased market power could potentially shut them out of the market, robust findings by Clougherty and Duso (2009) showed that non-merging rivals usually gained (i.e., showed an increase in CAR) when their rivals engaged in M&As, challenging the assumption that rivals might be imperiled.

For example, in 2015, the U.S. industrial automation and energy solutions firm Honeywell International Inc. acquired its German competitor Teaford GmbH, which specialized in thermal gas solutions for commercial, industrial, and residential heating systems, as well as gas, water, and electricity meters. The CAR of the merging firms' closest rivals, such as Siemens, Itron, and Emerson, all increased following the deal's announcement (Mataigne et al., 2021). Such gains could be attributed to two main reasons. First, by reducing competitive rivalry, horizontal M&As should contribute to increasing the pricing power for all firms in the market, not only the merging firms. Second, given M&As' high possibility of failure (King et al., 2004), the market might perceive that a horizontal M&A represents a competitive opportunity for the firm's rivals (Clougherty & Duso, 2009).

Conversely, vertical acquisitions involve deals representing a firm's backward or forward integration (i.e., the acquisition of a supplier or a customer, respectively). Backward integration can result in rationing, where rivals of the focal firm might need to cut production due to the lack of needed supplies or due to price increases of available suppliers, while forward integration can result in exclusive contracts, pricing discrimination, and shutting out customers completely (Kedia et al., 2011). For example, in 2016 the telecommunications firm AT&T announced the acquisition of Time Warner, a media and content creation firm. The purpose of the deal was to create a vertically integrated firm, streamlining content delivery and giving AT&T better control over the media pipeline. The CAR of AT&T's main rivals, such as Comcast and Charter Communications, decreased after the announcement of the deal, as the market anticipated higher content costs for them (Zimmerman et al., 2024). Other studies also provide evidence that rivals of firms engaging in vertical M&As do indeed suffer negative returns (Kedia et al., 2011).

Given that the findings of the initial decades of research on financial market reactions of rival firms to M&A announcements were somewhat inconsistent, scholars in the 2010s emphasized contextual factors affecting the deals, such as foreign acquisitions and the M&A landscape in countries other than the U.S. Early research focused on domestic deals in the U.S., but foreign acquisitions might substantially differ from those, as they create much larger consumer markets for the merging firms, increasing their bargaining power and the opportunity for synergies across the firms' businesses, which should decrease rivals' market value (Yilmaz, 2024). Yet, specific deal, industry, and country characteristics should also affect rivals' financial reactions. For instance, rivals' reactions may differ for rivals located in developed versus developing countries.

For example, in a study of U.S. takeovers in foreign countries, Burns and Liebenberg (2011) found that the targets' rivals reacted positively to acquisitions in developing countries, which the authors attributed to contagion effects, as foreign acquisitions might benefit the local market through innovation and knowledge spillovers. This finding contradicts the general assumption that competition from a developed country's firm might harm local firms in developing countries. Such positive returns are contingent on industry and institutional aspects, such as the level of economic development and shareholder protection. Nonetheless, when targets were in developed countries, their rivals' reactions were generally not significant. Instead, most of the factors explaining rivals' reactions in developed countries were at the firm level, such as rival size, efficiency, and leverage, which might be due to the signaling effects discussed earlier.

Likewise, Elango et al. (2019) analyzed foreign acquisitions of Indian firms, finding similar positive returns that could also be attributed to contagion effects. Such positive returns were contingent on foreign competition and business group competition, both increasing overall expectations for local firms, as well as institutional reforms. However, when these foreign acquisitions happened alongside institutional reforms aimed at facilitating business operations, the initial moderating effects of foreign competition and business group competition reversed, as the market might perceive that foreign firms could have a future advantage over local firms. This corroborates the idea that developing country firms benefit from knowing how to navigate the country's institutional environment, which coupled with the spillovers from foreign competition, should provide them with a competitive advantage.

Finally, and in accordance with the previous findings, a range of studies using both multi-country samples (Li et al., 2017) and samples from specific countries, such as India (Ranju & Mallikarjunappa, 2019) and China (Gaur et al., 2013), also corroborate the signaling effects theorized by early studies and tested in U.S. samples, showing that foreign M&As in developing countries attest to the growth potential of local firms. As with domestic M&As in the United States, however, nuances related to industry and firm level factors also exist in other countries. For example, in their study of Chinese acquisitions, Gaur et al. (2013) found that the positive returns experienced by rivals were higher in industries with less competition, as well as contingent on whether M&A were horizontal or vertical.

Further understanding these nuances continued in more recent research (i.e., from 2020 onwards), which has brought back some of the initial concerns of prior studies, addressing them with larger samples and many sensitivity and robustness tests. For example, Clougherty and Duso (2023) revisited the relatedness hypothesis, complementing initial findings that related deals outperformed unrelated deals and adding that highly related deals also undermined the stock price of rival firms. The timing of the M&A during a merger wave also matters (Gao et al., 2024; Haleblian et al., 2012). Moreover, the signaling effects continued to be addressed and further analyzed (e.g., Davis et al., 2022; Lee, 2022). For example, Guo et al. (2023) found that comparable peers of acquired firms might not experience change in returns right after announcement but tend to perform better in the long term and have significantly higher chances of becoming a takeover target in the years after the focal acquisition. Such a higher likelihood of future acquisition is also found in other studies concerning rivals whose risk is expected to reduce after the focal acquisition (Holcomb & Mason, 2021) and rivals possessing similar technological resources as the focal firm (Testoni, 2022).

Moreover, research continues to point to country-level aspects that contribute to either positive or negative rivals' returns, with inconclusive findings due to the particularities of each country and market. For example, rivals of Latin American firms in the banking industry were not affected by M&A announcements, but the insignificant results changed when analyzing subsamples of each country included in the analysis (Lozada et al., 2022). Rivals of Chinese manufacturing firms, however, suffered from a decrease in their long-term performance after a focal firm's international acquisition, although this was measured as the change in the firms' return on assets, which differs from the usual CAR used in most studies (Hu et al., 2020). The authors also found that different aspects moderated this relationship, including whether the acquisition was horizontal, targets were in the high-technology industry, and rivals used a cost-leadership strategy.

In sum, by analyzing the bulk of research on financial market reactions of rival firms to M&A announcements, as well as the specificities of each study, I find that rivals' positive returns tend to be more accentuated when the rivals are similar to the target (Gao et al., 2024), which sometimes includes horizontal M&As (Clougherty & Duso, 2009) and firms with technological overlaps (Cai et al., 2024). This effect is often due to signaling growth potential, which improves the liquidity of these firms' shares (Dunham & Obonyo, 2025). However, these results might vary when the focal merger or acquisition is a hostile takeover (Shahrur & Venkateswaran, 2009). Moreover, rivals might also experience negative returns, particularly when there is enough evidence to predict that they rivals might be negatively affected or even "shut out" by the new competitive landscape (Kedia et al., 2011; Yilmaz, 2024; Zimmerman et al., 2024), or when the acquiring firm realizes operational efficiencies (Bernile & Lyandres, 2019). Finally, results are much more nuanced in cross-border deals, which face an added layer of complexity due to cultural, institutional, and regulatory differences (Kolaric et al., 2024).

Strategic Responses

Studies analyzing strategic responses of rival firms to M&A announcements emphasize both higher-level corporate responses, such as engaging in M&As, alliances, or joint ventures (Fani et al., 2023), and operational responses, such as changing their financing and investment activities (Servaes & Tamayo, 2014). While some of these responses, particularly operational ones, are mostly driven by the firms' wish to signal their value to the market, given the threat of becoming targets themselves (Chatterjee, 1986; Eckbo, 1983), others seek to capitalize on the postmerger disruptions that might distract the newly merged managers. For example, rival firms can attempt to steal customers or employees of firms combining in an acquisition (Brown et al., 2008; Kato & Schoenberg, 2012; King & Schriber, 2016). Additionally, rivals may pursue changing the market by engaging and bolder and riskier moves that can lead to a competitive advantage in the future (Valentini, 2016). Three broad categories of strategic responses were identified, which are discussed below.

Corporate, operational, and competitive responses. In April 2012, Facebook announced the acquisition of Instagram, aiming at strengthening its position in mobile photo sharing and preempting a rising competitor. Six months later, in October 2012, Twitter (now X) acquired Vine, a short-form video app, just months after the firm's inception and before the platform had officially launched. Twitter's acquisition was widely interpreted as a strategic response to Facebook's aggressive expansion into adjacent social media domains (Cheredar, 2012; Geron, 2012).

Following this example, studies on corporate responses are mostly based on competitive dynamics research (Keil et al., 2013; Schriber et al., 2022), often focusing particularly on the awareness-motivation-capability (AMC) framework (Fani et al., 2023; Uhlenbruck et al., 2017). Fani et al. (2023) posited that financial and fiscal institutional differences across countries elicited more corporate responses from rivals—namely, acquisitions, alliances, and joint ventures—within two years of the focal international acquisition announcement in cases where financial institutional gains for the targets and fiscal institutional gains for the acquirers were expected. Such responses, nonetheless, were contingent on whether the rivals were aware of potential gains and motivated to act, measured by using R&D intensity and geographic position (i.e., whether the rival is located in either the acquired or the target's country). Corporate responses, however, might have either positive or negative effects of rivals' performance, which are also affected by industry-level aspects. For example, Keil et al. (2013) found that rivals of merging public software firms in the United States only benefited from responding to the merger or acquisition by acquiring a firm in a different segment, as rivals that responded by acquiring firms in the same segment experienced negative performance.

Although some firms might respond with higher-level corporate moves, rivals more often respond to M&A announcements by taking steps that would allow them to become more competitive at the industry level or even within specific market segments. Such steps usually involve a combination of competitive actions (Schriber et al., 2022; Uhlenbruck et al., 2017), including changes in pricing and marketing, new product releases and adaptations to their product mix (Mukherji et al., 2011), an increase in the firm's capacity, or taking legal action (Uhlenbruck et al., 2017). In highly competitive landscapes, these actions often involve a readjustment of the firm's operations, with a goal of improving efficiency and reducing costs (Evanoff & Ors, 2008; Feng & Rao, 2022), with actions such as laying off employees, readjusting or even decreasing production (Stiebale & Szücs, 2022), and reducing business expenses. Finally, improvements in corporate governance are also identified, which includes changing the firms' CEO and increasing board independence (Feng & Rao, 2022).

Innovation and Sustainability. In 2023, the pharmaceutical firm Merck & Co. more than doubled its investment in research and development (R&D), from $13.5 billion in 2022, to over $30 billion (Buntz, 2024). While this strategic move was influenced by internal factors such as impending patent cliffs, it was also made in the context of broader industry consolidation trends, as rivals such as Pfizer and Bristol Myers Squibb pursued significant acquisitions during the period (Sagonowsky, 2024).

Following this example, the general finding is that M&As have a positive effect on innovation-related activities and investments of rival firms, including R&D intensity (Xue et al., 2021), patent grants and citations (Kaufmann & Schiereck, 2023; Valentini, 2016), and a combination of both (Feng & Rao, 2022). Moreover, such a positive effect tends to be higher in competitive markets (Xue et al., 2021). Also, when rivals are innovative, the likelihood of their engaging in a subsequent acquisition for technology access increases (Kaufmann & Schiereck, 2023). These results suggest that rivals' intent to improve their products and processes as the market becomes more competitive, allocating more resources to innovative activities. A similar finding concerns sustainability practices, often accompanied by innovative activity (Adams et al., 2016). Kang and Ahn (2024) found that rivals increase their corporate social responsibility (CSR) commitments following M&As by high-level CSR acquirers, suggesting the same spillovers that exist for innovation. This positive relationship is also more pronounced in competitive markets, which shows that competitive pressures intensify the need for rivals to seek better and more innovative CSR practices.

Nonetheless, a couple of articles found a negative effect of M&A announcements on innovation-related activities and investments of rival firms, suggesting that nuances might exist in specific contexts. For example, such a negative effect was found in a sample of Chinese firms engaging in M&As with the specific purpose of obtaining patents, exclusive technologies, or key innovative human capital (Cao et al., 2023). The authors justified the finding by suggesting that, in this context, rivals became more conservative, reserving more cash holdings, as they anticipated fiercer competition ahead. A decrease in patent applications was also found by Stiebale and Szücs (2022), which could be attributed to the narrowly defined group of competitors in their sample of European firms; these rivals are so tightly linked to the focal firm that their initial objectives following the M&A announcement are to tighten operations and improve efficiency to face the new competition.

Finance, Accounting, and Disclosure Practices. In 2018, the telecommunication firms T-Mobile and Sprint announced a merger, with the goal of better competing against market leaders Verizon and AT&T. Following the deal's completion in 2020, the two rivals responded with earning signaling, including issuing optimistic forward guidance, expanding share buyback programs, and emphasizing their early investments in 5G infrastructure during earnings calls and public disclosures (e.g., AT&T, 2021; Verizon, 2020).

Following this example, and in accordance with signaling effects, rivals will engage in tactics that make them appear financially better. For example, Du et al. (2024) found that rivals engage in more real earnings management (REM), a practice where managers deliberately manipulate accounting choices and economic activities with the purpose of increasing earnings to make them appear financially better. The strategy seems to pay off, as their likelihood of being acquired in subsequent years increases, as well as to be sold at higher premiums. Conversely, Stiebale and Szücs (2022) found that rivals decreased their investments in tangible assets, while Servaes and Tamayo (2014) found that rivals reduced their capital spending, free cash flows, and cash holdings, as well as increased their leverage and payouts to shareholders following a rival firm's hostile takeover announcement, as a way of escaping the threat of control. These measures, nonetheless, tend to contribute to improvements in long-term performance, demonstrating the efficiency of the market for corporate control. In this vein,

The control threat also leads rivals to engage in tactics that are not related to the firm's operations, but rather to how the market perceives them. Chen et al. (2022) found that rivals facing a control threat might change their disclosure strategy to emphasize bad news, which includes delivering more bad news forecasts, bundling such forecasts with earnings announcements and using a more negative tone in earnings presentations, with the goal of increasing uncertainty over the firm value. Such tactics, nonetheless, are mostly used by firms that face a greater threat of a hostile takeover, which includes having a younger CEO or a CEO with higher compensation than peers.

In sum, research on strategic responses of rival firms to M&A announcements suggests a myriad of actions taken to increase these firms' own competitiveness or mitigate the threats imposed by the changes in the competitive landscape. Actions comprise corporate, operational, and competitive responses, changes in innovation and sustainability practices, and changes in finance, accounting, and disclosure practices. These actions and their long-term effect on performance are affected by firm-specific characteristics, industry structure, and, in the case of cross-border M&As, the acquirer and target's institutional context. Building on competitive dynamics, which is the most cited theoretical approach (Fani et al., 2023; Keil et al., 2013; Schriber et al., 2022; Uhlenbruck et al., 2017), the bulk of the research shows that the higher the similarity between the rival and the focal firm, in terms of firm-level resources (Cai et al., 2024), and the higher their rivalry, in terms of market concentration (Stiebale & Szücs, 2022), the higher the volume and complexity of the responses (Uhlenbruck et al., 2017). Moreover, responses aimed at reducing costs and increasing efficiency seem to pay off in the long term, as firms that take such actions tend to achieve better performance (Servaes & Tamayo, 2014). A summary of rival actions is presented on Table 1.

Table 1 Summary of rival actions

Financial market reactions	*Strategic responses*		
	Corporate, operational, and competitive responses	*Innovation and sustainability*	*Finance, accounting, and disclosure practices*
- Cumulative Abnormal Returns (CAR) - Long-term performance (e.g., ROA)	- Acquisitions - Alliances - Joint ventures - Changes in pricing and marketing - Increased capacity - Legal action - Improved efficiency - Cost reductions - Improvements in corporate governance	- R&D spending - Patent applications, grants, and citations - Increased CSR commitments	- Increased real earnings management - Decreased investments in tangible assets - Reduced capital spending, free cash flows, and cash holdings - Increased leverage - Increased payouts to shareholders - Changes in disclosure strategies

Discussion

Reviewing research underscores the increasingly complex and multifaceted nature of rivals' responses to acquisitions, reflecting both the strategic significance of these events. While early research predominantly focused on short-term financial market reactions, more recent studies have expanded consider an array of strategic responses, including corporate restructuring, operational adjustments, innovation initiatives, and changes in financial and disclosure practices. However, the knowledge on rival actions and impacts associated with acquisition activity remains fragmented. For example, rival responses vary considerably depending on deal characteristics, industry structure, firm-specific factors, and institutional environments. This diversity in findings points to the need for a more integrated theoretical and empirical approach to understanding how, when, and why rivals react to M&As—and what the long-term implications of these reactions are for firm performance. Additional implications for management research and practice are discussed next, as well as limitations that present opportunities for additional research.

Research Implications

Taking stock of the bulk of the research on rivals' responses to M&As allows us to better understand how these important but often overlooked stakeholders are affected and, in turn, react to either protect themselves from or take advantage of the changes in the competitive landscape. Given that rivals' responses and their performance implications are contingent on firm-, industry-, and country-level characteristics, I provide a framework that helps scholars navigate the findings, as well as identify opportunities for future research, see Fig. 2.

The framework summarizes the findings identified by previous research, showing that the bulk of the research analyzes how industry characteristics affect rival firms' reaction to M&A announcements, either in terms of short-term performance (e.g., abnormal returns), strategic responses, or a combination of both. Studies focused on cross-border acquisitions also emphasize institutional factors of the acquirer and target's countries (Fani et al., 2023). Firm-level factors and deal characteristics are most often included as moderators. Finally, changes in

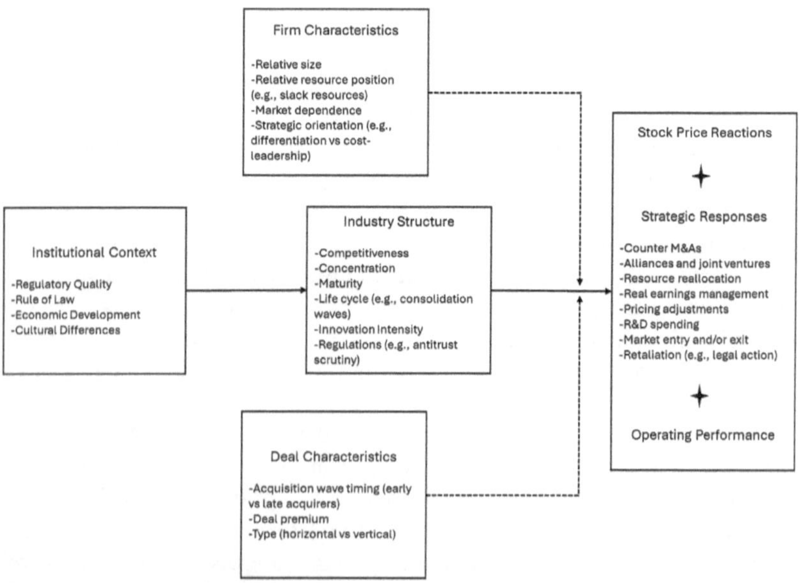

Fig. 2 Framework for understanding research on rival's responses to M&A

operating performance are usually included to explain the consequences of not only the merger or acquisition but, most importantly, the strategic responses taken by rivals. Operating performance usually covers many years following the focal M&A (Hu et al., 2020; Keil et al., 2013).

The framework allows us to suggest some paths for future research. First, three main theoretical approaches are used to explain rivals' responses to M&A announcements, namely signaling theory, competitive theory (i.e., efficiency versus collusion), and competitive dynamics. How can other theories, such as game theory and the resource-based view, increase our understanding of the topic, particularly concerning strategic responses? Relatedly, are there unexplored moderating or mediating variables that could complement or further explain the existing findings? Second, concerning financial market reactions, could the divergent findings (positive versus negative returns) be explained in one comprehensive framework? How can research conciliate the various market conditions and firm-level characteristics driving the spillover effects experienced by rival firms? Third, concerning strategic responses, how do rival firms strategically prioritize corporate, operational, and other competitive actions when responding to a focal firm's M&A? How does the type of synergies promised by the focal M&A (Feldman & Hernandez, 2022) and other strategy typologies determine variation in rivals' reactions? Fourth, concerning the temporal and longitudinal dynamics of rivals' responses and their effect on performance, how do rivals' immediate reactions and responses align with their longer-term strategic and operational adjustments, as well as their performance? How do response patterns evolve over M&A waves, and if shifts happen, what triggers them? Finally, with big data, machine learning, and generative artificial intelligence (AI) becoming more prevalent, there is a need to better understand if and how such advancements can alter rivals' abilities to predict and respond to M&As that shift their competitive environment.

Managerial Implications

The findings reviewed in this chapter offer several important implications for managers navigating M&As. First, managers of acquiring firms must recognize that M&A announcements affect rivals, which in turn engage in strategic responses that might even lower the acquiring firm's long-term performance (Schriber et al., 2022). As a result, managers should plan and take appropriate actions to mitigate the effectiveness of rival actions when making an acquisition (King & Schriber, 2016). Second, the research reveals that the nature and effectiveness of rival responses depend on several firm, deal, industry, and even country characteristics. Managers should closely monitor these factors to anticipate how rivals are likely to respond, adjusting their strategies accordingly. Third, firms not directly involved in an M&A should consider using rivals' acquisition announcements as opportunities to strengthen their own positioning (Uhlenbruck et al., 2017). Whether through innovating by launching new products or acquiring complementary technologies, emphasizing sustainability, or reallocating resources, rivals can leverage the disruption created by an M&A to reposition themselves competitively. Finally, the literature highlights that rivals might also respond through tactics that project financial strength and a stable market position, which suggests the importance of impression management in M&As. Managers on all sides of a deal should proactively shape stakeholder expectations through strategically communicating about the M&A and its possible consequences (Chen et al., 2022; Du et al., 2024).

Limitations

While the focus of this chapter is on rivals' reactions to M&As, there are additional ways that rivals can strategically use acquisitions. For example, firms may make acquisitions to preempt rival firms (Brito, 2003). Additionally, acquisitions can combine rival firms (Clark et al., 2010), and this complicates integration that can also potentially make other rival actions more effective. Another limitation is that this review focused on actions taken after an M&A, but rival firms can make competing bids to drive up the price an acquirer pays for a target firm (Uhlenbruck et al., 2017). Further, other factors such as media coverage may influence rivalry surrounding acquisitions (Tan, 2016). Overall, additional research is needed to understand the influence and impacts of rival actions surrounding M&As.

Appendix: Review Methodology

I conducted a systematic review of literature published until the end of 2024, following the procedure outlined by Denyer and Tranfield (2009). First, I formulated a specific review question, namely *How do rival firms respond to a focal firm's M&A*? I used two databases to locate relevant studies, Scopus and Web of Science. As the literature on M&As is interdisciplinary, I included research in not only management but also other business and related areas, such as accounting, finance, and economics. Also, researchers might use a variety of terms to define rivals, such as competitors and even market, which led us to use both specific and broad search terms. The initial search in Scopus included the terms *("merger* and acquisition*" OR "M&A*" OR "corporate acquisition*" OR "merger*" OR "acquisition*") AND ("rival* response*" OR "compet* response*" OR "compet* reaction*" OR "rival* strateg*" OR "compet* dynamic*" OR "market* reaction*" OR "peer*" OR "retaliat*")* in the *article title, abstract, and keywords*. I included the subject areas *Business, Management and Accounting* and *Economics, Econometrics, and Finance*, and restricted the search to *articles*. This initial search yielded 701 studies.

Then, I conducted a similar search on Web of Science (WoSc), including the terms *("merger* and acquisition*" OR "M&A*" OR "corporate acquisition*" OR "merger*" OR "acquisition*") AND ("rival* response*" OR "compet* response*" OR "compet* reaction*" OR "rival* strateg*" OR "compet* dynamic*" OR "market* reaction*" OR "peer*" OR "retaliat*")* in the *topics*. I included the research area *Business Economics* and restricted the search to *articles*. This search yielded 635 studies. This initial sample of 1,336 articles contained 465 duplicates that were excluded. The remaining 871 articles were assessed for possible inclusion in the review.

More specifically, the author reviewed the titles and abstracts of each study, to evaluate whether the articles addressed the review question (i.e., empirically analyzed rivals' responses to M&As) and were indeed published in academic journals. In cases where it was not clear, the author then read the article. Based on this analysis, only 38 of the 871 articles discussed rival firms' responses to M&As. In order to ensure that the searches did not leave out any relevant studies, the author tracked the citations of the most relevant articles using WoSc. This new search yielded 34 new articles (excluding duplicates), which were reviewed based on the review question. 15 of them addressed the review question and were included in the sample. Finally, the author proceeded to fully read these 53 articles to assess their quality and relevance (Rojon et al., 2021; Tranfield et al., 2003), ensuring that they empirically analyzed M&As and rivals' responses to them. A total of 52 studies matched the criteria (one study was conceptual and, thus, not included). As the author read these articles, four other relevant cited references concerning the research question were also included in the review, which comprises a total of 56 articles.

References

(*denotes study included in the review)

Adams, R., Jeanrenaud, S., Bessant, J., Denyer, D., & Overy, P. (2016). Sustainability-oriented innovation: A systematic review. *International Journal of Management Reviews, 18*(2), 180–205.

*Akhigbe, A., Borde, S., & Whyte, A. (2000). The source of gains to targets and their industry rivals: Evidence based on terminated merger proposals. *Financial Management*, 101–118.

AT&T. (2021, March 12). *AT&T provides long-term growth outlook and strategy update at analyst & investor day*. https://about.att.com/story/2021/att_analyst_day.html

Bernile, G., & Lyandres, E. (2019). The effects of horizontal merger operating efficiencies on rivals, customers, and suppliers. *Review of Finance, 23*(1), 117–160.

Brito, D. (2003). Preemptive mergers under spatial competition. *International Journal of Industrial Organization, 21*, 1601–1622.

Brown, C., Clancy, G., & Scholer, R. (2008). A post-merger IT integration success story: Sallie Mae. *MIS Quarterly Executive, 2*(1), 3.

Buntz, B. (2024, March 11). Why Merck shelled out $30B+ on R&D in 2023. *Drug Discovery & Development*. https://www.drugdiscoverytrends.com/why-merck-shelled-out-30b-on-rd-in-2023/

Burns, N., & Liebenberg, I. (2011). US takeovers in foreign markets: Do they impact emerging and developed markets differently? *Journal of Corporate Finance, 17*(4), 1028–1046.

Cai, X., De Cesari, A., Gao, N., & Peng, N. (2024). Acquisitions and technology value revision. *Management Science, 70*(7), 4283–4305.

Cao, Z., Hua, C., Tong, Y., & Wang, X. (2023). The crowding-out effects of innovation information disclosure on peers' innovation: Evidence from innovation-driven M&As in China. *Accounting & Finance, 63*(5), 4883–4908.

Campa, J., & Hernando, I. (2008). The reaction by industry insiders to M&As in the European financial industry. *Journal of Financial Services Research, 33*, 127–146.

Chatterjee, S. (1986). Types of synergy and economic value: The impact of acquisitions on merging and rival firms. *Strategic Management Journal, 7*(2), 119–139.

Chehab, A. (2002). Market reaction to large bank merger announcements in oligopolies. *Journal of Economics and Finance, 26*(1), 63–76.

Chen, S., Miao, B., & Valentine, K. (2022). Corporate control contests and the asymmetric disclosure of bad news: Evidence from peer firm disclosure response to takeover threat. *Accounting Review, 97*(1), 123–146.

Cheredar, T. (2012, October 10). Twitter takes aim at video, acquires video clip service Vine. *Reuters*. https://www.reuters.com/article/business/twitter-takes-aim-at-video-acquires-video-clip-service-vine-idUS4286695776/

Clark, S., Gioia, D., Ketchen, D., & Thomas, J. (2010). Transitional identity as a facilitator of organizational identity change during a merger. *Administrative Science Quarterly, 55*, 397–438.

Clougherty, J., & Duso, T. (2009). The impact of horizontal mergers on rivals: Gains to being left outside a merger. *Journal of Management Studies, 46*(8), 1365–1395.

Clougherty, J., & Duso, T. (2023). Revisiting the relatedness hypothesis: The impact of merger relatedness on acquiring and rival firm value. *Long Range Planning, 56*(6), Article 102325.

Davis, F., Davis, S., Sha, X., & Walker, T. (2022). The impact of takeover anticipation on rival firms. *Journal of Business Finance & Accounting, 49*(7–8), 1264–1288.

Denyer, D., & Tranfield, D. (2009). Producing a systematic review. In D. A. Buchanan & A. Bryman (Eds.), *The Sage handbook of organizational research methods* (pp. 671–689). Sage Publications.

*Du, L., Li, W., & Sun, J. (2024). The real effects of M&As on targets' peers. *Journal of Business Finance & Accounting*.

*Dunham, L., & Obonyo, T. (2025). Industry peers stock liquidity and M&A. *Review of Financial Economics*.

Eckbo, B. (1983). Horizontal mergers, collusion, and stockholder wealth. *Journal of Financial Economics, 11*(1–4), 241–273.

Elango, B., Dhandapani, K., & Giachetti, C. (2019). Impact of institutional reforms and industry structural factors on market returns of emerging market rivals during acquisitions by foreign firms. *International Business Review, 28*(5), Article 101493.

Evanoff, D. D., & Ors, E. (2008). The competitive dynamics of geographic deregulation in banking: Implications for productive efficiency. *Journal of Money, Credit and Banking, 40*(5), 897–928.

Fani, V., Kalanoski, D., & Bertrand, O. (2023). The competitive effects of financial and fiscal institutional arbitrage opportunities: Evidence from cross-border M&AS. *Long Range Planning, 56*(3), Article 102324.

Fee, E., & Thomas, S. (2004). Sources of gains in horizontal mergers: Evidence from customer, supplier and rival firms. *Journal of Financial Economics, 73*, 423–460.

Feldman, E., & Hernandez, E. (2022). Synergy in mergers and acquisitions: Typology, life cycles, and value. *Academy of Management Review, 47*(4), 549–578.

Feng, H., & Rao, R. P. (2022). The positive externalities of leveraged buyouts. *Journal of Banking & Finance, 135*, Article 106360.

Gao, X., An, Z., Li, D., & Xu, W. (2024). Does media affect the rival response to acquisition targets? *Journal of Empirical Finance, 76*, Article 101475.

Gaur, A., Malhotra, S., & Zhu, P. (2013). Acquisition announcements and stock market valuations of acquiring firms' rivals: A test of the growth probability hypothesis in China. *Strategic Management Journal, 34*(2), 215–232.

Geron, T. (2012, September 6). Facebook officially closes Instagram deal. *Forbes*. https://www.forbes.com/sites/tomiogeron/2012/09/06/facebook-officially-closes-instagram-deal/

Gomes, E., Alam, S., Tarba, S., & Vendrell-Herrero, F. (2020). A 27-year review of mergers and acquisitions research in 27 leading management journals. *Strategic Change, 29*(2), 179–193.

Gong, S., & Firth, M. (2006). The competitive effects of airline mergers and acquisitions: More capital market evidence. *Journal of Air Transportation, 11*(1), 88.

Guo, F., Liu, T., & Tu, D. (2023). Neglected peers in merger valuations. *Review of Financial Studies, 36*(8), 3257–3310.

Haleblian, J., McNamara, G., Kolev, K., & Dykes, B. (2012). Exploring firm characteristics that differentiate leaders from followers in industry merger waves: A competitive dynamics perspective. *Strategic Management Journal, 33*(9), 1037–1052.

Hankir, Y., Rauch, C., & Umber, M. (2011). Bank M&A: A market power story? *Journal of Banking & Finance, 35*(9), 2341–2354.

Holcomb, A., & Mason, P. (2021). The effect of industry restructuring on peer firms. *Journal of Risk and Financial Management, 14*(5), 205.

Hu, X., Yin, X., Jin, Z., & Li, J. (2020). How do international M&As affect rival firm's sustainable performance? Empirical evidence from an emerging market. *Sustainability, 12*(4), 1318.

King, D., Dalton, D., Daily, C., & Covin, J. (2004). Meta-analysis of post-acquisition performance: Indications of unidentified moderators. *Strategic Management Journal, 25*(2), 187–200.

*Kang, G., & Ahn, H. (2024). CSR spillover effects of corporate M&As by US Acquirers. *Industry and Innovation*, 1–27.

Kato, J., & Schoenberg, R. (2012). Customer and competitor responses to mergers and acquisitions: An empirical investigation in the logistics industry. *Advances in Mergers and Acquisitions, 11*, 155–180.

Kaufmann, M., & Schiereck, D. (2023). Acquiring for innovation: Evidence from the US technology industry. *Journal of Economic Dynamics and Control, 152*, Article 104673.

Kedia, S., Ravid, S., & Pons, V. (2011). When do vertical mergers create value? *Financial Management, 40*(4), 845–877.

Keil, T., Laamanen, T., & McGrath, R. (2013). Is a counterattack the best defense? Competitive dynamics through acquisitions. *Long Range Planning, 46*(3), 195–215.

King, D., & Schriber, S. (2016). Addressing competitive responses to acquisitions. *California Management Review, 58*(3), 109–124.

*Kolaric, S., Kiesel, F., & Schiereck, D. (2024). Banking market consolidation in Asia: Evidence from acquirers, targets, and rivals. *International Journal of Finance & Economics.*

Lee, S. (2022). Target shareholder gains, peer firm values, and merger and acquisition announcements. *International Journal of Finance & Economics, 27*(3), 3550–3563.

Li, D., Chen, Z., An, Z., & Murong, M. (2017). Do financial analysts play a role in shaping the rival response of target firms? International evidence. *Journal of Corporate Finance, 45*, 84–103.

Lozada, J., Cortés, L., & Velásquez-Gaviria, D. (2022). The stock market reaction to mergers and acquisitions: Evidence from the banking industry. *Latin American Business Review, 23*(3), 255–278.

Mataigne, V., Manigart, S., & Luypaert, M. (2021). Acquisitions: A curse or blessing for direct competitors? The impact of target ownership structure. *Journal of Corporate Finance, 69*, Article 101988.

Mukherji, P., Sorescu, A., Prabhu, J., & Chandy, R. (2011). Behemoths at the gate: How incumbents take on acquisitive entrants (and why some do better than others). *Journal of Marketing, 75*(5), 53–70.

Mullin, G., Mullin, J., & Mullin, W. (1995). The competitive effects of mergers: Stock market evidence from the US steel dissolution suit. *RAND Journal of Economics, 26*(2), 314–330.

Ranju, P., & Mallikarjunappa, T. (2019). Spillover effect of M&A announcements on acquiring firms' rivals: Evidence from India. *Global Business Review, 20*(3), 692–707.

Rojon, C., Okupe, A., & McDowall, A. (2021). Utilization and development of systematic reviews in management research: What do we know and where do we go from here? *International Journal of Management Reviews, 23*(2), 191–223.

Sagonowsky, E. (2024, February 5). Top 10 biopharma M&A deals of 2023. *Fierce Pharma*. https://www.fiercepharma.com/special-reports/top-10-biopharma-ma-deals-2023

Schriber, S., King, D., & Bauer, F. (2022). Retaliation effectiveness and acquisition performance: The influence of managerial decisions and industry context. *British Journal of Management, 33*(2), 939–957.

Servaes, H., & Tamayo, A. (2014). How do industry peers respond to control threats? *Management Science, 60*(2), 380–399.

Shahrur, H. (2005). Industry structure and horizontal takeovers: Analysis of wealth effects on rivals, suppliers and corporate customers. *Journal of Financial Economics, 76*, 61–98.

Shahrur, H., & Venkateswaran, A. (2009). Industry prospects and acquirer returns in diversifying takeovers. *Journal of Financial Research, 32*(1), 23–51.

Song, M., & Walkling, R. (2000). Abnormal returns to rivals of acquisition targets: A test of the acquisition probability hypothesis. *Journal of Financial Economics, 55*, 143–171.

Stiebale, J., & Szücs, F. (2022). Mergers and market power: Evidence from rivals' responses in European markets. *RAND Journal of Economics, 53*(4), 678–702.

Tan, D. (2016). Making the news: Heterogeneous media coverage and corporate litigation. *Strategic Management Journal, 37*(7), 1341–1353.

Testoni, M. (2022). The market value spillovers of technological acquisitions: Evidence from patent-text analysis. *Strategic Management Journal, 43*(5), 964–985.

Tranfield, D., Denyer, D., & Smart, P. (2003). Towards a methodology for developing evidence-informed management knowledge by means of systematic review. *British Journal of Management, 14*(3), 207–222.

Uhlenbruck, K., Hughes-Morgan, M., Hitt, M., Ferrier, W., & Brymer, R. (2017). Rivals' reactions to mergers and acquisitions. *Strategic Organization, 15*(1), 40–66.

Valentini, G. (2016). The impact of M&A on rivals' innovation strategy. *Long Range Planning, 49*(2), 241–249.

Verizon. (2020, February 11). *Verizon reaction to T-Mobile/Sprint merger approval*. https://www.verizon.com/about/news/verizon-reaction-t-mobile sprint-merger-approval

Wårell, L. (2007). A horizontal merger in the iron ore industry: An event study approach. *Resources Policy, 32*(4), 191–204.

Xue, H., Zeng, S., Sun, D., & Shi, J. (2021). Impacts of peers' mergers and acquisitions on firm innovation. *IEEE Transactions on Engineering Management, 71*, 598–613.

Yilmaz, U. (2024). The effects of foreign acquisitions on the value of industry peers. *Journal of Financial and Quantitative Analysis, 59*(4), 1849–1885.

Yin, X., & Shanley, M. (2008). Industry determinants of the "merger versus alliance" decision. *Academy of Management Review, 33*(2), 473–491.

Zimmerman, P., Chang, G., & Ulrick, S. (2024). A Prospective competitive effects analysis of the AT&T/time warner merger. *The Antitrust Bulletin, 69*(1), 44–73.

Understanding and Addressing Acquiring Firm Employee Concerns

Anjali Bansal, David R. King, and Ahmed Alsafwani

Introduction

Even though a lot of research has discussed the concerns of acquired company employees, during integration (Brannen & Peterson, 2009; King et al., 2020), the concerns and performance of acquiring company employees receive less attention. Still, existing managers and employees are also relevant stakeholders for acquiring firms (Martynova & Renneboog, 2008). For example, when a firm acquires, the reactions of its employees can play a pivotal role in shaping the future success of the merged organization. Employee responses to an acquisition may likely vary based on their position within an acquiring firm's hierarchy (Risberg, 2001). The differences in their responses may be caused by differences experienced in job security, power dynamics, involvement in decision-making processes, and perceived changes in job roles or responsibilities.

A. Bansal
Indian Institute of Management, Lucknow, India

D. R. King (✉) · A. Alsafwani
Florida State University, Tallahassee, FL, USA
e-mail: drking@fsu.edu

D. R. King and A. Bansal (eds.), *Navigating Stakeholder Dynamics Surrounding Acquisitions*,
https://doi.org/10.1007/978-3-032-03199-0_7

However, research largely considers acquiring firm employees as a single block, or it separates and examines the reactions of one employee group.

Expectations that acquiring firm employees react differently to acquisitions are reasonable. For example, senior leadership is often part of the acquisition process from the beginning. While they may experience some stress from having to adjust leadership dynamics and navigate the integration process, their position typically provides them with a sense of control and influence over how the acquisition unfolds. Meanwhile, lower-level employees of the acquiring firm often experience a range of emotions, from excitement to apprehension, as they face the uncertainty of new leadership, organizational changes, and potential shifts in company culture. Caught between these groups are middle managers that are expected to enact desired changes by senior managers, and lower-level employees seek guidance and support from middle managers. However, there is limited research on the interactions between senior and middle managers in general (Raes et al., 2011) and in acquisitions (King et al., 2020).

We summarize existing research on the effects of acquisitions on employees at different levels of an acquiring firm. The result is a summary of what is known the effects of acquisitions at different hierarchal levels, and, when available, their interactions. The intent is to provide a guide of available research and to identify avenues for additional research. However, we also make several contributions to existing research. For example, our findings underscore the importance of clear communication, strategic planning, and tailored support mechanisms to enhance employee adaptation and overall acquisition success. Additionally, we identify the need to consider differences in employees across hierarchical levels, as well as their interaction when planning or studying acquisitions. For acquired firm employees, please see Chapter "Acquired Firm Employees: Strategies for Engagement and Retention".

Acquiring Firm Employee Responses to Acquisitions

Again, understanding changes in an acquiring firm surrounding an acquisition likely can be aided by understanding the perspective of employees at different organizational levels. While acquisitions can be stressful for senior managers, they generally influence how an acquisition unfolds.

Meanwhile, middle managers are caught in a web of conflicting expectations. For example, they are expected to act as both change agents and stabilizing forces, as well as advocates for employees and loyal supporters of senior managers (Balogun & Johnson, 2004; Maitlis & Sonenshein, 2010). Finally, lower-level employees are the farthest removed from the decision-making processes during an acquisition. As a result, they can experience higher levels of uncertainty and anxiety if they perceive the acquisition as a potential threat to their job security or work environment. Ultimately, acquisitions can fail if too many managers and employees leave an acquiring firm (Tung, 2016). Next, we separately summarize research for employees at different levels of acquiring firms.

Senior Managers

Senior managers drive corporate strategy planning and implementation (Wright & Ferris, 1997), including acquisitions. For example, senior managers identify strategic goals leading to acquisitions and they lead target selection and negotiation. There are also advantages to senior managers setting the direction for integration (King et al., 2020; Kroon et al., 2022), but lack of planning for integration by top managers is a frequent source of failure (Gomes et al., 2013). As a result, senior managers are often held accountable with CEOs of poorly performing acquirers often losing their jobs (Lehn & Zhao, 2006). One problem is that after negotiating and closing an acquisition is that top managers often turn their attention to their own business and neglect the acquired business (Cording et al., 2008; Perry & Herd, 2004). Regardless, an important task for senior managers is to outline the desired organizational identity for combining firms (Empson, 2004; Hatch et al., 2015).

Acquisitions tend to immediately seek financial synergies by reducing redundancies. This can include laying off senior managers at both an acquiring and acquired firm (Bilgili et al., 2017), as there needs to be a mix of leadership in a combined firm (Graebner, 2004). In one report, 80 percent of acquiring firms initiated downsizing operations with most focusing on eliminating managers (Gutknecht & Keys, 1993). If not managed well, the workload for remaining acquiring company managers will increase due to increased responsibilities for additional product lines and geographic markets (Jacobs, 1988). Additional workload on acquiring firm managers can complicate integration (Lamont et al., 2019) and contribute to undesired turnover in managers that can degrade firm capabilities (Bilgili et al., 2017).

While acquiring a distressed firm often provides a sense of security for acquiring firm employees, they simultaneously impose significant strategic and managerial burdens on the leadership of the acquiring company. For instance, following the 2008 financial fraud orchestrated by B. Ramalinga Raju, the founder and chairman of Satyam Computer Services, it was acquired by Tech Mahindra in 2012 (Kalavalapalli, 2013). However, the combined firm continued to grapple with the reputational problems. For example, while lawsuits were settled with several stakeholders (e.g., U.S. Securities and Exchange Commission, U.S. class-action suits, and former investors), it remained entangled in legal disputes within India (Kanth, 2015).

Another critical challenge faced by senior managers of acquiring firms is managing the anxiety and demotivation of employees from the acquired company (Marks & Mirvis, 2001), including heightened job insecurity, anxiety, and unplanned turnover. Associated employee attrition can undermine acquisition goals and the means to achieve them. For example, in an interview with one of the authors, an acquiring firm senior manager stated: "we acquire companies for their talent, their network, and clientele, not for their walls and cubicles." Consequently, acquiring firm senior managers need to consider the potential exit of acquiring and acquired firm employees (Dionisi et al., 2017). Addressing this challenge places pressure on senior leadership to develop robust integration strategies, including effective onboarding programs, thorough communication strategies, and comprehensive retention plans.

Middle Managers

Middle managers have a significant impact on firm performance (Mollick, 2012), including that of acquisitions (Fried et al., 1996). Located between upper management and lower-level employees, middle managers must navigate and reconcile multiple, sometimes opposing, demands during acquisitions. For example, senior managers likely pursued an acquisition to enact change, and lower-level employees will desire stability. This drives sensemaking and giving by middle managers who communicate the need for change to lower-level employees and provide feedback to senior managers (Beck & Plowman, 2014). Further, senior managers will expect middle managers to maintain productivity during changes, and it will likely fall as employees adapt and potentially resist change.

This reflects that middle managers are responsible for enacting integration at the behest of senior managers (Maitlis & Sonenshein, 2010). For example, middle managers are often tasked with acquisition integration, including managing communication, aligning operational systems, and ensuring compliance with new organizational structures and processes. While employees will look to middle managers to explain the reasoning behind decisions, address their concerns, and guide them through uncertainty, middle managers will often not have needed information (Balogun & Johnson, 2004). In combination, changes following an acquisition alter middle manager organizational roles (Birollo & Teerikangas, 2019). As a result, middle managers can become frustrated by being responsible for outcomes for decisions made by senior managers.

Increased frustration likely results from less insight into acquisitions before they are announced (when compared to top managers), and middle managers having resulting change imposed on them at the same time they are asked to implement additional change on organizational structure and processes that impact other employees (Balogun & Johnson, 2004; Kavanagh & Ashkanasy, 2006). This creates ambiguity for middle managers when they are asked to implement integration to meet strategic goals (Correia et al., 2013), driving middle managers to simultaneously pursue sensemaking for themselves and sensegiving to lower-level employees (Bansal et al., 2022; Kroon & Reif, 2023). While sensemaking takes longer for middle managers and subsequently even longer in providing sensegiving to lower-level employees it remains important (Stensaker et al., 2008). For example, middle manager sensegiving to other employees is important as it influences their perceptions of justice (Monin et al., 2013) that can significantly impact acquisition outcomes. For example, perceived inequity following an acquisition can lower employee engagement and increase employee turnover (Bansal & King, 2022). As a result, it is important for middle managers to shield their employees from negative effects of an acquisition (Bellou, 2006) and manage employee emotions and fear (Huy, 2002; Meyer & Altenborg, 2008).

Still, it is traditionally assumed that middle managers follow the guidance of senior managers and act in the interest of the larger organization. However, research also shows that middle managers can resist or fail to implement strategic objectives after an acquisition (Meyer & Altenborg, 2008). Middle managers may feel angry about change driven by top managers (Huy, 2011), contributing to political behavior that may not align with corporate strategy (Burgelman, 1994). For example, acquirer firm managers show higher turnover in cases of diversification and geographic expansion that places higher value on target firm managers (Dionisi et al., 2017). A sense of competition may result in greater political behavior where different middle managers contest for outcomes consistent with their self-interest (Guh & MacMillan, 1986), resulting in managers displaying counterproductive behavior (Astley & Van de Ven, 1983). This can contribute to organizational disruption following an acquisition that hinders meeting strategic goals behind an acquisition.

Lower-Level Employees

Managers are often unprepared to handle employee concerns following an acquisition (Sinetar, 1981). Resistance to acquisitions often focuses on acquired employees, but it can also apply to employees of an acquiring firm because of associated changes that impact employees from both sides (Korsgaard et al., 2002; Larsson & Finkelstein, 1999). For example, one reason acquisitions fail is because of employee uncertainty relating to their current job and prospects (Csiszar & Schweiger, 1994; Ullrich et al., 2005). However, employees may resist change for either feeling that change does either too much or too little (Sonenshein, 2010).

Following an acquisition, employee concerns include changes in identity, a lack of information, and potential concerns over perceived losses (Schweiger et al., 1987; Ullrich & van Dick, 2007). This increases the relevance of communication and understanding how employees feel they are treated (Bansal & King, 2022; Giessner, 2011). Understanding employee feelings can be aided by considering perceived justice of acquiring firm actions, including interactional, distributive, and procedural justice. Interactional justice deals with the quality of an individual's treatment during the transition, including empathy, transparency, and respect from the leaders (Bansal, 2019). Distributive justice entails the perception of the fairness of outcomes like career growth opportunities, compensation adjustments, and job security. Procedural justice relates to fair and unbiased rules, procedures, and decision-making processes (Lucas et al., 2016). Higher perceptions of fairness can increase employee satisfaction and lower turnover after an acquisition (Bansal & King, 2022).

However, acquiring firm employees can remain resistant to change. For example, acquiring firm employees tend to prefer existing relationships over forming new relationships across preacquisition boundaries (Colman & Lunnan, 2024), and this may be more pronounced with veteran employees (Rousseau, 2001). This manifests in inertia in communication patterns following an acquisition (Steigenberger, 2017) that can hinder adoption of new work processes, as new relationships facilitate flexibility and coordination (Sarala et al., 2016). Inertia in relationships may be overcome through mutual respect and developing shared goals (Carmeli & Gittell, 2009), or by pairing acquired and target firm employees with a buddy system (Mayer & Kenney, 2004). The latter can help overcome the challenge of having employees cooperate over previously separate organizations (Ullrich & van Dick, 2007). However, conflict between acquiring and target firm employees can result from inconsistencies in human resource policies (Strobl et al., 2024).

Addressing employee anxiety can be addressed by communicating with employees about the implications of an acquisition early (Risberg, 2001). For example, firms can hold information sessions about planned changes (Rafferty & Restubog, 2010). Counterintuitively, a strategic pause after an acquisition can help acclimate employees and facilitate acceptance of change (Bansal et al., 2022). This may relate to increasing perceptions of employee justice or how employees feel they are treated (Bansal & King, 2022; Devers et al., 2020). Regardless, steps are needed to reduce employee uncertainty, as valuable employees often receive competing job offers following an acquisition (Meyer, 2008). Further, it is important to recognize that retained employees may suffer from merger syndrome related to emotional changes following an acquisition and seeing others lose their jobs (Fried et al., 1996; Sinkovics et al., 2011). A potential solution is helping employees through efforts to promote sensegiving (Bansal et al., 2022; Kroon & Reif, 2023; Sarala et al., 2019).

Cultural and human resource (HR) integration can smooth change for employees always leads to increased turnover and uncertainty. For example, HR can aid acquisition integration by providing skill development and onboarding (Correia et al., 2013). Additionally, cultural integration strategies to foster a shared organizational identity can help employees adapt to change smoothly (Bansal & King, 2022; Devers et al., 2020). For example, employee engagement can be aided by clear communication concerning workplace expectations and policy changes (Bansal & King, 2022). With effective communication along with HR alignment, firms can promote a cohesive work environment and increase lower-level employee support and commitment.

Mapping Affective and Cognitive Reactions of Acquiring Firm Employees

It is clear from research that understanding employee reactions across hierarchical levels in the acquiring firm is needed for acquisition success. While most research focuses on the acquired firm (please see Chapter "Acquired Firm Employees: Strategies for Engagement and Retention"), employees of the acquiring firm also experience significant disruption, ranging from strategic and role-based ambiguity to emotional strain, such as anxiety, fear, and resistance. We extensively draw from Affective Events Theory (Weiss & Cropanzano, 1996) and highlight how workplace events trigger emotional responses that influence acquiring firm employees' attitudes and behaviors. Additionally, we use Cognitive Appraisal Theory (Lazarus, 1991) and explain how individuals interpret and evaluate events mentally (cognitively) before or alongside emotional reactions. This distinction helps disentangle the multilayered nature of employee response, see Fig. 1. The figure shows cognitive responses reflect how employees make sense of organizational change, while emotional responses shape their affective engagement, morale, and behavior. Recognizing these factors across all levels of an acquiring firm can help managers design targeted communication strategies, leadership interventions, and cultural integration efforts to foster smoother transitions, retain key talent, and build post-merger commitment.

Discussion

The only thing consistent across acquisitions is uncertainty (Kvanagh & Ashkanasy, 2006), and managers may overlook internal risks by not sufficiently addressing this uncertainty (Elango et al., 2013). While research has predominantly focused on the concerns and management strategies for employees of the acquired firm during the post-merger integration phase, relatively little attention has been given to its implications for

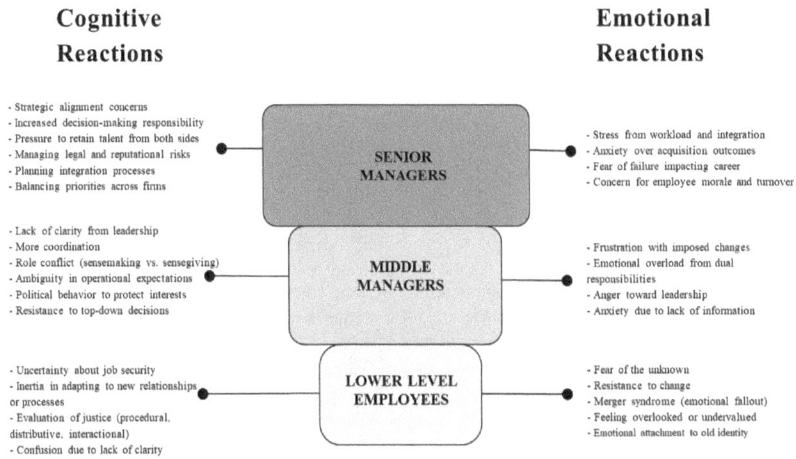

Fig. 1 Contrasting cognitive and emotional reactions across hierarchical levels

employees of the acquiring organization. This oversight limits a comprehensive understanding of the challenges faced by the acquiring firm's workforce, which may serve as a critical impediment to the merger's success. To address this gap, we identify and examine the concerns of acquiring firm employees at three hierarchical levels (i.e., senior managers, middle managers, and lower-level employees). Associated concerns and remedies are summarized for acquiring firm employees are shown in Table 1. In the following subsections, we also discuss research and managerial implications, as well as avenues for future research.

Research Implications

We offer a scholarly synthesis of multifaceted challenges encountered by different level employees in the acquiring firm. Senior managers tasked with setting strategic direction often grapple with balancing priorities between the parent and acquired firm while mitigating talent attrition and revitalizing struggling units. Middle managers, caught between leadership directives and lower-level realities, must execute integration plans while fostering stability amid uncertainty (Raes et al., 2011). Lower-level employees, the most vulnerable to change, face job insecurity, resistance, and cultural disconnects. Better understanding and managing the impact

Table 1 Acquiring firm employee concerns and remedies

Acquiring company employees	*Key concerns*	*Strategic recommendations*	*Implementation approaches*
Senior Managers	–Aligning acquisition with strategic goals –Setting long-term direction –Balancing focus between parent and acquired entity –Increased workload and decision-making pressure –High attrition of talent	–Leadership alignment to ensure stability –Clear communication strategy –Comprehensive integration planning –Align HR policies and incentives to increase employee retention	–Conduct regular strategy meetings –Develop structured onboarding for acquired employees –Offer performance-based retention packages –Assign dedicated integration teams
Middle Managers	–Lack of clarity from senior leadership –Dual responsibility of managing expectations of senior management and lower-level employees –Operational disruptions and workflow integration –Standardizing processes and aligning organizational culture	–Leadership and change management training –Acting as a buffer to shield employees from uncertainties –Strengthening employee communication –Active role in integration management –Hands-on support for a smoother transition	–Organize town halls and Q&A sessions –Implement structured transition plans –Assign change management leads –Develop managerial training programs for handling uncertainty

(continued)

Table 1 (continued)

Acquiring company employees	*Key concerns*	*Strategic recommendations*	*Implementation approaches*
Lower-level Employees	–Resistance to change and fear of the unknown –Job security concerns –Struggle to build relationships with new colleagues –Lack of information about changes and their motivation	–Frequent and transparent communication –Reassurances and early engagement –Encouraging team collaboration –Establishing open forums for feedback	–Create joint task teams –Provide autonomy in decision-making –Provide timely updates through internal newsletters –Introduce mentorship programs for smoother transition –Create an anonymous feedback mechanism

of acquisitions on acquiring firm employees and identifying the means for retaining them needs additional research (Ng & Stuart, 2022). The goal of associated research should enable crafting targeted strategies to navigate acquisition complexities and increase their success.

Differences in the effect of acquisition experience on acquiring firm performance may result from different effects of prior acquisitions on different levels of employee, and this is not consistently recognized in existing research. For example, senior managers are involved more during preacquisition phases that are more time constrained and repeatable. Meanwhile, middle managers and lower-level employees are more involved in acquisition integration that takes longer and is more idiosyncratic. Specifically, relevant experience for completing and integrating acquisitions may be based at different levels of a firm's hierarchy and have different levels of transferability to subsequent acquisitions. It is likely that senior manager experience with acquisition completion may be more relevant between acquisitions than for middle manager or employee experience with integration. Still, senior managers trying to apply similar integration strategies may hinder meeting the goals of different acquisitions (Colman & Lunnan, 2024). Additionally, while senior managers are more likely to be involved with each acquisition, middle managers may not be impacted by each acquisition and have less experience with acquisitions.

Considering different levels of experience with acquisitions across organizational levels is relevant as manager capability retention likely varies (Rahmandad & Repenning, 2016) with the potential that each acquisition may be treated as novel by middle managers and employees. This has implications for expectations for acquisition experience, and it may begin to explain conflicting research findings of acquisition experience on acquiring firm performance (King et al., 2021).

Managerial Implications

Senior managers should recognize the challenges middle managers face and provide them with the resources, training, and clear communication they need to successfully navigate the complex demands of an acquisition, as managerial problems contribute to the failure of acquisitions (Lockett, 2005). This process likely can begin with senior managers recognizing that their experience differs from middle managers and lower-level employees of a firm (Harwood & Ashleigh, 2005). Additionally, senior managers need to recognize differences in their roles with middle managers (King et al., 2020). We suggest that senior managers primarily focus on aligning acquisitions with strategic goals, formulating long-term plans, and addressing sources of employee turnover to improve acquisition success. Relevant options for pursuing these aims include conducting regular strategic meetings, deploying dedicated integration teams, and ensuring clear, consistent, and direct communication with employees and stakeholders (Ashkenas et al., 1998; Bansal & King, 2022; Giessner, 2011). Meanwhile, middle managers can help mitigate lower-level employee concerns amidst the uncertainties associated with the acquisitions. However, middle managers entrusted with the change implementation may lack required training for handling and directing change (Kvanagh & Ashkanasy, 2006). Additionally, middle managers may focus on functional synergies and give less attention to strategic goals (Bauer & Friesl, 2024).

Lower-level employees bear the greatest burden in acquisitions, as they must align with their counterparts from the acquired firm, adapt to new workflows, and navigate job security concerns. Thus, when considering acquisition goals, senior managers need to prioritize employee motivation (Foss & Lindenberg, 2013). To ease employee transition into a combined firm, management should center on timely and transparent communication to actively address employee concerns. Additionally, managers can aid integration by creating joint task teams, providing formal and informal interaction opportunities, and granting autonomy in decision-making (Bansal, 2015).

Effective communication can mitigate challenges for acquiring firm employees following an acquisition (Giessner, 2011). Conveyance of sensitive information should be done through direct, in-person communication to reduce uncertainty and increase trust. However, communication strategies should be tailored to different employee groups. For example, strategic insights and guidance can be provided to middle managers to aid their solving team issues, and to also provide lower-level employees clear expectations (Ashkenas et al., 1998; Bansal & King, 2022). With a well-structured communication strategy, long-term success will be supported by fostering alignment in goals and processes and reducing resistance after an acquisition.

Limitations and Future Research

The ability of employees to adapt to change varies (Bellou, 2006), and this is not considered outside our differentiation of employees at different organizational levels. For example, we do not discuss specialized firm employees, such as scientists involved in R&D (Hess & Rothaermel, 2011; Ranft & Lord, 2002). Our coverage of acquiring firm employees may have additional limitations. Specifically, our selection of covered research may reflect potential author bias, as well as a lack of comprehensiveness due to problems in identifying relevant research. For example, all studies were limited to those published in English. We also did not consider the methods used in reviewed studies or critically evaluate them. Despite these recognized limitations, we raise awareness on the need to study and separately consider differences in acquiring firm employees. Overall, our hope is to encourage greater understanding of acquisitions and management practices to improve their performance.

References

Ashkenas, R., DeMonaco, L., & Francis, S. (1998). Making the deal real: How GE Capital integrates acquisitions. *Harvard Business Review, 76*(1), 165–170.

Astley, W., & Van de Ven, A. (1983). Central perspectives and debates in organization theory. *Administrative Science Quarterly*, 245–273.

Balogun, J., & Johnson, G. (2004). Organizational restructuring and middle manager sensemaking. *Academy of Management Journal, 47*(4), 523–549.

Bansal, A. (2015). Understanding the integration mechanisms practiced during organizational change: Evidence from five M & A transactions. *Journal of Organizational Change Management, 28*(6), 929–947.

Bansal, A. (2019). Thinking of mergers and acquisitions? Think of justice: A people perspective. *International Journal of Manpower, 41*(4), 435–456.

Bansal, A., & King, D. (2022). Communicating change following an acquisition. *The International Journal of Human Resource Management, 33*(9), 1886–1915.

Bansal, A., King, D., & Meglio, O. (2022). Acquisitions as programs: The role of sensemaking and sensegiving. *International Journal of Project Management, 40*(3), 278–289.

Bauer, F., & Friesl, M. (2024). Synergy evaluation in mergers and acquisitions: An attention-based view. *Journal of Management Studies, 61*(1), 37–68.

Beck, T., & Plowman, D. (2014). Temporary, emergent interorganizational collaboration in unexpected circumstances: A study of the Columbia space shuttle response effort. *Organization Science, 25*(4), 1234–1252.

Bellou, V. (2006). Psychological contract assessment after a major organizational change: The case of mergers and acquisitions. *Employee Relations, 29*(1), 68–88.

Bilgili, T., Calderon, C., Allen, D., & Kedia, B. (2017). Gone with the wind: A meta-analytic review of executive turnover, its antecedents, and postacquisition performance. *Journal of Management, 43*(6), 1966–1997.

Birollo, G., & Teerikangas, S. (2019). Integration projects as relational spaces: A closer look at acquired managers' strategic role recovery in cross-border acquisitions. *International Journal of Project Management, 37*(8), 1003–1016.

Brannen, M., & Peterson, M. (2009). Merging without alienating: Interventions promoting cross-cultural organizational integration and their limitations. *Journal of International Business Studies, 40*, 468–489.

Burgelman, R. (1994). Fading memories: A process theory of strategic business exit in dynamic environments. *Administrative Science Quarterly*, 24–56.

Carmeli, A., & Gittell, J. (2009). High-quality relationships, psychological safety, and learning from failures in work organizations. *Journal of Organizational Behavior, 30*(6), 709–729.

Colman, H., & Lunnan, R. (2024). Pulling together while falling apart: A relational view on integration in serial acquirers. *Journal of Management, 50*(2), 588–619.

Cording, M., Christmann, P., & King, D. (2008). Reducing causal ambiguity in acquisition integration: Intermediate goals as mediators of integration decisions and acquisition performance. *Academy of Management Journal, 51*(4), 744–767.

Correia, M., e Cunha, R., & Scholten, M. (2013). Impact of M&As on organizational performance: The moderating role of HRM centrality. *European Management Journal, 31*(4), 323–332.

Csiszar, E., & Schweiger, D. (1994). An integrative framework for creating value through acquisition. *Handbook of Business Strategy*, 93–115.

Devers, C., Wuorinen, S., McNamara, G., Haleblian, J., Gee, I., & Kim, J. (2020). An integrative review of the emerging behavioral acquisition literature: Charting the next decade of research. *Academy of Management Annals, 14*(2), 869–907.

Dionisi, B., Dutt, N., Gambardella, A., & Snoeren, P. M. (2017). Adding assets, losing people: The contingent relationship between M&A and managerial mobility. In *Academy of Management Proceedings* (Vol. 2017, No. 1, p. 15335). Briarcliff Manor, NY 10510: Academy of Management.

Elango, B., Lahiri, S., & Kundu, S. (2013). How does firm experience and institutional distance impact ownership choice in high-technology acquisitions? *R&D Management, 43*(5), 501–516.

Empson, L. (2004). Organizational identity change: Managerial regulation and member identification in an accounting firm acquisition. *Accounting, Organizations and Society, 29*(8), 759–781.

Foss, N., & Lindenberg, S. (2013). Microfoundations for strategy: A goal-framing perspective on the drivers of value creation. *Academy of Management Perspectives, 27*(2), 85–102.

Fried, Y., Tiegs, R., Naughton, T., & Ashforth, B. (1996). Managers' reactions to a corporate acquisition: A test of an integrative model. *Journal of Organizational Behavior, 17*(5), 401–427.

Giessner, S. (2011). Is the merger necessary? The interactive effect of perceived necessity and sense of continuity on post-merger identification. *Human Relations, 64*(8), 1079–1098.

Gomes, E., Angwin, D., Weber, Y., & Tarba, S. (2013). Critical success factors through the mergers and acquisitions process: Revealing pre-and post-M&A connections for improved performance. *Thunderbird International Business Review, 55*(1), 13–35.

Graebner, M. (2004). Momentum and serendipity: How acquired leaders create value in the integration of technology firms. *Strategic Management Journal, 25*(8–9), 751–777.

Guth, W., & MacMillan, I. (1986). Strategy implementation versus middle management self-interest. *Strategic Management Journal, 7*(4), 313–327.

Gutknecht, J., & Keys, J. (1993). Mergers, acquisitions and takeovers: Maintaining morale of survivors and protecting employees. *Academy of Management Perspectives, 7*(3), 26–36.

Harwood, I., & Ashleigh, M. (2005). The impact of trust and confidentiality on strategic organizational change programmes: A case study of post-acquisition integration. *Strategic Change, 14*(2), 63–75.

Hatch, M., Schultz, M., & Skov, A. (2015). Organizational identity and culture in the context of managed change: Transformation in the Carlsberg Group, 2009–2013. *Academy of Management Discoveries, 1*(1), 58–90.

Hess, A., & Rothaermel, F. (2011). When are assets complementary? Star scientists, strategic alliances, and innovation in the pharmaceutical industry. *Strategic Management Journal, 32*(8), 895–909.

Huy, Q. (2002). Emotional balancing of organizational continuity and radical change: The contribution of middle managers. *Administrative Science Quarterly, 47*(1), 31–69.

Huy, Q. (2011). How middle managers' group-focus emotions and social identities influence strategy implementation. *Strategic Management Journal, 32*(13), 1387–1410.

Jacobs, D. (1988). Maintaining morale during and after downsizing. *Management Solutions, 33*(4), 5–13.

Kalavalapalli, Y. (2013). Tech Mahindra completes merger with Satyam Computer. *Mint*. https://www.livemint.com/Companies/xtpLdB4y08b9CjolKFj36K/Tech-Mahindra-completes-merger-with-Satyam-Computer.html

Kanth, K. (2015). Satyam shadow still haunts Tech Mahindra. *Business Standard*: https://www.business-standard.com/article/companies/satyam-shadow-still-haunts-tech-mahindra-115040801043_1.html

Kavanagh, M., & Ashkanasy, N. (2006). The impact of leadership and change management strategy on organizational culture and individual acceptance of change during a merger. *British Journal of Management, 17*(S1), S81–S103.

King, D., Bauer, F., Weng, Q., Schriber, S., & Tarba, S. (2020). What, when, and who: Manager involvement in predicting employee resistance to acquisition integration. *Human Resource Management, 59*(1), 63–81.

King, D., Wang, G., Samimi, M., & Cortes, A. (2021). A meta-analytic integration of acquisition performance prediction. *Journal of Management Studies, 58*(5), 1198–1236.

Korsgaard, M., Sapienza, H., & Schweiger, D. (2002). Beaten before begun: The role of procedural justice in planning change. *Journal of Management, 28*(4), 497–516.

Kroon, D., Noorderhaven, N., Corley, K., & Vaara, E. (2022). Hard and soft integration: Towards a dynamic model of post-acquisition integration. *Journal of Management Studies, 59*(5), 1132–1161.

Kroon, D., & Reif, H. (2023). The role of emotions in middle managers' sensemaking and sensegiving practices during post-merger integration. *Group & Organization Management, 48*(3), 790–832.

Lamont, B., King, D., Maslach, D., Schwerdtfeger, M., & Tienari, J. (2019). Integration capacity and knowledge-based acquisition performance. *R&D Management, 49*(1), 103–114.

Larsson, R., & Finkelstein, S. (1999). Integrating strategic, organizational, and human resource perspectives on mergers and acquisitions: A case survey of synergy realization. *Organization Science, 10*(1), 1–26.

Lazarus, R. S. (1991). Progress on a cognitive-motivational-relational theory of emotion. *American Psychologist, 46*(8), 819.

Lehn, K., & Zhao, M. (2006). CEO turnover after acquisitions: Are bad bidders fired? *Journal of Finance, 61*(4), 1759–1811.

Lockett, A. (2005). Edith Penrose's legacy to the resource-based view. *Managerial and Decision Economics, 26*(2), 83–98.

Lucas, T., Kamble, S., Wu, M., Zhdanova, L., & Wendorf, C. (2016). Distributive and procedural justice for self and others: Measurement invariance and links to life satisfaction in four cultures. *Journal of Cross-Cultural Psychology, 47*(2), 234–248.

Marks, M., & Mirvis, P. (2001). Making mergers and acquisitions work: Strategic and psychological preparation. *Academy of Management Perspectives, 15*(2), 80–92.

Martynova, M., & Renneboog, L. (2008). A century of corporate takeovers: What have we learned and where do we stand. *Journal of Banking and Finance, 32*, 2148–2177.

Maitlis, S., & Sonenshein, S. (2010). Sensemaking in crisis and change: Inspiration and insights from Weick (1988). *Journal of Management Studies, 47*(3), 551–580.

Mayer, D., & Kenney, M. (2004). Economic action does not take place in a vacuum: Understanding Cisco's acquisition and development strategy. *Industry and Innovation, 11*(4), 299–325.

Meyer, C. (2008). Value leakages in mergers and acquisitions: Why they occur and how they can be addressed. *Long Range Planning, 41*(2), 197–224.

Meyer, C., & Altenborg, E. (2008). Incompatible strategies in international mergers: The failed merger between Telia and Telenor. *Journal of International Business Studies, 39*, 508–525.

Mollick, E. (2012). People and process, suits and innovators: The role of individuals in firm performance. *Strategic Management Journal, 33*(9), 1001–1015.

Monin, P., Noorderhaven, N., Vaara, E., & Kroon, D. (2013). Giving sense to and making sense of justice in postmerger integration. *Academy of Management Journal, 56*(1), 256–284.

Ng, W., & Stuart, T. (2022). Acquired employees versus hired employees: Retained or turned over? *Strategic Management Journal, 43*(5), 1025–1045.

Perry, J., & Herd, T. (2004). Reducing M&A risk through improved due diligence. *Strategy & Leadership, 32*(2), 12–19.

Raes, A., Heijltjes, M., Glunk, U., & Roe, R. (2011). The interface of the top management team and middle managers: A process model. *Academy of Management Review, 36*(1), 102–126.
Rafferty, A., & Restubog, S. (2010). The impact of change process and context on change reactions and turnover during a merger. *Journal of Management, 36*(5), 1309–1338.
Rahmandad, H., & Repenning, N. (2016). Capability erosion dynamics. *Strategic Management Journal, 37*(4), 649–672.
Ranft, A., & Lord, M. (2002). Acquiring new technologies and capabilities: A grounded model of acquisition implementation. *Organization Science, 13*(4), 420–441.
Risberg, A. (2001). Employee experiences of acquisition processes. *Journal of World Business, 36*(1), 58–84.
Rousseau, D. (2001). Schema, promise and mutuality: The building blocks of the psychological contract. *Journal of Occupational and Organizational Psychology, 74*(4), 511–541.
Sarala, R., Junni, P., Cooper, C., & Tarba, S. (2016). A sociocultural perspective on knowledge transfer in mergers and acquisitions. *Journal of Management, 42*(5), 1230–1249.
Sarala, R. M., Vaara, E., & Junni, P. (2019). Beyond merger syndrome and cultural differences: New avenues for research on the "Human Side" of Global M&As. *Journal of World Business, 54*(4), 307–321.
Schweiger, D., Ivancevich, J., & Power, F. (1987). Executive actions for managing human resources before and after acquisition. *Academy of Management Perspectives, 1*(2), 127–138.
Sinetar, M. (1981, November). Mergers, morale and productivity. *Personnel Journal*, 863–867.
Sinkovics, R., Zagelmeyer, S., & Kusstatscher, V. (2011). Between merger and syndrome: The intermediary role of emotions in four cross-border M&As. *International Business Review, 20*(1), 27–47.
Sonenshein, S. (2010). We're changing—Or are we? Untangling the role of progressive, regressive, and stability narratives during strategic change implementation. *Academy of Management Journal, 53*(3), 477–512.
Steigenberger, N. (2017). The challenge of integration: A review of the M&A integration literature. *International Journal of Management Reviews, 19*(4), 408–431.
Stensaker, I., Falkenberg, J., & Grønhaug, K. (2008). Implementation activities and organizational sensemaking. *Journal of Applied Behavioral Science, 44*(2), 162–185.
Strobl, A., Bauer, F., Shepherd, N., Lou, B., Tarba, S., & Dao, M. (2024). Dynamic capabilities in acquisitions: When acquirer and target employees face

contradictory and complementary human resource signals. *British Journal of Management*. https://doi.org/10.1111/1467-8551.12889

Tung, R. (2016). New perspectives on human resource management in a global context. *Journal of World Business, 51*(1), 142–152.

Ullrich, J., & van Dick, R. (2007). The group psychology of mergers & acquisitions: Lessons from the social identity approach. *Advances in Mergers and Acquisitions, 6*, 1–15.

Ullrich, J., Wieseke, J., & van Dick, R. (2005). Continuity and change in mergers and acquisitions: A social identity case study of a German industrial merger. *Journal of Management Studies, 42*(8), 1549–1569.

Weiss, H. M., & Cropanzano, R. (1996). Affective events theory. *Research in Organizational Behavior, 18*(1), 1–74.

Wright, P., & Ferris, S. (1997). Agency conflict and corporate strategy: The effect of divestment on corporate value. *Strategic Management Journal, 18*(1), 77–83.

Acquired Firm Employees: Strategies for Engagement and Retention

Ahmed Alsafwani, Princess Anya, and Destiny Cole

Introduction

Acquisitions receive considerable attention from management researchers and practitioners. A primary motive for acquiring another firm is to gain access to its resources (King et al., 2003; King et al., 2008; Makri et al., 2010). However, associated target firm capabilities are primarily embedded in the firm's employees, and the underlying value sought can be easily destroyed or lost (Graebner, 2004; Ng & Stuart, 2022; Ranft & Lord, 2000). For example, acquired employees often possess unique skills, cultural knowledge, and institutional memory that can enhance the acquiring company's competitive advantage. As a result, research highlights employee retention, engagement, and adaptation into a combined organization as essential inputs into post-acquisition success (Bansal & King, 2022). While the importance of these employees is well-recognized, the nuances across different levels of employees have been examined separately.

A. Alsafwani (✉) · P. Anya · D. Cole
Florida State University, Tallahassee, USA
e-mail: aha24a@fsu.edu

D. R. King and A. Bansal (eds.), *Navigating Stakeholder Dynamics Surrounding Acquisitions*,
https://doi.org/10.1007/978-3-032-03199-0_8

Despite extensive research examining acquired employees' reactions, significant gaps persist in understanding how the experiences of acquired employees differ based on their roles and positions within an organization. For instance, we know more about top executives and their decision-making processes during acquisitions (e.g., Cuypers et al., 2017) and less about mid-level managers and lower-level employees' perspectives and challenges. Different levels of research attention and fragmentation across varying levels of acquired firm employees create a limited view of employee adaptation and overall acquisition effectiveness, possibly leading to oversimplified answers without integration.

We review the current state of knowledge on acquired firm employees to identify findings, trends, and standard methodologies. Please see Chapter 7 for a discussion of acquiring firm employees. By combining literature at different levels of acquired employees, we isolate consistent themes and conflicting results to understand better the factors that influence employee integration and retention. Further, we identify limitations and areas for additional research. Our combined intent is to consolidate existing knowledge and provide a foundation for advancing research on acquired firm employees that can contribute to improved acquisition success.

Our review offers additional contributions. Beyond providing a more holistic understanding of the employee experience following acquisitions, we inform theory and practice by showing variance in acquisition impacts for target firm employees at different organizational levels. This offers insights into developing strategies for acquired employee engagement and retention. Further, we recognize the unique challenges in managing various levels of acquired firm employees. As M&A activities continue to shape the business environment, better understanding the impact on acquired firm employees can improve integration and organizational outcomes.

Review

Like broader acquisition research, the examination of target firm employees is fragmented. For example, research generally considers target firm employees at different levels; see Table 1. At best, research tends to divide target employees into two groups, such as senior and middle managers (King et al., 2020) or middle managers and lower-level employees (Graebner, 2004). Additionally, the research topics focused

Table 1 Acquired firm employee attributes by level and acquisition stage

	Pre-acquisition	*Post-acquisition*
Senior managers	Prior experience social ties	Decision-making turnover
Middle managers	Role clarity and preparation for change	Sensemaking & sense giving alignment and feedback emotions and motivation
Lower-level employees	Job security concerns, uncertainty	Justice communication, resistance, and turnover employee satisfaction

on different levels of employees at target firms show limited overlap. In the following subsections, we summarize major themes identified in our review of research on acquired firm employees before discussing implications for management research and practice.

Senior Managers

Acquisitions are essential for executing strategic management initiatives and achieving competitiveness (Heyden et al., 2017). However, the performance of an acquisition is influenced by how senior managers of an acquired firm identify key acquisition targets and develop relevant strategies (Devers et al., 2020). The role of the target firm's senior managers displays conflict as they play an essential interface between their firm's stability and its need to adapt. Differences in the influence of acquired firm managers can be seen in pre-acquisition and post-acquisition processes.

Pre-acquisition. Factors associated with the senior managers of a target firm can influence an acquisition and its later performance beforehand. For example, the experience of target firm managers can give them an advantage in negotiations to obtain higher premiums (Cuypers et al., 2017). Additionally, if target firm senior managers lead acquisitions by their firms, it can complicate their being acquired (Zorn et al., 2019). Additionally, the social ties of a target firm's CEO can contribute to acquisitions by influencing not only the pre-acquisition process but also the post-acquisition integration. Savov (2013) illustrates that the CEOs' affiliation is another essential consideration in acquisition as prior working connections between the chief executives of both parties heavily influenced the cooperation between Nokia and Microsoft. There is always a trusting relationship between two organizations involved in an acquisition, as risk is part of the process. This was the case with Nokia, where several managers previously worked with Microsoft, facilitating integration as both parties shared common ground (Savov, 2013). However, pre-existing relationships may also pose problems after an acquisition, as CEOs may have preconceived notions, contradictory interests, and non-aligning goals (Devers et al., 2020).

Post-Acquisition. More is known about the impact of acquisitions on target firm senior manager retention, but target firm senior managers also contribute to post-acquisition strategic decision-making. For strategic decision-making, senior managers better appreciate the context of the target firm needed to export expertise into a combined firm (Junni et al., 2015). According to Devers et al. (2020), leadership changes during acquisitions are shown to be affected by power relations in senior management, where these dynamics resemble a determinant of the extent to which senior managers can adequately adapt to leadership changes. Still, efforts to retain key talent can increase conflict (Cuypers et al., 2017).

Research on turnover and retention suggests that the rate of turnover and senior manager retention are significant concerns in acquisitions. For instance, turnover of target senior managers after an acquisition has a noticeable impact on target senior managers and may negatively affect the acquiring firm performance (Krug & Shill, 2008). For example, employees may leave with important technology, employee knowledge, and firm culture, and the risk of losing key information (Devers et al., 2020; Graebner, 2004). Bilgili et al. (2017) also outline how retaining target firm senior managers is necessary to maintain operations continuity. Senior managers accepting new corporate cultures and direction must retain if acquiring organizations are to benefit from their retention. According to Capron and Guillén (2009), incentives can enable the realignment of the acquired firm's management team to the strategic orientation of the acquirer.

In contrast, senior manager turnover is exacerbated by cultural differences due to the lowered acceptance of strategic change, putting one more up for the exit (Krug & Hegarty, 1997). This can be mitigated using clear communication that recognizes senior managers' authority and their influence on decision-making (Devers et al., 2020). For example, Cisco reduced turnover by not firing any employees following an acquisition unless both the acquiring and target firm CEO agreed (Mayer & Kenney,

2004). This can increase the confidence of target firm senior managers in the leadership of the acquirer, boosting their retention (Heyden et al., 2017).

Middle Managers

Middle managers are pivotal in merging organizational operations, cultures, and strategies as they receive and transmit information up and down organizational hierarchies. This role allows them to align senior management's strategic vision with lower-level employees' practical challenges. Still, their position can be discouraging, as middle managers may feel they have little control over the firm's fate and their subordinates. For example, middle managers can react to acquisition integration with resistance when concerned about maintaining their units' autonomy (Vaara, 2003). Research on middle managers focuses on their sensemaking and sensegiving and their roles in alignment, feedback, and managing emotions. Another example is during the acquisition of Daimler-Benz by Chrysler, middle managers played a crucial role in aligning the two companies' cultures. However, many struggled with conflicting expectations from senior management and employees (Graebner, 2004).

Sensemaking and Sense-Giving. A dual responsibility for sensemaking and sensegiving for middle managers requires flexibility, patience, and empathy. As part of sensemaking, middle managers adapt strategic directions from senior management to meet the practical needs of their teams (Balogun & Johnson, 2004; Nguyen, 2011). In addition to sensemaking, middle managers actively engage in sensegiving, guiding their teams through the changes that come with acquisitions. For instance, they translate high-level strategies into clear, actionable steps that help employees grasp new goals and limit confusion (Balogun & Johnson, 2004; Rouleau, 2005; Rouleau & Balogun, 2011). In this process, middle managers are active participants who adapt procedures and management styles to help their teams understand and adjust to organizational changes (Currie & Procter, 2005; Kroon & Reif, 2023) and create a shared understanding of objectives (Maitlis, 2005).

Alignment and Feedback. Middle managers'interpretive roles aim to reconcile differences between senior management's directives and employee concerns (Lüscher & Lewis, 2008) using alignment and feedback. For alignment, middle managers transform strategic goals into practical steps to increase connection and coherence across organizational levels (Gioia & Chittipeddi, 1991) to reduce uncertainty (Dutton et al., 2001). Additionally, middle managers provide feedback to senior managers, including implementation challenges, gaps, and any resistance encountered (Reitzig & Maciejovsky, 2015). This feedback allows fine-tuning strategies, organizational agility, and responsiveness to challenges (Maitlis & Lawrence, 2007; Steigenberger & Mirc, 2020). When practical, middle managers serve as role models for change, demonstrating that challenges with new systems or practices are manageable (Chreim & Tafaghod, 2012). However, the alignment and feedback processes are rarely straightforward, as they involve emotions (Klok et al., 2023).

Emotions and Motivation. Acquisitions bring uncertainty and fear, leading to employee stress and demotivation, and middle managers are uniquely positioned to influence their teams as they act as a "hub" of strategic information (Beck & Plowman, 2009; Maitlis & Sonenshein, 2010). During acquisitions, middle managers act as emotional guides to ensure employees remain engaged, resilient, and committed to organizational goals (Currie & Procter, 2005; Graebner, 2004; Kroon & Reif, 2023). For example, middle managers can employ participatory decision-making to involve employees in the integration process, encouraging them to take responsibility and control their roles (Dutton et al., 2001; Floyd & Wooldridge, 1997). Additionally, middle managers can mitigate turnover intentions and manage this resistance by clarifying roles, providing reassurance, actively managing employee concerns (King et al., 2020), and increasing a sense of organizational justice that reduces employee resistance and turnover (Bansal & King, 2022; Monin et al., 2013).

Lower-Level Employees

An acquisition can create anxiety for lower-level employees of acquired firms due to the fear of job loss (Ng & Stuart, 2022), change of culture (Bastien, 1992), lack of trust in new management (Bhattacharya & Ghosh, 2010; Nikandrou & Papalexandris, 2008), hostile relations with new coworkers (Nikandrou & Papalexandris, 2008), and role inconsistencies (Kanbur & Canbek, 2017). Acquired employees usually do not have much say in how the acquisition will go, instilling further fear due to a lack of control or understanding of the process. For instance, Kim (2024) finds that acquired employees have average turnover rates of 33 percent within the first year compared to 12 percent of regular hires of the same level in that year. Moreover, in the case of Microsoft's acquisition of LinkedIn, lower-level employees were initially concerned about job security. Still, Microsoft took proactive steps to alleviate these concerns by providing clear communication and integration strategies (Bansal & King, 2022). The following sections explore how management can address these concerns by ensuring procedural justice, fostering transparent communication, and providing support during integration. These elements play a crucial role in helping lower-level employees adapt to the changes and feel more secure in the post-acquisition environment.

Justice. The attractiveness of the new organization's HR practices, mode of takeover, and collaboration history significantly influence employee trust after the acquisition (Stahl et al., 2012), highlighting the need to consider perceptions of justice (Bansal & King, 2022). For instance, Gomes et al. (2017) find a strong association between how an employee perceives justice and commitment to the new organization. Specifically, procedural justice (i.e., the level of fairness in the evaluation procedures used to determine factors in the workplace, such as raises, punishments, and promotions; Greenberg, 1986) can improve commitment to the new organization (Gomes et al., 2017). In contrast, micromanaging a newly acquired firm with a strong culture can harm performance (Strategic Direction, 2021).

Perceptions of fairness often shape employee concerns during acquisitions. Transparency in procedures and procedural justice, or fairness of the decision process that frees employees from being treated disrespectfully, are important in nurturing justice. According to Bansal (2019), employees' commitment and satisfaction with decision-making greatly depend on perceived fairness in decision-making and can impact post-merger integration outcomes. In addition, distributive justice—the perceived fairness of outcomes, such as compensation, job security, and career advancement opportunities—is also important to employees' reactions to acquisitions. Research proves that employees are more likely to resist change when they feel they are fairly compensated or rewarded for work and responsibilities (Bansal & King, 2022). The distribution of rewards, especially of responsibility, serves as the touchstone of equity; for example, those who view the distribution of rewards and responsibilities dealt out after an acquisition to be fair are more likely to accept organizational changes and remain loyal to the company. Finally, interactional justice—the quality of interpersonal treatment employees receives, such as respect and discernibility in communication— is extremely important for engagement and employee trust. According to Bansal and King (2022), how managers present decision-making and respect during acquisition plays a crucial role in employee satisfaction and turnover. This combination of three forms of justice, procedural, distributive, and interactional, decreases uncertainty and negative emotions and reduces negative emotions, thus aiding in a smoother transition for employees.

HR and Cultural Integration. Communication and justice alone may not fully address the concerns of frontline employees. Other key decisions regarding HR practices and cultural integration are determinants in reducing turnover and improving employee fear. Bansal and King (2022) suggest that communication regarding changes' rationale and perceived fairness will alleviate employee anxiety. However, well-structured HR practices are not in place in a company (i.e., job security assurances, role clarity, and supportive training programs). In that case, employees may still be left in doubt regarding the company's future. These practices are since HR plays a vital role in designing such practices so that employees become aware of their position within the new organizational structure and feel supported during integration.

In addition, cultural integration is important to dealing with organizational change issues. Mergers and acquisitions tend to come together with companies of different cultures, and employees are concerned about how these will affect the work environment and the relationship with their colleagues. According to Bansal (2019), HR should prioritize cultural integration in the acquisition process. Employees may feel alienated or resistant to the changes when cultural differences are not addressed, resulting in higher turnover rates. Employees can sense more belonging and ease the adjustment by offering resources to ride these cultural changes, from cultural training programs to team-building activities. Bringing together HR and culture can overcome resistance to change and make a more coherent workforce that leads to lower turnover and better organizational performance.

Communication, Resistance, and Turnover. Information shared with employees varies and should be delivered in a manner specific to either acquired or acquired employees (Zhu et al., 2004) to avoid fragmenting social groups (Colman & Lunnan, 2024). Communication following an acquisition shares information and can limit employee dissatisfaction (Bansal & King, 2022), which can turn into resistance (Larsson &

Finkelstein, 1999). Employee resistance involves pushback on changes following an acquisition due to fear of the unknown or misalignment of values (Ford & Ford, 2010). Passive resistance can turn into active steps by employees, including turnover or employees that result in a loss of knowledge (Horton et al., 2024).

Effective communication is essential in ensuring a successful acquisition and addressing employee concerns. Communication needs to be clear, complete, and transparent, but the mode, frequency, and even points in in-person communication also play a critical part, especially in the case of sensitive information. Bansal and King (2022) indicate that communication should be made face-to-face, via emails, or by virtual meetings depending on the context and type of the information being shared. Particularly, in-person communication maintains a sense of trust and respect as you talk about things that might make you nervous, such as job security and changing roles. According to research, most employees will feel more supported and valued when sensitive information is shared in person, providing instant feedback and smoothing out any confusion (Bansal, 2019). Communication frequency is also equally important. While it can even be with no new information, regular updates help to decrease the uncertainty and keep the transparency of information on the table.

According to Bansal and King (2022), in the context of an acquisition, employees who communicate consistently and timely have high confidence in their future with the company. On the other hand, infrequent or no communication can create rumors and dissatisfaction, making people doubt management. The structure consists of going finally, while clear messaging is critical, and the mode and frequency should be considered in harmony with the timing of the communication. For instance, large communication of changes in person, yet continuing with regular updates so that employees do not act by themselves over that information, will only augment tension and unwillingness. When leaders communicate sensitive information, this information should be communicated consistently in person where possible and where they give employees opportunities to ask questions and raise any concerns.

Employee Satisfaction. Management styles (Puranam et al., 2009; Teerikangas, 2012) can affect better employee outcomes after acquisitions. For instance, Raukko (2009) indicates that people actively changing key positions are associated with acquisition and organizational commitment perceptions. This is consistent with research suggesting that leaders implementing moderate levels of integration and expedited resolution of employee concerns during an acquisition can help mitigate turnover effects and loss of acquired knowledge (Graebner, 2004). Additionally, employee retention may be facilitated by transformational leadership (Babić et al., 2014), which aligns employee values and goals (MacKenzie et al., 2001) and maintains employee satisfaction (Nikandrou & Papalexandris, 2008).

Discussion

It is generally accepted that managers use acquisitions to increase performance (Heyden et al., 2017; King et al., 2021). However, this can only be achieved with proper planning and implementation by an acquiring firm's management team (Remanda, 2016), see Table 2. Efforts to assuage employee concerns can be aided by communication and collaboration to facilitate transparency in decision-making (Chreim & Tafaghod, 2012). If not well executed, acquiring firm managers will face poor performance and potential job loss (Ng & Stuart, 2022). Another consideration raised by our review is that the effects of acquisitions on target firms are felt differently across organizational levels. To further explore the dynamics between hierarchical levels in the acquisition process, research could benefit from applying Social Identity Theory (Tajfel, 1974) to explore how change processes unraveled and what inter-relationships existed between different levels of the hierarchy within the context of post-acquisition integration. For example, Van Knippenberg and Hogg (2003) explain the roles of the identifications of organizational roles and groups of employees on the way they respond to the acquisitions and changes in leadership styles.

The most obvious impacts of an acquisition on target firm employees are on senior managers, who exhibit higher turnover following an acquisition (Krug & Hegarty, 1997; Krug & Shill, 2008), which can have adverse effects. As a result, pre- and post-acquisition plans should be evaluated to increase cooperation and lower target firm senior manager turnover to prevent information loss (Devers et al., 2020; Graebner, 2004; Savov, 2013). Associated efforts can also help to maintain business continuity that can aid employees in combining firms and relations with external stakeholders (Bilgili et al., 2017; King & Schriber, 2016). Still,

Table 2 Acquired firm employee concerns and their mitigation

Employee Concerns	*Remedial Measures*
Job security concerns due to the acquisition.	Transparent communication from management about job security, precise role definitions, and HR support.
Fear of cultural differences between the merging companies.	Implement cultural integration programs, team-building activities, and artistic training for employees.
Uncertainty about role changes and career progression.	Role clarity from HR, training opportunities, and career development programs to ensure job stability.
Lack of trust in new management.	In-person communication and transparency from leadership to foster trust, as well as involving employees in decision-making.
Negative impact on employee morale.	Regular updates from leadership, recognition programs, and efforts to ensure fair treatment (interactional justice).

upper-echelon theory (Hambrick & Mason, 1984) would help deconstruct how the features of senior leadership teams determine strategic responses and integration results.

While middle managers have received limited research attention, what exists suggests they should not be overlooked (Graebner, 2004). For example, middle managers help implement acquisitions and align goals between senior managers and lower-level employees (Balogun & Johnson, 2004; Nguyen, 2011). Associated processes that can go up and down an organization's hierarchy involve sensemaking and sensegiving (Currie & Procter, 2005; Kroon & Reif, 2023). Better alignment of a guiding vision and management responsibilities across organizational levels can limit employee resistance after an acquisition (King et al., 2020; Monin et al., 2013).

Finally, lower-level employees may fear acquisition due to a lack of trust in the new management (Bhattacharya & Ghosh, 2010; Nikandrou & Papalexandris, 2008). However, increasing the perception of justice, such as procedural, can improve organizational commitment (Bansal & King, 2022; Gomes et al., 2017). One method of gaining organizational commitment following an acquisition is for managers to use communication to increase employee satisfaction (Bansal & King, 2022). Additional implications for management research and practice, as well as future research, are discussed below.

Research Implications

Mergers and acquisitions can be described as complex processes where two or more organizations undergo vigorous stages of planning, consultations, and integrations (Makri et al., 2010). However, there is also complexity within target firms that has not been comprehensively addressed. To this end, our review offers theoretical and practical implications for acquisition research, which we discuss in the following paragraphs.

Integrating research across target firms' senior managers, middle managers, and lower-level employees offers some theoretical contributions that can inform future research. First, we outline the need for a multilevel perspective that contrasts with a traditional focus on isolated groups (e.g., executives or frontline workers). Our review outlines an interdependence in the reaction of target firm employees where decisions and behaviors at one level influence others. For instance, senior manager vision and subsequent strategic alignment directly affect middle managers'ability to translate goals into actionable steps that, in turn, shape lower-level employees' perceptions of justice and job security. This integrated view suggests organizational change theories in M&A contexts should address interdependencies across hierarchies.

In addition to showing how target firm employees are interdependent, we identify that they face unique challenges related to different management theories. For example, senior managers face strategic and cultural realignment, middle managers navigate sensemaking and sensegiving under uncertainty, and lower-level employees contend with job security and cultural integration. This differentiation challenges one-size-fits-all models of employee response to acquisitions. It highlights the need for tailored strategies and additional theory development to better reflect the complexity of acquisitions.

From a more practical standpoint, future research on the impact of acquisitions on target firm employees is needed, and we have identified three areas where it can focus. First, current research primarily examines executive-level responses in M&As, leaving gaps in understanding how middle and lower-level employees adapt to acquisitions. Future studies should explore each organizational level's unique experiences and retention factors to provide a more nuanced understanding of employee integration. We need to learn more about the effectiveness of retention strategies for organizational performance and how sustained power relations shape the learning of organizational leaders.

Next, most acquisition research is done with samples in Europe or North America (Meglio & Risberg, 2010), and differences are observed between these regions. For example, hostile acquisitions are much less common in Europe (Moschieri & Campa, 2009). Still, many studies assume that integration strategies are universally effective across cultural contexts when we know that cultural differences impact acquisition performance, including employee retention (Bauer et al., 2018; Bauer et al., 2024; Stahl & Voigt, 2008). Research could examine how cross-cultural dimensions influence the effectiveness of various integration approaches in M&As, especially regarding retention and job satisfaction. It is essential to gain more empirical data on how these relations influence integration and knowledge transfer across industries and cultures.

As a result, research can investigate how employees respond to cultural integration challenges in cross-border acquisitions. The dimensions of culture, like power distance and individualism, can play an important role in moderating how employees perceive and respond to HR practices and communications during integration. To illustrate, Cartwright and Cooper (1993) point to the significance of cultural comparability in catalytic mergers. Weber et al. (1996) show how national and organizational cultural conflicts can lead to harmful results in the acquisition process. Through such cultural variables, research in the future can assist in producing more efficient integration practices in international environments and help minimize cultural-based resistance based on cultural misunderstandings.

Finally, research often reports a "snapshot" of the effects of being acquired on target firm employees. Patterns identified in longitudinal research, such as an acquisition where retention may change based on the evolution of organizational dynamics, could be identified. Thus, for example, Mayer and Kenney (2004) acknowledge the need for human resources to actively engage with the target firm's employees just a month after an acquisition. Further, longitudinal work could follow employee satisfaction, commitment, and retention over extended periods to determine long-term factors that may lead to successful integration.

Managerial Implications

To retain high-value employees given an acquisition, firm managers should begin at the top by defining specific retention and engagement strategies in advancing such employees' special needs and challenges. Senior leaders may find fostering inclusion in strategic planning effective; mid-level managers may be helped with resources to align and communicate better as a team. However, trying to retain managers should not neglect lower-level employees since worrying about their concerns during implementation would help increase acquisition success (Nkemakolam et al., 2021). For example, implementing techniques such as motivation creation, development of justice, and culture analysis can help acquisition success. Managers should look closely at the implications of acquisitions for lower-level employees to make necessary adjustments to create value (Chun & Davies, 2010).

A decentralized leadership style can enable middle managers to function as localized leaders who meet strategic goals by adapting to the unique dynamics of their departments (Mangaliso, 1995; Nguyen et al., 2002). Further, giving middle managers the autonomy to decide how best to implement senior management directives allows them to tailor integration strategies to their teams' specific needs (Chreim & Tafaghod, 2012). Progress is possible with transparent communication that can reduce anxiety and turnover, as well as resistance. The information provided should cover employee roles, expectations, and integration timelines.

Since power relations between senior managers of the acquiring and acquired firms affect organizational stability and acquisition integration, it warrants attention. Stakeholder management should efficiently communicate with all internal and external stakeholders impacted so that their interests are represented in acquisition decisions (Bosse et al., 2022). Finally, leadership development and training could make organizations more resilient by helping managers apply prior lessons to future situations (Bauer et al., 2024).

Additionally, the strategic and operational roles of middle managers as agents of change deserve deeper investigation. Middle managers are not mere recipients of strategy but are instrumental in interpreting the top-level mandates into action-oriented results following the acquisition. Their interpretive, communicative, and flexible skills render them active change agents. Nonetheless, their roles are usually underappreciated in the literature on M&A. Future research should look into how middle managers balance agendas between the top management and the immediate employees and how their involvement in the strategic aspects influences integration success (Wooldridge et al., 2008).

Limitations and Future Research

The current chapter reflects new limitations that can offer opportunities for additional research. For example, the summarized study may be limited by bias in overlooking relevant research that compromises its ability to be comprehensive. Additionally, summarized research on specific firms, industries, and nations where acquisitions are common may limit the generalizability of our conclusions. Additional research is needed to examine the generalizability of findings on employee reactions following an acquisition. Further, our review works to integrate research across different organizational levels of target firms. However, research prioritizes executive-level experience, providing less insight into how target firm middle managers and lower-level employees experience acquisitions.

Research that examines different organizational levels together is needed. For example, this would allow insights into the interconnected relationships and communication across organizational levels following an acquisition. Additionally, considering the communication and relationships of employees could offer insights into the emotional and psychological responses of employees and how they can be addressed. Again, this highlights the potential importance of middle managers, and research can work to better understand middle managers' effects before and after acquisitions on senior managers, lower-level employees, and general firm performance. For example, it may be interesting to see how middle managers' communication effectiveness varies depending on when they are notified about the acquisition occurring.

Future research can also examine how different dimensions of organizational justice—namely procedural, distributive, and interactional justice—affect employee outcomes such as trust, commitment, and turnover intentions across various organizational levels (Bansal & King, 2022). For example, fairness in the decision-making process and communicating the decisions can also affect the emotional level of the employees and their tendency to stay within the organization. According to Cropanzano et al. (2007), the key to employee motivation and engagement in the change setting is the effective management of the justice processes.

Similarly, Greenberg (1990) points out that employee judgements of fairness influence the immediate attitude and the long-term organizational commitment. Future studies can provide a more subtle account of how leadership perceptions of justice determine post-acquisition integration outcomes by examining how the various dimensions of justice play out among senior leaders, middle managers, and frontline employees.

In closing, acquiring companies should adopt tailored strategies to address the distinct needs of each level of target firm employees. For senior managers, effective communication and role alignment are vital to reducing turnover and preserving essential institutional knowledge. Middle managers must be empowered to effectively translate strategic goals into practical actions that benefit their teams to help minimize employee resistance and foster commitment (Balogun & Johnson, 2004; Rouleau, 2005). Lower-level employees require open communication and reassurance, as this can reduce anxiety and improve their engagement with new organizational objectives (Schweiger & Denisi, 1991). A continued focus on understanding the unique responses of acquired employees at various levels can improve acquisition integration effectiveness.

References

Babić, V., Savović, S., & Domanović, V. (2014). Transformational leadership and post-acquisition performance in transitional economies. *Journal of Organizational Change Management, 27*(6), 856–876.

Balogun, J., & Johnson, G. (2004). Organizational restructuring and middle manager sensemaking. *Academy of Management Journal, 47*(4), 523–549.

Bansal, A., & King, D. (2022). Communicating change following an acquisition. *The International Journal of Human Resource Management, 33*(9), 1886–1915.

Bansal, A. (2019). Thinking of mergers and acquisitions? Think of justice: A people perspective. *International Journal of Manpower, 41*(4), 435–456.

Bastien, D. (1992). Change in organizational culture: Using linguistic methods in a corporate acquisition. *Management Communication Quarterly, 5*(4), 403–442.

Bauer, F., King, D., Friesl, M., Schriber, S., & Weng, Q. (2024). Acquisition integration capabilities and organizational design. *Long Range Planning, 57*(6), 102479.

Bauer, F., Schriber, S., Degischer, D., & King, D. (2018). Contextualizing speed and cross-border acquisition performance: Labor market flexibility and efficiency effects. *Journal of World Business, 53*(2), 290–301.

Beck, T., & Plowman, D. (2009). Experiencing rare and unusual events richly: The role of middle managers in animating and guiding organizational interpretation. *Organization Science, 20*(5), 909–924.

Bhattacharya, S., & Ghosh, D. (2010). Impact of acquisition and trust as perceived by the acquiring and acquired employees of a multinational telecommunication company in Kolkata. *ASBM Journal of Management, 3*(1/2), 101–111.

Bilgili, T., Calderon, C., Allen, D., & Kedia, B. (2017). When do CEO departures lead to post-acquisition performance? *Journal of Management Studies, 54*(5), 564–594.

Bosse, D., Harrison, J., & Hoskisson, R. (2022). Acquisitions, stakeholder economies of scope, and stakeholder orientation. *Strategic Management Review, 3*(1), 35–65.

Capron, L., & Guillén, M. (2009). National corporate governance institutions and post-acquisition target reorganization. *Strategic Management Journal, 30*(8), 803–833.

Cartwright, S., & Cooper, C. (1993). The role of culture compatibility in successful organizational marriage. *Academy of Management Executive, 7*(2), 57–70.

Chreim, S., & Tafaghod, M. (2012). Contradiction and sensemaking in acquisition integration. *Journal of Applied Behavioral Science, 48*(1), 5–32.

Chun, R., & Davies, G. (2010). The effect of a merger on employee views of corporate reputation: Time and space-dependent theory. *Industrial Marketing Management, 39*(5), 721–727.

Colman, H., & Lunnan, R. (2024). Pulling together while falling apart: A relational view on integration in serial acquirers. *Journal of Management, 50*(2), 588–619.

Cropanzano, R., Bowen, D., & Gilliland, S. (2007). The management of organizational justice. *Academy of Management Perspectives, 21*(4), 34–48.

Currie, G., & Procter, S. (2005). The antecedents of middle managers' strategic contribution: The case of a professional bureaucracy. *Journal of Management Studies, 42*(7), 1325–1356.

Cuypers, I., Cuypers, Y., & Martin, X. (2017). When the target may know better: Effects of experience and information asymmetries on value from mergers and acquisitions. *Strategic Management Journal, 38*(3), 609–625.

Devers, C., Wuorinen, S., McNamara, G., Haleblian, J., Gee, I., & Kim, J. (2020). An integrative review of the emerging behavioral acquisition literature: Charting the next decade of research. *Academy of Management Annals, 14*(2), 869–907.

Dutton, J., Ashford, S., O'Neill, R., & Lawrence, K. (2001). Moves that matter: Issue selling and organizational change. *Academy of Management Journal, 44*(4), 716–736.

Floyd, S., & Wooldridge, B. (1997). Middle management's strategic influence and organizational performance. *Journal of Management Studies, 34*(3), 464–485.

Ford, J., & Ford, L. (2010). Stop blaming resistance to change and start using it. *Organizational Dynamics, 39*(1), 24–36.

Gioia, D., & Chittipeddi, K. (1991). Sensemaking and sense giving in strategic change initiation. *Strategic Management Journal, 12*(6), 433–448.

Gomes, E., Mellahi, K., Sahadev, S., & Harvey, A. (2017). Perceptions of justice and organizational commitment in international mergers and acquisitions. *International Marketing Review, 34*(5), 582–605.

Graebner, M. (2004). Momentum and serendipity: How acquired leaders create value in integrating technology firms. *Strategic Management Journal, 25*(8–9), 751–777.

Greenberg, J. (1986). Determinants of perceived fairness of performance evaluations. *Journal of Applied Psychology, 71*(2), 340–342.

Greenberg, J. (1990). Organizational justice: Yesterday, today, and tomorrow. *Journal of Management, 16*(2), 399–432.

Hambrick, D., & Mason, P. (1984). Upper echelons: The organization as a reflection of its top managers. *Academy of Management Review, 9*(2), 193–206.

Heyden, M. L., Kavadis, N., & Neuman, Q. (2017). External corporate governance and strategic investment behaviors of target CEOs. *Journal of Management, 43*(7), 2065–2089.

Horton, K., King, D., Bauer, F., Lamont, B., & Schriber, S. (2024). Integration, employee resistance, and acquisition performance. *European Management Journal*.

Junni, P., Sarala, R., Tarba, S., & Weber, Y. (2015). The role of strategic agility in acquisitions. *Scandinavian Journal of Management, 31*(2), 142–153.

Kanbur, E., & Canbek, M. (2017). Examining effects of role stressors (role ambiguity and role conflict) on intention to leave, organizational identification and perceived individual performance. *International Journal of Disciplines Economics & Administrative Sciences Studies, 3*(4), 363–375.

Kim, J. (2024). Startup acquisitions as a hiring strategy: Turnover differences between acquired and regular hires. *Strategy Science, 9*(2), 118–134.

King, D., Bauer, F., Weng, Q., Schriber, S., & Tarba, S. (2020). What, when, and who: Manager involvement in predicting employee resistance to acquisition integration. *Human Resource Management, 59*(1), 63–81.

King, D., Covin, J., & Hegarty, W. (2003). Complementary resources and the exploitation of technological innovations. *Journal of Management, 29*(4), 589–606.

King, D. R., & Schriber, S. (2016). Addressing competitive responses to acquisitions. *California Management Review, 58*(3), 109–124.

King, D., Slotegraaf, R., & Kesner, I. (2008). Performance implications of firm resource interactions in the acquisition of R&D-intensive firms. *Organization Science, 19*(2), 327–340.

King, D. R., Wang, G., Samimi, M., & Cortes, A. F. (2021). A meta-analytic integration of acquisition performance prediction. *Journal of Management Studies, 58*(5), 1198–1236.

Klok, Y., Kroon, D., & Khapova, S. (2023). The role of emotions during mergers and acquisitions: A review of the past and a glimpse into the future. *International Journal of Management Reviews, 25*(3), 587–613.

Kroon, D., & Reif, H. (2023). The role of emotions in middle managers' sensemaking and sensegiving practices during postmerger integration. *Group and Organization Management, 48*(3), 790–832.

Krug, J., & Hegarty, W. (1997). Post-acquisition turnover among US top management teams: An analysis of the effects of foreign vs. domestic acquisitions of US targets. *Strategic Management Journal, 18*(8), 667–675.

Krug, J., & Shill, W. (2008). The big exit: Executive churn in the wake of M&as. *Journal of Business Strategy, 29*(4), 15–21.

Larsson, R., & Finkelstein, S. (1999). Integrating strategic, organizational, and human resource perspectives on mergers and acquisitions: A case survey of synergy realization. *Organization Science, 10*(1), 1–26.

Lüscher, L., & Lewis, M. (2008). Organizational change and managerial sensemaking: Working through paradox. *Academy of Management Journal, 51*(2), 221–240.

MacKenzie, S., Podsakoff, P., & Rich, G. (2001). Transformational and transactional leadership and salesperson performance. *Journal of the Academy of Marketing Science, 29*, 115–134.

Makri, M., Hitt, M., & Lane, P. (2010). Complementary technologies, knowledge relatedness, and invention outcomes in high technology mergers and acquisitions. *Strategic Management Journal, 31*(6), 602–628.

Maitlis, S. (2005). The social processes of organizational sensemaking. *Academy of Management Journal, 48*(1), 21–49.

Maitlis, S., & Lawrence, T. (2007). Triggers and enablers of sensegiving in organizations. *Academy of Management Journal, 50*(1), 57–84.

Maitlis, S., & Sonenshein, S. (2010). Sensemaking in crisis and change: Inspiration and insights from Weick (1988). *Journal of Management Studies, 47*(3), 551–580.

Mangaliso, M. (1995). The strategic usefulness of management information as perceived by middle managers. *Journal of Management, 21*(2), 231–250.

Mayer, D., & Kenney, M. (2004). Economic action does not take place in a vacuum: Understanding Cisco's acquisition and development strategy. *Industry and Innovation, 11*(4), 299–325.

Meglio, O., & Risberg, A. (2010). Mergers and acquisitions—Time for a methodological rejuvenation of the field? *Scandinavian Journal of Management, 26*(1), 87–95.

Monin, P., Noorderhaven, N., Vaara, E., & Kroon, D. (2013). Giving sense to and making sense of justice in postmerger integration. *Academy of Management Journal, 56*(1), 256–284.

Moschieri, C., & Campa, J. (2009). The European M&a industry: A market in the process of construction. *Academy of Management Perspectives, 23*(4), 71–87.

Ng, W., & Stuart, T. (2022). Acquired employees versus hired employees: Retained or turned over? *Strategic Management Journal, 43*(5), 1025–1045.

Nguyen, H. (2011). How middle managers' group-focus emotions and social identities influence strategy implementation. *Strategic Management Journal, 32*(13), 1387–1410.

Nguyen, H., Angelmar, R., Brendl, M., Demers, C., Doz, Y., Dragonetti, N., Gimeno, J., Langley, A., Mintzberg, H., Prochno, P., Schnei-der, S., Smith, K., Tran, V., Van Wassenhove, L., & Westley, F. (2002). Emotional balancing of organizational continuity and radical change: The contribution of middle managers. *Administrative Science Quarterly, 47*, 31–69.

Nikandrou, I., & Papalexandris, N. (2008). Employee responses to acquisitions: Evidence from Greek firms. *Employee Relations, 30*(2), 104–120.

Nkemakolam, J., Igbolekwu, C., Nwogu, E., Nnanna, N., Asaleye, A., Bamidele, R., & Arisukwu, O. (2021). Psychosocial predictors of emotional labor among employees of merged and acquired banks in Ibadan, south-west. *Nigeria. Heliyon, 7*(9).

Puranam, P., Singh, H., & Chaudhuri, S. (2009). Integrating acquired capabilities: When structural integration is (un) necessary. *Organization Science, 20*(2), 313–328.

Ranft, A., & Lord, M. (2000). Acquiring new knowledge: The role of retaining human capital in acquisitions of high-tech firms. *Journal of High Technology Management Research, 11*(2), 295–319.

Raukko, M. (2009). Organizational commitment during organizational changes. *Baltic Journal of Management, 4*(3), 331–352.

Reitzig, M., & Maciejovsky, B. (2015). Corporate hierarchy and vertical information flow inside the firm: A behavioral view. *Strategic Management Journal, 36*(13), 1979–1999.

Remanda, L. C. (2016). A review of organizational culture in the mergers and acquisitions process. *Journal of Media Critiques, 2*(8), 99–110.

Rouleau, L. (2005). Micro-practices of strategic sensemaking and sense giving: How middle managers interpret and sell changes daily. *Journal of Management Studies, 42*(7), 1413–1441.

Rouleau, L., & Balogun, J. (2011). Middle managers, strategic sensemaking, and discursive competence. *Journal of Management Studies, 48*(5), 953–983.

Savov, V. (2013). *Microsoft buys Nokia's phone division as Steve Ballmer plans his exit*. Verge.

Schweiger, D., & Denisi, A. (1991). Communication with employees following a merger: A longitudinal field experiment. *Academy of Management Journal, 34*(1), 110–135.

Stahl, G., Chua, C., & Pablo, A. (2012). Does national context affect target firm employees' trust in acquisitions? *Management International Review, 52*(3), 395–423.

Stahl, G., & Voigt, A. (2008). Do cultural differences matter in mergers and acquisitions? A tentative model and examination. *Organization Science, 19*(1), 160–176.

Steigenberger, N., & Mirc, N. (2020). Should I stay or should I go? Multi-focus identification and employee retention in post-acquisition integration. *Human Relations, 73*(7), 981–1009.

Strategic Direction. (2021). *The elusive practice of driving post-acquisition company performance, 37*(1), 29–31.

Tajfel, H. (1974). Social identity and intergroup behaviour. *Social Science Information, 13*(2), 65–93.

Teerikangas, S. (2012). Dynamics of acquired firm pre-acquisition employee reactions. *Journal of Management, 38*(2), 599–639.

Vaara, E. (2003). Post-acquisition integration as sensemaking: Glimpses of ambiguity, confusion, hypocrisy, and politicization. *Journal of Management Studies, 40*(4), 859–894.

Van Knippenberg, D., & Hogg, M. A. (2003). A social identity model of leadership effectiveness in groups. *Research in Organizational Behavior, 25*, 243–295.

Weber, Y., Shenkar, O., & Raveh, A. (1996). National and organizational culture in mergers/acquisitions: An exploratory study. *Management Science, 42*(8), 1201–1216.

Wooldridge, B., Schmid, W., & Floyd, S. (2008). The middle management perspective: Its impact on strategy and involvement. *Strategic Management Journal, 29*(11), 1199–1221.

Zhu, Y., May, S., & Rosenfeld, L. (2004). Information adequacy and job satisfaction during merger and acquisition. *Management Communication Quarterly, 18*(2), 241–270.

Zorn, M., Sexton, J., Bhussar, M., & Lamont, B. (2019). Unfinished business: Nested acquisitions, managerial capacity, and firm performance. *Journal of Management, 45*(4), 1488–1516.

The Societal Impacts of Mergers and Acquisitions

Silvia Gordano and Daniel Torchia

Introduction

Acquisitions are pervasive organizational events with far-reaching societal implications. By reshaping resource allocation across firms, acquisitions can redefine the geographies of production and consumption, financial resources, and employment. As such, they can both create value and bear negative impacts on society at large. For instance, acquisitions may lead to efficiencies, innovation, and financial market development, but they can also result in resource depletion, job losses, increased market concentration, and inequality in wealth distribution.

We examine the relationship between acquisitions and society, providing a framework on how acquisitions can positively and negatively affect society. In this context, *society* is referred to as the interconnected system of individuals, institutions, and ecosystems that collectively shape and are shaped by economic activities, such as acquisitions. The ideal

S. Gordano (✉)
University of Turin, Turin, Italy
e-mail: silvia.gordano@unito.it

D. Torchia
University of Milano-Bicocca, Milan, Italy

D. R. King and A. Bansal (eds.), *Navigating Stakeholder Dynamics Surrounding Acquisitions*,
https://doi.org/10.1007/978-3-032-03199-0_9

contribution of businesses to society is enclosed in the Sustainable Development Goals (SDGs). The SDGs are a set of 17 objectives, adopted by United Nations (UN) member states in 2015 as part of the 2030 Agenda (UN, 2015), to advance global sustainability and, thus, meet the needs of the present without compromising the ability of future generations to meet their own needs (WCED, 1987). More specifically, the SDGs address a wide range of societal issues (Kolk et al., 2017), comprising *environmental* (e.g., natural-resource depletion, biodiversity loss, and climate change), *social* (e.g., social inequality, gender discrimination, human-health deficiencies, and education deficits), and *economic* (e.g., financial instability, unemployment, income disparities, and poverty) grand challenges. Although the SDGs are extensive goals set at the country-level by governments, business organizations are considered crucial actors for their achievement (Montiel et al., 2021; UN, 2015; van Zanten & van Tulder, 2021). This is consistent with the notion that businesses can successfully balance their economic activities with environmental and social objectives (the so-called Triple-Bottom-Line approach), thus "doing well while doing good" (Elkington, 1994).

Based on the above, we map extant research on the societal impacts of acquisitions across the three pillars of sustainability (economic, social and environmental). To do so, we conduct a traditional literature review (Jesson et al., 2011) to provide a comprehensive, narrative-based synthesis of academic articles. After selecting potentially relevant studies using keywords drawn from the SDGs framework, we restrict our review to studies on acquisition effects. In examining both contributions and unintended consequences of business acquisitions on sustainable development, we recognize that macro-level impacts can be ultimately caused by firm-level outcomes, which collectively may carry significant broader sustainability implications. Accordingly, our review encompasses studies that analyze acquisition effects at the macro- (i.e., country) and firm-level (i.e., acquirer and/or target firms). A thematic analysis is performed to uncover emerging themes, which are then positioned across the *economic*, *social*, and *environmental* dimensions, to facilitate the systematization of literature. In doing so, we acknowledge that the three dimensions, along with the related SDGs, cannot be understood as mutually exclusive (Nilsson et al., 2018); rather, they show natural areas of overlap. In this vein, studies investigating, the socioeconomic effects of acquisitions in emerging markets lie at the intersection of social and economic interests. Therefore, while we recognize that acquisitions can generate cascading impacts across multiple dimensions, we present them in isolation for simplicity, without claiming that such categorization captures all the correlated impacts. Finally, we employ the lens of the SDGs to provide a comprehensive framework on how acquisitions can contribute and/or hamper the achievement of society-level goals, thus offering insights for future research and government interventions in line with the 2030 Agenda.

The Economic Impacts of Acquisitions

Acquisition deals represent a global economically significant phenomenon, which involves more than three trillion dollars of worldwide assets each year (Broughton, 2023). As such, acquisitions not only serve as a critical mechanism for corporate adaptation and external growth, but also for driving broader economic outcomes. We summarize the main sources of economic value creation and destruction stemming from acquisitions, as emerging from reviewed articles.

Economic Growth

The market for corporate control plays a crucial role in enhancing economic growth and resource allocation optimization. By reallocating productive assets to firms that can use them more efficiently, it helps improve capital allocation across the economy (Manne, 1965), thus enhancing productivity. More specifically, evidence suggests that acquisition activity contributes about 14% to productivity and 4% to consumption (David, 2021). The productivity growth is driven by an approximately 9% increase in the productivity of existing firms and by nearly 6% improvement due to higher selection resulting from changes in equilibrium prices. Acquisition activity can foster efficiency among existing firms, for instance, by reallocating human capital to more productive firms (Siegel & Simons, 2010) and replacing inefficient management teams (Manne, 1965). Simultaneously, acquisitions can encourage the exit of less productive businesses by altering the incentives for firm entry and exit and thereby promoting a more competitive market where only the most efficient ones survive.

While acquisitions can be a significant source of value creation, research highlights the *acquisition paradox*—a persistent trend in which many acquisitions fail to deliver their expected value. Acquisitions are inherently high-risk and complex organizational events, with notable failure rates arising from various factors, including managerial opportunism (King et al., 2004). Inefficiencies in the broader market for corporate control may also contribute to suboptimal outcomes. For instance, changes in equilibrium prices can lead to an increased rate of business failures and, consequently, inefficient resource allocation that could be more effectively directed toward consumption (David, 2021). Additionally, productivity gains may be undermined by fiscal advantages, as tax differentials between acquiring and target firms can distort the efficient allocation of resources, particularly in horizontal deals (Todtenhaupt & Voget, 2021).

Market Concentration

Efficiency gains may be offset by counterbalancing effects from acquisitions. Most notably, there is a threat that the increased market power and concentration resulting from acquisitions hinders fair market competition. Indeed, while a higher market concentration can lead to reduced costs of goods and services because of economies of scale, it can also result in higher prices and fewer choices for consumers due to reduced competition (Mehta et al., 2020). There is indeed evidence that acquisitions are mostly associated with increases in average markups (Blonigen & Pierce, 2016), leading to lower consumer surplus and decreased incentives to innovate. Economically significant acquisitions are therefore monitored by antitrust authorities. In the United States, for instance, companies pursuing acquisitions valued at $126.4 million or more are subject to review by US antitrust enforcers. For example, in recent times, Facebook (now Meta) strategically acquired Instagram (in 2012) and WhatsApp (in 2014), solidifying its dominance in social media services and raising concerns about anti-competitive behavior. On the one hand, existing competition policies are demonstrated to generate gains in growth and social wealth (Cavenaile et al., 2021). On the other hand, some scholars advocate that antitrust enforcement may be motivated by economic nationalism, rather than competition-related concerns (Serdar Dinc & Erel, 2013). This is especially relevant when strategic sectors, such as oil and gas, are involved.

Technological Development

Beyond efficiency gains, acquisitions can also drive innovation and technological progress by facilitating the transfer of knowledge, capabilities, and technologies, which are difficult to replicate and generate internally (Hitt et al., 1996). Innovation-driven acquisitions are particularly valuable strategies for companies operating within high-technology industries, to get access to critical resources that can complement the company's own research activity (Ahuja & Katila, 2001) and enhance their innovative performance (Puranam et al., 2006). Microsoft and Cisco represent cases of successful outcomes that can be derived from the combination of internal R&D efforts and acquired complementary technologies in the high-tech sector. Learning and innovation can also transcend national boundaries through cross-border acquisitions (Christofi et al., 2019), benefiting both foreign and local firms. This effect is particularly pronounced in more advanced host countries, where the economic and technological infrastructure facilitates the absorption and utilization of innovative advancements brought by foreign acquirers (Ashraf et al., 2016). Technological capabilities acquired can be leveraged to pursue *inter-alia* green transformation (Li et al., 2020) and digitalization (Chen et al., 2023).

Nonetheless, the transfer of innovative capabilities can be hindered due to acquisition integration (Graebner, 2004), particularly when it comes to human integration (Bauer et al., 2016). For instance, integration may negatively impact inventors' productivity, leading to declines in patent output (Paruchuri et al., 2006) and the loss of key talent from the acquired company (Ernst & Vitt, 2000). As a result, innovative performance may suffer, especially when cultural differences between the merging entities are significant (Bauer et al., 2016).

Capital Flows Across Developed and Emerging Economies

Foreign acquisitions play a pivotal role in the global economy, as they direct capital toward specific regions, fostering cross-border investment flows, and economic integration across developed (DE) and emerging economies (EE). For instance, through cross-border acquisitions, DE-firms can extend the benefits associated with superior institutions to emerging markets (Chari et al., 2010). However, firms from DEs may be reluctant to acquire targets in countries with high political risk, corruption, and legal uncertainties, as these factors increase transaction costs, such as due diligence, negotiations, and post-acquisition integration. Empirical evidence shows indeed that host countries with better quality institutions tend to attract larger acquisition inflows (Hur et al., 2011) and firms from politically stable countries are less likely to invest in countries that pose a significant political risk (Holburn & Zelner, 2010). This hinders the flow of capital from "rich" to "poor" countries (Alfaro et al., 2008), which is further exacerbated when acquisitions in EEs are primarily motivated by the exploitation of cheap labor, abundant natural resources, and weak regulations (Bose et al., 2021).

On the other side, the phenomenon of outward foreign direct investment by EEs (e.g., Brazil, Russia, India, and China (BRIC)) is on the rise. Notable examples include Lenovo's acquisitions of IBM's personal computer business in 2005 and Motorola Mobility in 2014 (China), Geely's acquisition of Volvo in 2010 (China), and HCL's acquisition of the UK-based Axon Group in 2008 (India). These acquisitions can offset competitive weaknesses and help EE-firms to overcome the "latecomer disadvantage" (Luo & Tung, 2007; Rui & Yip, 2008). Further, they can benefit target firms in DEs by means of tangible resource redeployment and asset divestiture (Buckley et al., 2014).

Social Impacts of Acquisitions

We refer to the social dimension as the impact of acquisitions on people (or social capital). Acquisitions are not only an organizational and economic process, but they also have a strong "human" side. Given the relatively large number of people involved and the intense emotional context, the potential for negative consequences and organizational conflicts is high. Indeed, most of the issues that adversely impact acquisition success are suggested to derive from human integration (Dao & Bauer, 2021). Nonetheless, human-related factors are often undermanaged, as "soft" issues are perceived as less relevant, more unpredictable, and difficult to measure in quantitative terms (Marks & Mirvis, 2011). Hence, there is a compelling need to examine acquisitions from a social, or human, point of view (Sarala et al., 2019).

Employment and Working Conditions

Acquiring and target firms' employees are the most directly impacted by these operations. Because acquisitions are major events that bring uncertainties, they can result in high levels of stress, tension, anxiety, and resentment among organization members (Sarala et al., 2019), which are in turn associated with reduced productivity and innovation (Ernst &

Vitt, 2000). In addition, acquisitions are often cited as the cause of waves of layoffs, which is why they often face strong opposition from labor unions and attract widespread, often negative, media attention. It is common that acquisitions aim to achieve economies of scale by eliminating overlapping activities, which almost always includes workforce downsizing (Bauer et al., 2018). There is indeed evidence of reductions in labor demand and employment after acquisitions (Conyon et al., 2002), especially where labor protection rules are weaker (Gugler & Yurtoglu, 2004).

By contrast, other studies, building on the argument that acquisitions allow for a more efficient use of resources, support that acquisitions can positively affect employment and workforce productivity (Oberhofer, 2013; Taguchi & Yanagawa, 2013). For instance, according to Siegel and Simons (2010), acquisitions constitute a mechanism that promotes human capital by improving the sorting and matching of workers and managers to firms and industries that best suit their skills. In particular, acquisitions lead to a reduction of unproductive workers, an upgrading of existing workers' skills through knowledge transfer, and the hiring of new employees whose skills benefit the organization (ibid).

Network Relationships

When companies pursue acquisitions, there can be anticipated or unexpected effects on customers and suppliers (Anderson et al., 2001). Acquiring firms gain access not only to an individual, independent organization, but also to its established network of market relationships. While the transfer of customer base, access to critical suppliers and innovative networks, and increase in bargaining power are motives for acquisitions, indirect impacts on customers and suppliers can derive from these transactions. In doing so, acquisitions can strengthen or jeopardize existing business relationships. For example, research suggests that acquisitions can reduce customer satisfaction (Umashankar et al., 2022) and raise consumers' betrayal perception (Yu et al., 2022). The latter leads to psychological reactance and brand shift, especially when acquired brands have strong local roots (Yu et al., 2022). On the other side, consumers of the acquiring firm may feel a sense of national pride in a cross-border acquisition, resulting in an increased willingness to pay or demand certain products (Chu, 2013).

Some studies also outline that impacts may not be confined solely to the relationship between the combining entities but spread into connected relations and generate more extensive network effects (Anderson et al., 2001; Havila & Salmi, 2000). For instance, Öberg et al. (2007) show that acquisitions lead customers and suppliers to reassess the way they perceive their network of business relationships, to position themselves strategically, and react by changing their perceptions of networking options. Moreover, acquisitions among suppliers can be a driver for acquisitions among customers, and vice versa (Öberg & Holtström, 2006).

Cultural Integration and Identity

Acquisitions have also effects on the cultural environment at both the organizational and national levels, particularly in cross-border deals where firms from diverse cultural backgrounds merge. First, the cultural integration process in acquisitions is inherently complex and multifaceted, as corporate culture permeates almost all organizational practices, including leadership styles, decision-making processes, and communication norms. Hence, cultural issues of combining companies are determining factors of the success or failure of cross-border acquisitions (Zhang et al., 2011). In particular, cultural fit (i.e., the extent to which the cultures of the acquiring and target firms are compatible), is crucial for sociocultural integration, synergy realization, and shareholder value (Bauer & Matzler, 2014).

Second, cross-border acquisitions also face cultural complexities at the national level. Differences in national culture can serve as both a barrier and an opportunity for integration. On one hand, they can facilitate mutual learning and drive innovation by combining diverse perspectives (Bauer et al., 2016). On the other hand, national cultural differences can be even more challenging to reconcile than organizational ones, as they are deeply rooted in societal values, traditions, and historical experiences (Stahl & Voigt, 2008). These differences can evoke both attraction and apprehension, influencing how employees and local stakeholders perceive and respond to the acquisition. For example, if the acquirer is from a historically dominant country, discourses related to imperialism and colonialism are likely to emerge in the target (Sarala et al., 2019). Hence, foreign entrants may be received with diffidence and distrust from local communities.

Corporate Social Responsibility (CSR)

Some burgeoning literature highlights the importance of adopting a stakeholder-oriented approach in acquisitions to attenuate potential cultural conflicts by reducing the probability of a breach in implicit contracts (Arouri et al., 2019). This approach is reflected in the implementation of corporate socially responsible (CSR) practices by acquiring firms (Dmytriyev et al., 2021). CSR can help gaining legitimacy from local stakeholders and to "balance relationships and interests across a geographically dispersed network of stakeholders" (Park et al., 2019). Hence, the social outcomes of acquisitions are affected by the socially (ir)responsible way an acquisition is managed, and the extent to which the broader interests of multiple stakeholders are considered. For instance, while some acquirers may actively engage with local communities, others may prioritize restructuring and downsizing to streamline operations at the expense of social considerations. Research suggests that the adoption of CSR practices leads to financial benefits. For example, there is evidence that stronger CSR attributes reduce arbitrage spread (Arouri et al., 2019) and lead to long-term acquisition gains (Bettinazzi & Zollo, 2017). By contrast, negative media coverage of corporate irresponsible practices is associated with a lower likelihood of deal completion and longer duration (Hawn, 2021). Hence, acquirers can signal their commitment toward CSR to respond to diverse stakeholder demands and strengthen acquisition performance (Chen et al., 2023).

The Environmental Impacts of Acquisitions

The environmental dimension relates to the consequences of acquisitions on the natural environment (or natural capital). Environmental considerations in acquisitions encompass issues such as pollution, resource depletion, and climate change, which can impact business operations.

Carbon Footprint

In the face of the growing attention to environmental protection and regulatory pressures, acquisitions have emerged as a viable strategy for companies to reduce their emissions and maintain their legitimacy (Yang & Chi, 2023). For instance, the enactment of the *Environmental Protection Law* (2015) establishing strict limits on the discharge of pollutants into air, water, and soil in China, has promoted corporate engagement in green acquisitions (Han et al., 2022). *Green* (or also *low-carbon*) *acquisitions* refer to acquisitions carried out by highly polluting enterprises to obtain green resources and clean technologies (Lu, 2021). The volume of green deals valued at over $100 million has increased of 66%, rising from 5.3% to 8.9% since 2013 (Raberger et al., 2024). These acquisitions are particularly relevant in highly polluting sectors, like mining, which are subject to stricter environmental regulations and policies than other industries (Leon-Gonzalez & Tole, 2015). Therefore, green deals offer polluting firms a strategic way to lower compliance costs (Li et al., 2020). Much research focuses indeed on the financial impacts of green acquisitions, particularly in the Chinese context, where heavy polluting firms often face severe financial restrictions. In this regard, green acquisitions can help companies gain trust from stakeholders, reduce resource constraints, and improve reputation (Li et al., 2020; Wei & Pujari, 2023; Zhang et al., 2024). These acquisitions are found to enhance environmental governance and support a green transformation. Li and Geng (2024), for instance, show that green acquisitions increase environmental protection investments, especially in horizontal deals. Additionally, spillover effects can be observed, as firms in the same industry tend to improve their green performance following an acquisition (Zhang et al., 2024).

In parallel, research also suggests that the acquisition of polluting ("brown") firms by environmentally responsible acquirers can lead to positive environmental outcomes. These acquisitions create opportunities for the acquiring firm to transfer its environmental capabilities to the target company (Gordano et al., 2024). This capability transfer can lead to significant improvements in the target's environmental performance, including reductions in pollution levels, particularly when the target operates in a chemically related industry (Patel & King, 2022).

While acquisitions can be used by acquirer to upgrade their green performance or to drive meaningful improvements in the environmental performance of acquired firms, they can be also used strategically to bypass stricter regulations by shifting polluting operations to countries with weaker environmental policies and enforcement mechanisms (Bose et al., 2021). As a result, these countries become "pollution havens" victims. For instance, studies indicate that India is experiencing such effects, suggesting the need to strengthen anti-corruption measures to prevent foreign companies from exploiting regulatory weaknesses (Chandrika et al., 2022). This phenomenon raises concerns about the global redistribution of environmental harm, where sustainability commitments in DEs may come at the expense of ecological degradation in less regulated markets.

Contributions to the SDGs

According to the UN, acquisitions, especially foreign deals, are relevant for their potential to "transfer knowledge and technology, create jobs, boost overall productivity, enhance competitiveness and entrepreneurship, and ultimately eradicate poverty through economic growth and development" (UN, 2003, p. 9). Having provided a synthesis of the main acquisition impacts on key societal dimensions, as emerged from our review work, we use the SDGs (see Table 1) as an integrative framework to highlight missing research perspectives and implications for policy. Next, we discuss implications for future research and policy.

Implications for Research

Table 2 summarizes the main societal impacts as emerging from the reviewed literature and highlights missing perspectives in existing research. While the economic implications of acquisitions, such as growth, efficiency, and capital reallocation, have been extensively examined, the social and environmental consequences of acquisition activity and their interconnectedness with economic outcomes remain rather neglected. For instance, there is still limited understanding of how acquisition-driven efficiency gains are distributed beyond firm boundaries in the economic domain. For example, further research is needed to examine whether such gains lead to inclusive growth, such as reducing poverty and social inequalities, and how economic benefits are distributed across space and stakeholders. Additionally, the potential for life-cycle rebound effects, where efficiency in one area leads to increased resource use elsewhere, remains an overlooked factor in assessing the environmental consequences associated with expansion through acquisitions.

On the social side, while research has mainly focused on employees and employment effects, other social dimensions are lacking. This gap can be attributed to the inherent difficulty in evaluating and measuring impacts, such as communities' well-being, cultural identity, and cohesion.

Table 1 Sustainable development goals

#	*Goal*	*Description*
1	No poverty	End poverty in all its forms everywhere
2	Zero hunger	End hunger, achieve food security and improved nutrition, and promote sustainable agriculture
3	Good health and well-being	Ensure healthy lives and promote well-being for all at all ages
4	Quality education	Ensure inclusive and equitable quality education and promote lifelong learning opportunities for all
5	Gender equality	Achieve gender equality and empower all women and girls
6	Clean water and sanitation	Ensure availability and sustainable management of water and sanitation for all
7	Affordable and clean energy	Ensure access to affordable, reliable, sustainable, and modern energy for all
8	Decent work and economic growth	Promote sustained, inclusive and sustainable economic growth, full and productive employment, and decent work for all
9	Industry, innovation and infrastructure	Build resilient infrastructure, promote inclusive and sustainable industrialization, and foster innovation
10	Reduced inequalities	Reduce inequality within and among countries
11	Sustainable cities and communities	Make cities and human settlements inclusive, safe, resilient and sustainable
12	Responsible consumption and production	Ensure sustainable consumption and production patterns
13	Climate action	Take urgent action to combat climate change and its impacts
14	Life below water	Conserve and sustainably use the oceans, seas and marine resources for sustainable development
15	Life on land	Protect, restore and promote sustainable use of terrestrial ecosystems, manage forests, combat desertification, and halt biodiversity loss
16	Peace, justice and strong institutions	Promote peaceful and inclusive societies, provide access to justice for all, and build effective, accountable and inclusive institutions
17	Partnerships for the goals	Strengthen the means of implementation and revitalize the global partnership for sustainable development

Table 2 Societal impacts of acquisitions

Sustainability dimensions	*Positive societal impacts*	*Negative societal impacts*	*Main SDGs impacted*	*Missing perspectives*
Economic				Economic and financial impacts of acquisitions still overplay the other two dimensions.
Economic growth	Efficient resource allocation, disciplinary mechanism.	Market for corporate control inefficiencies, managerial opportunism	Goal 8	*Inclusive growth*: How do acquisition-driven financial gains translate into poverty reduction, wage growth at the bottom of the income scale, or greater economic inclusion for vulnerable groups?
Market concentration	Reduced costs for consumers.	Anti-competitive behaviors	Goals 8, 10, 16	How do technology transfers through acquisitions affect access and equity for marginalized groups?
Technological advancement	Complementary knowledge transfer, green transformation and digitalization.	Loss of technological capabilities in the integration process	Goals 8, 9	*Regional development and spillovers*: How are efficiency gains from acquisitions distributed among stakeholders and dispersed spatially? Do acquisitions exacerbate or alleviate inequalities across regions and countries? How do acquisitions impact labor rights, resource use, and institutional power in emerging economies?

(continued)

Table 2 (continued)

Sustainability dimensions	*Positive societal impacts*	*Negative societal impacts*	*Main SDGs impacted*	*Missing perspectives*
Capital flows across developed and emerging economies	Economic and institutional development of EEs, efficiency gains for DE-target firms.	Exploitation of labor and natural resources of EEs	Goals 8, 10	*Life-cycle rebound effects*: How do efficiency improvements in one operational area trigger increased resource consumption elsewhere in the combined entity value chain? What is the net environmental impact?
Social				Social dimension still lacks a multi-stakeholder perspective
Employment and working conditions	Job creation, higher work productivity, human capital valorization	Job losses, worse workers'performance, higher stress and lower morale	Goals 3, 8	*Participatory community voices:* In what ways can acquisitions incorporate dialogic approaches to engage with local communities, particularly in EEs?
Network relationships	Customer base expansion, customer satisfaction, supply network expansion	Customer betrayal perception, worse supply contract conditions	Goals 11, 17	*Gender and diversity:* How do acquisitions differentially affect layoffs, promotions, and representation in management for women and other under-represented groups?
Cultural integration and identity	Mutual learning and synergy realization	Cultural clashes, negative public sentiment	Goals 10, 11	*Cultural impacts:* What are the long-term effects of acquisitions on cultural erosion, loss of identity, and preservation of local cultural practices?

Sustainability dimensions	*Positive societal impacts*	*Negative societal impacts*	*Main SDGs impacted*	*Missing perspectives*
Corporate social responsibility (CSR)	Trust from local communities, improved acquisition performance	-	Goal 11	***Social value creation:*** How can CSR move beyond compliance and reputation management to embed social value creation? Environmental concerns are filtered through economic and financial considerations
Environmental				
Carbon footprint	Pollution reduction through green acquisitions or green capabilities' transfer	Pollution offshoring	Goal 13	***Proactive vs. reactive environmental governance:*** To what extent do acquirers adopt green practices, such as through green acquisitions, as genuine strategic commitments versus reactive compliance or even greenwashing? ***Circular economy and climate change:*** How do acquisitions promote circular economy principles? How acquisitions can support organizational transformation for adaptation to and mitigation of climate change? ***Biodiversity and natural ecosystems:*** Beyond carbon footprint, how do acquisitions—especially in resource-intensive industries—affect land use, habitat fragmentation, and biodiversity through changes in siting, sourcing, and logistics? ***Environmental justice and equity:*** How are the environmental benefits and burdens resulting from acquisitions distributed socio-economically? Do they disproportionately impact marginalized communities?

This reflects a still missing multi-stakeholder perspective, where voices of local communities, marginalized groups, and non-market actors are often neglected. A more participatory approach is needed to integrate financial data with voices and narratives from local communities affected by acquisitions, particularly in emerging economies, where power asymmetries and institutional weaknesses often limit stakeholder engagement. Likewise, the gendered and diversity-related consequences of acquisitions remain underexplored, including how mergers affect representation, workplace equity, and the distribution of risks and opportunities among women and other marginalized groups. Another neglected area is the long-term cultural impact of acquisitions. While integration challenges are acknowledged, broader issues such as cultural erosion, identity loss, and the reshaping of organizational culture are rarely addressed, despite their relevance for sustainable social cohesion. In parallel, although research has started to investigate the integration of CSR in acquisition decisions and processes, their effectiveness in generating tangible social value—beyond reputation management or compliance—remains largely unexamined. Future research could investigate how different CSR strategies (e.g., education programs, digital inclusion, stakeholder dialog) contribute to community well-being and resilience.

On the environmental side of acquisitions, we note that most studies focus on the business case for green acquisitions, often overlooking broader environmental consequences. This calls for a more critical investigation of whether green practices are genuinely embedded in strategic intent or simply represent reactive compliance measures or, in some cases, even serve as greenwashing to enhance corporate image (Todaro & Torelli, 2024). Oil and gas companies, for example, might invest in renewable energy ventures to wash their image, while their core business remains fossil fuel dependent. Moreover, sustainability research in acquisitions focuses on the effects on carbon footprint, underemphasizing broader ecosystem impacts. For instance, there is also a lack of studies on the role of acquisitions in promoting circular economy principles (i.e., reduce, reuse and recycle) in the management of waste, water, energy, and materials. Acquisitions offer opportunities to streamline production processes, minimize waste, and redesign supply chains for greater environmental efficiency and closed resource loops, but these potential gains are rarely evaluated systematically. At the same time, little is known about how acquisitions contribute to climate change adaptation and mitigation beyond emissions reduction. For instance, firms may acquire or transfer green capabilities but the extent to which these acquisitions support climate resilience remains underexplored. Further, acquisitions can significantly alter land use, disrupt habitat connectivity, and accelerate biodiversity loss through shifts in facility locations, raw material sourcing, and logistics strategies. These dimensions remain largely absent from current studies, yet they are central to understanding the full ecological footprint of corporate consolidation. Finally, the issues of environmental justice and equity are rarely addressed. There is limited understanding of how the environmental benefits and burdens resulting from acquisitions are distributed across different socioeconomic and demographic groups. Often, marginalized or low-income communities disproportionately bear the impacts of increased pollution, resource depletion, or land degradation, while receiving fewer benefits from improvements in infrastructure or employment opportunities. Future research should investigate these disparities and evaluate whether acquisitions can exacerbate or alleviate environmental inequalities.

Implications for Policy

At a policy level, acquisitions can offer significant opportunities for lagging countries by attracting capital and fostering economic development. However, institutional weaknesses can hinder capital flows. Therefore, governments bear the responsibility of enhancing the institutional framework and strengthening law enforcement to attract capital flows through acquisitions. It is indeed often beneficial for the home (or host) country government to address regulatory gaps and institutional weaknesses, engaging in institutional diplomacy and regional cooperation, and ensuring a corruption-free regulatory environment, particularly in countries with high corruption levels, weak law enforcement, and political instability. Establishing such a solid institutional foundation is crucial to prevent environmentally harmful business practices from being outsourced to more vulnerable areas, thereby protecting both local communities and ecosystems.

Further, given the targets set by the European Green Deal of reducing net greenhouse gas emissions by at least 55% by 2030 (compared to 1990 levels) and net zero by 2050 (European Commission (EC), 2019), enterprises must undergo substantial transitions in their business models. In particular, the recent EU Directive on Corporate Sustainability Due

Diligence (CSDD; EC, 2024) marks a pivotal advancement in corporate regulation by mandating that companies proactively identify, prevent, mitigate, and account for adverse impacts on human rights and the environment throughout their operations and value chains. This directive extends its reach beyond European borders, holding companies accountable for the effects of their activities worldwide. By embedding sustainability considerations into due diligence, the CSDD compels firms to take responsibility not only for direct impacts but also for those occurring in their supply chains and acquired entities. Further, significant changes may be driven by the Corporate Sustainability Reporting Directive (CSRD; EC, 2022), which requires, among other things, that large companies adopt a "double materiality" perspective in their reporting. This approach requires companies to evaluate sustainability issues on two fronts: 1) how their business decisions and acquisition activities affect the environmental and stakeholders (i.e., impact materiality), and 2) how these same stakeholders and sustainability factors, in turn, influence the company's financial performance, risk exposure, and long-term viability (i.e., financial materiality). This regulation can promote the integration of a double materiality perspective into acquisition processes. By adopting this holistic framework, acquiring firms would be equipped to conduct a more comprehensive and nuanced assessment of potential risks and opportunities associated with acquisitions. For example, understanding the financial consequences of the environmental footprint of a target company, the social dynamics of local communities, or the institutional context of the host country can reveal hidden liabilities or value-creating opportunities that conventional analyses might overlook. This integrated evaluation thus supports more responsible investment decisions, aligning corporate growth strategies with broader SDGs by encouraging companies to internalize environmental and social costs and benefits of acquisitions.

Conclusion

Acquisitions have the potential to drive not only economic growth but also social and environmental progress. However, the full potential of acquisitions is often constrained by siloed approaches and an imbalance that prioritizes economic outcomes over social and environmental considerations, limiting a comprehensive evaluation of their far-reaching effects. Such an integrated perspective reflects SDG 17, which calls for global partnerships to support and achieve all other SDGs. In this context, acquisitions represent a powerful mechanism to catalyze the spirit of SDG 17: by leveraging acquisitions, organizations can transcend traditional boundaries, pooling resources, expertise, and innovations to drive holistic, inclusive, and sustainable progress on a global scale.

References

Ahuja, G., & Katila, R. (2001). Technological acquisitions and the innovation performance of acquiring firms: A longitudinal study. *Strategic Management Journal, 22*(3), 197–220.

Alfaro, L., Kalemli-Ozcan, S., & Volosovych, V. (2008). Why doesn't capital flow from rich to poor countries? An empirical investigation. *Review of Economics and Statistics, 90*(2), 347–368.

Anderson, H., Havila, V., & Salmi, A. (2001). Can you buy a business relationship?: On the importance of customer and supplier relationships in acquisitions. *Industrial Marketing Management, 30*(7), 575–586.

Arouri, M., Gomes, M., & Pukthuanthong, K. (2019). Corporate social responsibility and M&a uncertainty. *Journal of Corporate Finance, 56*, 176–198.

Ashraf, A., Herzer, D., & Nunnenkamp, P. (2016). The effects of greenfield FDI and cross-border M&as on total factor productivity. *The World Economy, 39*(11), 1728–1755.

Bauer, F., & Matzler, K. (2014). Antecedents of M&a success: The role of strategic complementarity, cultural fit, and degree and speed of integration. *Strategic Management Journal, 35*(2), 269–291.

Bauer, F., Matzler, K., & Wolf, S. (2016). M&a and innovation: The role of integration and cultural differences—A central European targets perspective. *International Business Review, 25*(1), 76–86.

Bauer, F., Schriber, S., Degischer, D., & King, D. (2018). Contextualizing speed and cross-border acquisition performance: Labor market flexibility and efficiency effects. *Journal of World Business, 53*(2), 290–301.

Bettinazzi, E., & Zollo, M. (2017). Stakeholder orientation and acquisition performance. *Strategic Management Journal, 38*(12), 2465–2485.

Blonigen, B., & Pierce, J. (2016). *Evidence for the effects of mergers on market power and efficiency* (Vol. No. w22750). National Bureau of Economic Research.

Bose, S., Minnick, K., & Shams, S. (2021). Does carbon risk matter for corporate acquisition decisions? *Journal of Corporate Finance, 70*, 102058.

Broughton, K. (2023, December 29). What Happened in M&A in 2023, and what's Ahead, in Five Charts. *Wall Street Journal*. https://www.wsj.com/articles/what-happened-in-m-a-in-2023-and-whats-ahead-in-five-charts-236b2dbf

Buckley, P., Elia, S., & Kafouros, M. (2014). Acquisitions by emerging market multinationals: Implications for firm performance. *Journal of World Business, 49*(4), 611–632.

Cavenaile, L., Celik, M., & Tian, X. (2021). The dynamic effects of antitrust policy on growth and welfare. *Journal of Monetary Economics, 121*, 42–59.

Chandrika, R., Mahesh, R., & Tripathy, N. (2022). Is India a pollution haven? Evidence from cross-border mergers and acquisitions. *Journal of Cleaner Production, 376*, 134355.

Chari, A., Ouimet, P., & Tesar, L. (2010). The value of control in emerging markets. *The Review of Financial Studies, 23*(4), 1741–1770.

Chen, X., Liang, X., & Wu, H. (2023). Cross-border mergers and acquisitions and CSR performance: Evidence from China. *Journal of Business Ethics, 183*(1), 255–288.

Christofi, M., Vrontis, D., Thrassou, A., & Shams, S. (2019). Triggering technological innovation through cross-border mergers and acquisitions: A micro-foundational perspective. *Technological Forecasting and Social Change, 146*, 148–166.

Chu, J. (2013). Quantifying nation equity with sales data: A structural approach. *International Journal of Research in Marketing, 30*(1), 19–35.

Conyon, M., Girma, S. T., & Wright, P. (2002). The impact of mergers and acquisitions on company employment in the United Kingdom. *European Economic Review, 46*, 31–49.

Dao, M., & Bauer, F. (2021). Human integration following M&a: Synthesizing different M&a research streams. *Human Resource Management Review, 31*(3), 100746.

David, J. (2021). The aggregate implications of mergers and acquisitions. *The Review of Economic Studies, 88*(4), 1796–1830.

Dmytriyev, S., Freeman, R., & Hörisch, J. (2021). The relationship between stakeholder theory and corporate social responsibility: Differences, similarities, and implications for social issues in management. *Journal of Management Studies, 58*(6), 1441–1470.

Elkington, J. (1994). Towards the sustainable corporation: Win-win-win business strategies for sustainable development. *California Management Review, 36*(2), 90–100.

Ernst, H., & Vitt, J. (2000). The influence of corporate acquisitions on the behaviour of key inventors. *R&D Management, 30*(2), 105–120.

European Commission (EC). (2019, December 11). *The European Green Deal.* https://eur-lex.europa.eu/resource.html?uri=cellar:b828d165-1c22-11ea-8c1f-01aa75ed71a1.0002.02/DOC_1&format=PDF

European Commission (EC). (2022, December 14). *Directive (EU) 2022/2464 of the European Parliament and of the Council of 14 December 2022.* http://data.europa.eu/eli/dir/2022/2464/oj

European Commission (EC). (2024, June 13). *Directive (EU) 2024/1760 of the European Parliament and of the Council of 13 June 2024.* https://eur-lex.europa.eu/legal-content/EN/TXT/PDF/?uri=OJ:L_202401760

Gordano, S., Bauer, F., & King, D. (2024). Environmental, social, and governance (ESG) acquisitions: Deal structure and outcome. *Business Strategy and the Environment*, *33*(6), 6010–6028.

Graebner, M. (2004). Momentum and serendipity: How acquired leaders create value in the integration of technology firms. *Strategic Management Journal, 25*(8–9), 751–777.

Gugler, K., & Yurtoglu, B. (2004). The effects of mergers on company employment in the USA and Europe. *International Journal of Industrial Organization, 22*(4), 481–502.

Han, Z., Wang, Y., & Pang, J. (2022). Does environmental regulation promote green merger and acquisition? Evidence from the implementation of China's newly revised environmental protection law. *Frontiers in Environmental Science, 10*, 1042260.

Havila, V., & Salmi, A. (2000). Spread of change in business networks: An empirical study of mergers and acquisitions in the graphic industry. *Journal of Strategic Marketing, 8*(2), 105–119.

Hawn, O. (2021). How media coverage of corporate social responsibility and irresponsibility influences cross-border acquisitions. *Strategic Management Journal, 42*(1), 58–83.

Hitt, M., Hoskisson, R., Johnson, R., & Moesel, D. (1996). The market for corporate control and firm innovation. *Academy of Management Journal, 39*(5), 1084–1119.

Holburn, G., & Zelner, B. (2010). Political capabilities, policy risk, and international investment strategy: Evidence from the global electric power generation industry. *Strategic Management Journal, 31*(12), 1290–1315.

Hur, J., Parinduri, R., & Riyanto, Y. (2011). Cross-border M&a inflows and quality of country governance: Developing versus developed countries. *Pacific Economic Review, 16*(5), 638–655.

Jesson, J., Matheson, L., & Lacey, F. (2011). *Doing your literature review: Traditional and systematic techniques* (1st ed.). SAGE Publications.

King, D., Dalton, D., Daily, C., & Covin, J. (2004). Meta-analyses of post-acquisition performance: Indications of unidentified moderators. *Strategic Management Journal, 25*(2), 187–200.

Kolk, A., Kourula, A., & Pisani, N. (2017). Multinational enterprises and the sustainable development goals: What do we know and how to proceed? *Transnational Corporations, 24*(3), 9–32.

Leon-Gonzalez, R., & Tole, L. (2015). The determinants of mergers & acquisitions in a resource-based industry: What role for environmental sustainability? *Review of Economic Analysis, 7*(2), 111–134.

Li, B., Xu, L., McIver, R., Wu, Q., & Pan, A. (2020). Green M&a, legitimacy and risk-taking: Evidence from China's heavy polluters. *Accounting & Finance, 60*(1), 97–127.

Li, Y., & Geng, X. (2024). Analyzing the role of mergers and acquisitions and environmental investment in achieving energy transition and sustainability. *Economic Change and Restructuring, 57*(3), 1–27.

Lu, J. (2021). Can the green merger and acquisition strategy improve the environmental protection investment of listed company? *Environmental Impact Assessment Review, 86*, 106470.

Luo, Y., & Tung, R. (2007). International expansion of emerging market enterprises: A springboard perspective. *Journal of International Business Studies, 38*(4), 481–498.

Manne, H. (1965). Mergers and the market for corporate control. *Journal of Political Economy, 73*, 110–120.

Marks, M., & Mirvis, P. (2011). A framework for the human resources role in managing culture in mergers and acquisitions. *Human Resource Management, 50*(6), 859–877.

Mehta, M., Srinivasan, S., & Zhao, W. (2020). The politics of M&a antitrust. *Journal of Accounting Research, 58*(1), 5–53.

Montiel, I., Cuervo-Cazurra, A., Park, J., Antolín-López, R., & Husted, B. (2021). Implementing the United Nations' sustainable development goals in international business. *Journal of International Business Studies, 52*(5), 999–1030.

Nilsson, M., Chisholm, E., Griggs, D., et al. (2018). Mapping interactions between the sustainable development goals: Lessons learned and ways forward. *Sustainability Science, 13*, 1489–1503.

Öberg, C., Henneberg, S., & Mouzas, S. (2007). Changing network pictures: Evidence from mergers and acquisitions. *Industrial Marketing Management, 36*(7), 926–940.

Öberg, C., & Holtström, J. (2006). Are mergers and acquisitions contagious? *Journal of Business Research, 59*(12), 1267–1275.

Oberhofer, H. (2013). Employment effects of acquisitions: Evidence from acquired European firms. *Review of Industrial Organization, 42*, 345–363.

Park, K., Meglio, O., & Schriber, S. (2019). Building a global corporate social responsibility program via mergers and acquisitions: A managerial framework. *Business Horizons, 62*(3), 395–407.

Paruchuri, S., Nerkar, A., & Hambrick, D. (2006). Acquisition integration and productivity losses in the technical core: Disruption of inventors in acquired companies. *Organization Science, 17*(5), 545–562.

Patel, P., & King, D. (2022). Capability transfer: Improved performance from acquiring polluting targets. In *Acquisitions and corporate strategy* (pp. 128–156). Routledge.

Puranam, P., Singh, H., & Zollo, M. (2006). Organizing for innovation: Managing the coordination-autonomy dilemma in technology acquisitions. *Academy of Management Journal, 49*(2), 263–280.

Raberger, N., Rompen, F., Tanoli, T., & Van Oostende, M. (2024). *Creating value from green M&a*. McKinsey & Company. https://www.mckinsey.com/capabilities/m-and-a/our-insights/creating-value-from-green-m-and-a

Rui, H., & Yip, G. (2008). Foreign acquisitions by Chinese firms: A strategic intent perspective. *Journal of World Business, 43*(2), 213–226.

Sarala, R., Vaara, E., & Junni, P. (2019). Beyond merger syndrome and cultural differences: New avenues for research on the "human side" of global mergers and acquisitions (M&as). *Journal of World Business, 54*(4), 307–321.

Serdar Dinc, I., & Erel, I. (2013). Economic nationalism in mergers and acquisitions. *The Journal of Finance, 68*(6), 2471–2514.

Siegel, D., & Simons, K. (2010). Assessing the effects of mergers and acquisitions on firm performance, plant productivity, and workers: Newl evidence from matched employer-employee data. *Strategic Management Journal, 31*(8), 903–916.

Stahl, G., & Voigt, A. (2008). Do cultural differences matter in mergers and acquisitions? A tentative model and examination. *Organization Science, 19*(1), 160–176.

Taguchi, H., & Yanagawa, T. (2013). The dynamic impacts of M&a on employment in Japan. *Journal of Management & Governance, 17*(2), 511–533.

Todaro, D., & Torelli, R. (2024). *From greenwashing to ESG-washing: A focus on the circular economy field*. Corporate Social Responsibility and Environmental Management.

Todtenhaupt, M., & Voget, J. (2021). International taxation and productivity effects of M&as. *Journal of International Economics, 131*, 103438.

Umashankar, N., Bahadir, S., & Bharadwaj, S. (2022). Despite efficiencies, mergers and acquisitions reduce firm value by hurting customer satisfaction. *Journal of Marketing, 86*(2), 66–86.

United Nations (2003), *'Financing for Development', Monterrey Consensus of the International Conference on Financing for Development*. Available at: http://www.un.org/esa/ffd/monterrey/MonterreyConsensus.pdf

United Nations (2015). *Transforming our world: the 2030 Agenda for Sustainable Development*. https://sdgs.un.org/sites/default/files/publications/21252030%20Agenda%20for%20Sustainable%20Development%20web.pdf

Van Zanten, J., & van Tulder, R. (2021). Improving companies' impacts on sustainable development: A nexus approach to the SDGS. *Business Strategy and the Environment, 30*(8), 3703–3720.

Wei, Y., & Pujari, D. (2023). Does buying green pay off? Stock market reactions to green acquisitions. *Industrial Marketing Management, 114*, 137–151.

World Commission on Environment and Development (WCED). (1987). *Our common future*. Oxford University Press.

Yang, Y., & Chi, Y. (2023). Path selection for enterprises' green transition: Green innovation and green mergers and acquisitions. *Journal of Cleaner Production, 412*, 137397.

Yu, H., Legendre, T., & Jung, I. (2022). Brand betrayal and moral judgment: Consumers' responses to M&a of local foodservice brands. *International Journal of Contemporary Hospitality Management, 34*(12), 4592–4608.

Zhang, J., Zhou, C., & Ebbers, H. (2011). Completion of Chinese overseas acquisitions: Institutional perspectives and evidence. *International Business Review, 20*(2), 226–238.

Zhang, Y., Sun, Z., Sheng, A., Zhang, L., & Kan, Y. (2024). Can green technology mergers and acquisitions enhance sustainable development? Evidence from ESG ratings. *Sustainable Development*, *32*(6), 6072–6087.

Ecosystem Acquisitions: Integrating External Perspectives on Acquisition Environments

Svante Schriber and Olimpia Meglio

Introduction

Corporate acquisitions, when one firm acquires another one, represent a common tool to increase competitiveness and achieve synergies (Feldman & Hernandez, 2022) by adding new markets (Lee & Lieberman, 2010), resources, and organizational capabilities (King, Slotegraaf & Kesner, 2008) that would otherwise take years of risky investments to develop organically. Such benefits contribute to making acquisitions an increasingly popular phenomenon across most economies and industries, revealed by the frequency and total global values of acquisitions over the last decades.

Unfortunately, the popularity of acquisitions is contradicted by their performance, as there are indications that most acquisitions fail (King et al., 2021). The reason is that acquisitions are complex, ambiguous, and multitemporal processes (Jemison & Sitkin, 1986). For example, acquirers

S. Schriber (✉)
Stockholm Business School, Stockholm University, Stockholm, Sweden

O. Meglio
University of Naples Federico II, Naples, Italy
e-mail: olimpia.meglio@unina.it

D. R. King and A. Bansal (eds.), *Navigating Stakeholder Dynamics Surrounding Acquisitions*,
https://doi.org/10.1007/978-3-032-03199-0_10

experience information asymmetries before a deal as they often have very limited and uncertain insights into the target (Coff, 1999). Additionally, negotiations and valuation add to difficulties as the involved parties can withhold or distort relevant information (Graebner, 2009). Later, in the post-acquisition stage, synergies require careful integration between the involved organizations (Chatuverdi & Weigelt, 2024) associated with employee anxiety and stress, cultural, and other conflicts (van Marrewijk, 2016). As a result, managers confront issues before, during completion, and after acquisitions.

Beyond the internal aspects of acquisitions that relate to the parties involved, research increasingly points to the importance of a firm's external environment (Battisti et al., 2024) for several reasons. If acquisitions aim to increase competitiveness, then clearly success is evaluated against the environment. This environment in turn is dynamic, as external actors act in accordance with their interests which can diverge from those of the acquiring firm. For example, customers and suppliers may decide to terminate their relationships with the merging firm (Anderson, Havila & Salmi, 2001; Öberg, 2014). Others may act directly against the aims of the acquisition by making competing bids (Ruback, 1983) or poach employees (King & Schriber, 2016). Still, attention to the external environment remains scattered with different issues addressed in isolation. This is unfortunate as it risks leaving important factors unattended.

Our aim is to contribute to acquisition research focusing on the dynamics surrounding acquisitions. We achieve this aim by combining the ecosystem perspective (Adner, 2017) and the acquisition literature to investigate actors surrounding a focal acquisition (Schriber & Meglio, 2024). This offers a structured way to approach the wider environment, and how relations play out in acquisitions. The term "ecosystem"has gained prominence in management research to describe the competitive environment. It usually refers to a network of interconnected firms (Jacobides, Cennamo & Gawer, 2018). In a seminal article, Moore (1993: 76) describes how ecosystems evolve around innovations, stating that "[i]n a business ecosystem, companies coevolve capabilities around a new innovation: they work cooperatively and competitively to support new products, satisfy customer needs, and eventually incorporate the next round of innovations." The ecosystem metaphor illustrates a varied set of relations to a complex environment, where actors are interdependent and entertain competitive, collaborative, or coopetitive relationships. Therefore, we find it a suitable lens to connect the stakeholder and competitive dynamics perspectives and better capture the dynamics surrounding acquisitions.

Theoretical Framework

We take a strategic management view emphasizing that firms can survive and thrive if they have sufficient fit with their environment and control necessary resources and capabilities (Barney, 1991; Helfat et al., 2007; Porter, 1980). In this context, acquisitions are primarily driven by a firm's attempt to secure relevant positions, resources, and capabilities, and to provide attractive services or products to increase competitiveness. Accordingly, acquisition research has centered on how the merging firms relate to each other to predict and explain performance, often taking different perspectives.

While most of these typologies look at ex ante conditions, such as the degree of relatedness between the merging parties (King et al., 2021), there are other typologies considering also the integration required. While the former aim to understand which typology performs better (Lubatkin et al., 1997; Lien & Klein, 2006; Park, 2003), the latter offer managerial guidance on how to achieve the acquisition's intended benefits (Angwin & Meadows, 2005; Birkinshaw, Bresman & Håkanson, 2000; Haspeslagh & Jemison, 1991). Below we summarize existing research highlighting the dominance of either a stakeholder or a competitive dynamics perspective on the external environment of acquisitions, before we show how they can be integrated using an ecosystems perspective.

The Stakeholder Perspective on Acquisitions

Research on an acquisition's environment largely describes acquisition environments focusing on valuable relations, which, if harmed, also risk harming the performance of the acquisition. This is consistent with a stakeholder perspective (Freeman, 1984; Donaldson & Preston, 1995) that presents firms as entertaining relationships with a broad range of internal and external actors (the stakeholders, indeed). Consequently, the task of acquisition management is to handle a complex web of relations to many interested groups within and outside the firm (Meglio & Schriber, 2023). Specifically, this approach is crucial to understand how acquisitions unfold, as acquisitions put positive relations with such stakeholders at risk (Anderson et al., 2001). This manifests in growing attention to for instance the risk of customer or supplier loss following acquisitions (e.g., Kato & Schoenberg, 2014; Öberg, 2014), and it makes the management of customer relations an important explanation to acquisition success (Dalziel, 2007). In short, in this perspective, acquisitions are seen as a threat to essentially benevolent external actors.

The Competitive Dynamics Perspective on Acquisitions

More recently, a different strand of research has challenged this essentially benevolent view of acquisition environments. Competitive dynamic research revolves around the idea that firms act to increase their competitiveness, and that rivals will react with retaliatory actions (Smith et al., 2001). Chen and Miller (1994) propose that retaliation can be predicted based on three factors, awareness, motivation, and capability, labeled the A-M-C framework (Chen, 1996). It assesses the degree to which (a) the competitor is aware of the focal action, (b) the focal action motivates the competitor to retaliate, and (c) to which rivals are capable to respond. This framework has provided associated insights, such as a smaller firm relying only on one industry may perceive an action in its market as more of a threat than a larger competitor that operates in multiple markets (Chen, 1996). Moreover, competitors can develop mutual forbearance (Baum & Korn, 1996; Gimeno & Woo, 1996). For example, Baum and Korn (1999) show how firms in the airline industry can act vigorously against certain competitors, while living placidly alongside others with the difference explained in part by the relative size of involved firms.

These considerations have been extended to an acquisition context. Research suggests that competitors can launch several competitive actions to strengthen one's position at the expense of an acquisition (King & Schriber, 2016). The actions taken can vary in complexity and intensity (Uhlenbruck et al., 2017). Still, the competitive dynamics perspective concentrates on hostile relationships. For instance, Keil and colleagues (2013) found that firms behave according to competitive dynamics theory by responding to acquisitions in their industry, and this lowers acquisition performance.

An Integrating Ecosystem Perspective on Acquisitions

While advancing research of contextual issues surrounding acquisitions, stakeholder and competitive dynamics research also have weaknesses. Stakeholder theory considers a broad number of actors who share an interest in a focal firm and can influence it; however, it disregards competitive relations. Meanwhile, competitive dynamics focuses on hostile relations and often reduces the complexity of actors surrounding acquisitions to dyads (Chen & Miller, 2015). In short, there is potential for combining these outlooks, building on their respective strengths and balancing their relative weaknesses.

We argue ecosystems can provide an integrative role that goes beyond merely combining stakeholders and competitive dynamics. In management research, the term "ecosystem" usually refers to a network of interconnected firms that depend on each other (Jacobides, Cennamo & Gawer, 2018). We consider ecosystems populated by a range of actors with different interests, information about, and perceptions of reality, in relation to a focal firm, including other firms, authorities, consumers, regulators, and the like.

While some use ecosystems to explain the elements necessary for a certain value creation to occur drawing on the notion of ecosystem-as-structure (Adner, 2017), our focus is on expanding the view of the environment surrounding acquisitions, including those actors tangentially affecting or affected by but also adversaries to a focal deal, in line with the Ecosystems-as-affiliation view (Adner, 2017; Jacobides, Cennamo & Gawer, 2015). This concept has been applied to a wide range of situations, including business, innovative (Adner & Kapoor, 2010) or platform ecosystems (Iansiti & Levien, 2004); see Jacobides, Cennamo and Gawer (2018) for an overview. Still, in acquisition research the ecosystems perspective has primarily been applied to understand platform acquisitions (cf. Gawer, 2021).

As a further advantage, ecosystems relax assumptions of equilibria, or that environments are inherently stable. Instead, events are seen as evolving in chains of actions and reactions, shaping how firms grow, decline, and perish in an ongoing process without clear beginning or end (Ferrier & Lee, 2002). In other words, each action can be seen as a reaction to a firm's existing situation. Following Moore (1993), we consider ecosystems as inherently evolving, indeed exemplified by acquisitions. As relations between a focal firm and other constituents are unique, more generic ecosystem frameworks have been provided (e.g., Schriber & Meglio, 2024). Based on these insights, we summarize an ecosystems framework in Table 1.

The table illustrates an ecosystem where a focal acquisition involving acquirer and target forms the base or focal layer which is populated by other organizational actors. To structure these, the ecosystem can be analytically separated based on proximity to the focal acquisition. The first layer, closest to the acquisition, displays the firms traditionally considered industry actors (Porter, 1980), including customers, suppliers, competitors, and so on. Next, we find the second layer, involving suppliers' suppliers, complementors, and the like, while the third layer includes, for instance, standardizing bodies, regulators, and investors. While serving analytical purposes, acquisitions can differ significantly, and the framework can aid in identifying important differences. Moreover, these layers should not be confused with strict relations between acquisitions and other actors. While acquirers likely have more intense relations, e.g., with suppliers (first layer), they may also interact closely with actors in other

Table 1 Acquisition ecosystem layers

Layer	*Actors*
Focal acquisition	• Acquirer and target
First	• Competitors • Suppliers • Customers • Non-related firms
Second	• Complementors • Customers' customers • Suppliers' suppliers • Substitute providers
Third	• Regulators • Standardizing bodies • Investors • Media • Local communities • Non-governmental organizations • Labor unions • Natural environment and resources

layers. For instance, unions (third layer) can be heavily involved in an acquisition.

When considering acquisitions, it is important to emphasize that ecosystems differ from industries (e.g., Porter, 1980). First, ecosystems are wider and include more actors. Second, in the context of acquisitions, unrelated acquisitions can span different industries. Moreover, even if ecosystem models are often read from the center out, they may equally well be considered the other way around, or, as we shall see, used to consider certain actors or actor constellations in combination, and their relations to acquisitions. Importantly, an ecosystem can involve a multitude of relationships, each of which can be competitive, cooperative, or both between firms (Brandenburger & Nalebuff, 1996; Chen & Miller, 2015).

In sum, an ecosystem lens allows combining stakeholder competitive dynamic approaches to illuminate relationships between acquisitions and their environment. We next proceed with analyzing acquisitions, both pointing to and categorizing what has been done, but primarily pointing to hitherto-overlooked competitive effects in the ecosystem surrounding acquisitions, to illustrate the usefulness of an ecosystem framework on competitive dynamics surrounding acquisitions.

Ecosystem Acquisitions

We develop how acquisitions can shape their surrounding ecosystem to address effects often overlooked in prior research. Our analysis takes place at the ecosystem level where acquisitions can be seen as vehicles for creating change (cf. DaSilva & Trkman, 2014). We address both effects from acquisitions (acquisitions causing effects) and competitive reactions to acquisitions (acquisitions being affected). We also discuss the notion of retaliation considering a competitive ecosystem perspective. Our considerations elaborate upon Chen and Miller (2015), who argue that acquisitions and their competitive dynamics effects are overlooked.

Because of the almost endless combinations of reactions or competitive effects that can unfold following acquisitions, our analysis has no ambition to be exhaustive, but rather illustrative with examples serving to break new ground. We focus on deals that do not readily fit into traditional concepts, such as related or unrelated acquisitions, but which still provide distinctive advantages to acquirers by involving one or more external actors. We tentatively label them ecosystem acquisitions, as they share traits of aspiring for benefits by influencing the ecosystem in ways not described in extant acquisition research. Despite their variation, they collectively demonstrate the usefulness of the ecosystem view as they illustrate how acquisitions use external actors, or a third party, to influence a competitor or other actors. Together, this highlights novel benefits and purposes beyond those normally ascribed to acquisitions.

Acquisitions of Natural Resources orStrategic Infrastructure

Acquisitions can provide access to valuable resources (e.g., Capron & Mitchell, 2009; King et al., 2008). However, strategy research has largely focused on intangible resources, such as knowledge or organizational capabilities (cf. Barney, 1991), downplaying tangible assets (Schriber & Löwstedt, 2015). While technology acquisitions remain important for competition (Graebner & Eisenhardt, 2010; Puranam & Srikanth, 2007) the dynamics surrounding acquisitions of scarce tangible resources (e.g., oil or rare minerals) appear often taken for granted and overlooked. Likewise, acquisitions that involve strategic assets like a railway or telecommunication infrastructure can constitute a competition-changing move. Importantly, there are ecosystem consequences beyond the concentration of control over natural resources or strategic infrastructure in the hands of a few oligopolists.

As for the oil industry, since Standard Oil set off the first wave of mergers and acquisitions more than 100 years ago, acquisitions have contributed to industry concentration. Today, key production units are large oil companies generally referred to as "the machineries for maintaining the limits to the supply of oil." Oil is not only a commodity but also a strategic natural resource. As a result, acquisitions involving oil companies also entail geopolitical games (Guo, Yang & Wang, 2021). However, acquisitions also target other fixed assets. For example, in 2016, the Chinese firm Cosco acquired majority ownership of the main port of Greece. Subsequently, Pireus was described in 2019 by President Xi Jinping as an important building block in the Chinese-European trade route. The harbor thus forms an integrated part in the Belt and Road Initiative, also labeled the New Silk Road. Stretching from China to Africa, and Europe, an initiative aiming to strengthen China's position in the global markets. In contrast to many other ports where several firms co-locate, Pireus is fully owned and run by its Chinese owners (DW, 2022).

In part, the effects reflect traditional competitive gains. For instance, the Pireus acquisition led to reduced trade in competing ports in the Mediterranean. However, seen from an ecosystem lens, broader effects appear. The acquisitions of natural resources and strategic infrastructure had effects on several actors in the ecosystem; the Greek government, trade routes, customers and consumers, but also the workers' unions reacted to the Chinese acquisition. Effects went further still; calls were made for the EU to intervene against the complete divestments of ports. The concerns raised were visible both in US interest in securing ownership of another Greek port, Alexandropoulous, and subsequent Greek decision to maintain state ownership of the port (*Seatrade Maritime News*, 2022). These acquisitions illustrate how effects of acquisitions propagate across ecosystems' boundaries and influence international relations among states. In short, although traditional effects were seen on competitors, this captures only part of the acquisition effects, which helped redesign global trading routes.

Regulation-Evading Acquisitions

Several industries are influenced by technological regulations, and acquisitions may allow unexpected ways to increase competitiveness in such industries. Industries like pharmaceuticals, hospital, medicine-technology, nuclear power industries, but also oil, air traffic, and food production, are all highly regulated (Lisam, 2024). Such regulations can have very different effects depending on how they are defined. For instance, they can create output limits (e.g., on production levels per year), reduce the number of producers (e.g., concretely via controlled issuing of licenses, or indirectly via regulatory hurdles creating barriers to entry). They also can add costs per emission or define maximum emissions per product. In such situations, acquisitions can offer competitive benefits.

One such regulation increasingly pressing producers in many industries relates to carbon emissions. For instance, the European Union puts requirements on car producers relating to the amount of emission which their cars emit. Specifically, the EU Regulation 2019/631 states that "[i]t is, therefore, appropriate to pursue the objectives of Regulations (EC) No 443/2009 and (EU) No 510/2011 by setting new EU fleet-wide

CO_2 emissions reduction targets for passenger cars and light commercial vehicles for the period up to 2030" (EU, 2019).

One way to deal with such pressures is to invest in capabilities to better meet regulations. It is well-known that firms can acquire technology—patents or capabilities for instance in R&D—to better master existing or future market requirements, to improve operations and fulfill regulations (King et al., 2008). Another, less commonly recognized benefit of acquisitions is acquiring a firm which allows offsetting the acquirer's regulatory challenges. As an example, car producers can acquire a small-car producer, to lower average carbon dioxide emissions per car.

This latter idea can be illustrated by Daimler AG, the German car producer (then Daimler-Benz AG) investment in the car venture Smart. Smart was founded in 1982 on the idea of Nicolas Hayek, the founder of Smart (the watch brand), of producing a small, light, city car with very limited petrol consumption, and extremely low carbon dioxide emissions. After a cooperation with VW, Hayek approached several other car producers, and in 1994 Daimler-Benz AG announced the launch of the first cars based on the technology to the market in 1998. The acquisition thus reveals an ecosystem benefit. To Daimler, owning Smart meant spreading the high emissions of Daimler's typically large and heavy luxury cars across a larger fleet of small, energy-efficient vehicles. In this sense, the aim differed from capability acquisitions (King et al., 2008); rather than acquiring technology making the large cars more fuel-efficient, it avoided the overall corporation exceeding EU limits on carbon emissions through lowering the per car average emission. In the context of ecosystems, the acquisition illustrates how an acquisition allows handling pressures from actors in the ecosystem other than competitors, and more specifically, of regulators.

Standard-Setting Acquisitions

As mentioned, a traditional view is that acquisitions can improve firm competitiveness by offering important new capabilities to the acquirer (King et al., 2008). Organizational capabilities have come to the fore in strategic management thinking as other resources increasingly have turned into commodities. The consequence is that valuable organizational capabilities become attractive to access through acquisitions. However, acquiring a capability might be crucial also in other ways. Specifically, institutional theory describes how norms and standards shape firm behavior (e.g., Meyer & Rowan, 1977; Scott, 2003). This offers an opportunity for acquirers.

That is, rather than merely acquiring a unique capability which surpasses that of competitors, acquirers may benefit if it can leverage upon that capability to impose a standard on all actors in the industry that better suits the owning firm than others. This may be more common than expected and can be illustrated by Intel's acquisition of Mobileye (Reuters, 2024). The US acquirer is a leading producer of microprocessors, or microchips, and paid 15.3 billion USD in 2017 to access the technology of Israeli Mobileye. The target has developed autonomous vehicle technology, which would bring Intel into the growing industry of developing new vehicles. Arguably more interestingly, the acquirer brought Intel into a position where its acquired technology came to influence the technological standards. For instance, Mobileye technology has colored the requirements for tests of self-driving vehicles in the United States. Specifically, technology has shaped tests for the ability of a vehicle to handle unexpected situations. The example shows, by influencing the very standards applied to test products in an industry, an acquirer can gain an advantage over competitors, compared to if their technology would have been standard setting. In other words, acquisitions can be used to gain competitive benefits through affecting external actors in an ecosystem outside a firm's immediate market.

Substitute Products and Technologies Acquisitions

Acquisition research has paid more attention to certain types of acquisitions than others. Research has emphasized the benefits from various degrees of relatedness in knowledge bases, or technological overlap, between the involved firms (Ahuja & Katila, 2001; Sears & Hoetker, 2014). For instance, research has yet to reach consistent results on performance implications from the target's technological capabilities complementing (Cassiman & Veugelers, 2006) or substituting (King et al., 2008) the acquirer's technological capabilities. Similarly, the similarity of markets and gaining access to new markets has been given much research attention (Homburg & Bucerius, 2006; Lee & Lieberman, 2010). A common thread in this dominating view of acquisitions is the assumption that acquirers pay to utilize the target's resources such as technology or market.

In contrast, *not* utilizing target resources has been given relatively less attention. Still, from an ecosystem perspective, this appears a valid motive. When a firm's very livelihood is threatened by new technology, one option is to acquire control over that technology to ensure it does not reach the market. One way to do so is acquiring a firm with the technology, or creating a real option (Smit & Moraitis, 2010) for the acquirer to benefit from the new technology at a later stage. Alternatively, an acquirer may simply try to prevent a technology from reaching the market. In these cases, the benefit to the acquirer is the preservation of a lucrative ecosystem. Adner and Snow (2010) illustrate this point by showing how incumbent firms with old technology resist changing tech environments and capabilities by using different strategies to preserve their "outdated" technology.

The real motives behind acquisitions are difficult to detect, and valid motives can intermix with those that are dubious or illegal. While suppressing target technology may not be readily visible (Ivaldi, Petit & Unekbas, 2024), empirical studies suggest such "killer acquisitions" occur. They are more likely when a target firm's technology overlaps with an acquirer, there is a lack of competition, or technology is protected by patents, and the acquisition value is below regulatory thresholds (Cunningham, Ederer & Ma, 2021). Thus, under certain circumstances, acquisitions can benefit from not utilizing a superior technology, if the loss to competitors is even greater (Letina, Schmutzler & Seibel, 2024).

Acquisitions of Media Platforms

The increasing impact of media permeates many societies. Press coverage has moved from passively reporting what firms do to actively influencing firm actions and performance. For example, in 2010, an explosion on BP's oil rig Deepwater Horizon in the Gulf of Mexico caused a large environmental catastrophe. In the media, BP was severely criticized for its inability to handle the tangible consequences of the catastrophe. However, concerns were also raised over the initial failure to communicate the incident, including critique that expressions by Chairman Tony Hayward failed to reflect the scale of the accident both in terms of lives lost and environmental damage (BBC, 2010). The implication is that media is no longer a mere reflection of acquisition achievements or failures, but is itself an important arena to firms.

If firms previously needed to consider press coverage the rise of social media creates new challenges. First, rather than being controlled by a relatively small number of journalists, media impact is now literally in the hands of every individual with a smartphone. Second, global reach means news can have immediate effects far exceeding traditional subscription numbers or national borders.

While prior research has considered the role of media in reporting about acquisitions (e.g., Hellgren et al., 2002), gaining control of social media platforms constitutes a key type of acquisitions affecting the acquisition ecosystem. Media tycoon Rupert Murdoch's empire grew primarily in the media business; however arguably Elon Musk's acquisition of Twitter, later X, represents both a shift in industry, and an even greater impact. By paying $44 billion (NY Times, 2022), Musk gained control over an influential social media platform, raising concerns over his influence from the platform and relationships with political leaders. Regardless, the acquisition provided possibilities to favorably shape the ecosystem for Musk's businesses. In short, as media— and social media in particular— increase in influence, acquiring social media platform represents a striking example of ecosystem consequences arising from acquisitions.

Discussion

Over time, calls have been made to expand the research scope beyond the merging companies and include also the external environment (Rouziés et al., 2019; Meglio, 2022). We have argued this implies not only considering actors beyond the acquirer and the target, but it also analyzing the effects on and from the emerging dynamics surrounding acquisitions. This makes the challenge of strategic managers in acquisitions more complex as the benchmark against which an acquisition is to be evaluated is changing. We address how acquisitions can be regarded when considered from an ecosystem perspective to reveal several additional acquisition types and associated benefits, extending beyond traditional acquisition research, see Table 2.

As shown in Table 2, drawing on the ecosystem framework complements and advances beyond the multifaceted nature of environments surrounding acquisitions identified in current research (Rouziés et al., 2019). Rather than considering only a narrow set of actors, the ecosystem framework suggested here offers a broader and more detailed map of the actors surrounding acquisitions. As inherent in the suggested framework,

Table 2 Ecosystem acquisitions

Type	*Characteristics*	*Benefits*	*Illustrative examples*
Acquisitions of natural resources/strategic infrastructure	Acquiring rare physical asset	Target offering sources of competitive advantage	• Standard oil acquiring oil acquiring smaller competitors. • Cosco acquiring Pireus port
Regulation-evading acquisitions	Acquisitions enhancing regulation adherence	Target helps acquirer pass regulation, e.g., by lowering merged firm average emission	• Daimler acquisition of smart
Standard-setting acquisitions	Acquisitions influencing standards	De facto or perceived market power influencing perceived or explicit standards	• Intel acquisition of Mobileye
Substitute products and technologies acquisitions	Acquiring, controlling, or closing down threatening substitutes	Avoiding substitute threatening acquirer profits	• (typically kept secret)
Acquisitions of media platforms	Acquiring media platforms to influence public mindset	Achieving, e.g., financial gains, reputational benefits, political advantages	• Elon musk's acquisition of twitter (later X)

each actor can have a variety of relations, directly to an acquisition, and indirectly via other actors. This is important as it ties in with multilateral views, suggesting a more complex and less predictable environment than typically suggested in traditional strategic management frameworks (e.g., Porter, 1980).

We discuss five types of acquisitions that extend beyond traditional competitor dyads (Chen, 1996) or supplier-customer relationships (Kato & Schoenberg, 2014). By drawing on the ecosystem framework, we extend the scope to include a richer variety of actors. As our framework illustrates, acquisitions can encompass actors also in the outer ecosystem layers. The consequence is to contextualize otherwise rather narrow concepts of industry or competition analysis, to include actors traditionally left aside. For instance, targeting media platforms illustrates the power of acquisitions for shaping the ecosystem extending beyond competitors or customers. We have only begun to sketch possible types of acquisitions and their effects, and more are likely to exist. Collectively, we propose the term ecosystem acquisitions to signify deals that do not readily fit into traditional concepts such as related or unrelated acquisitions, but which still offer specific types of advantages to acquirers.

Beyond expanding on actors to consider, our study begins to show additional avenues for how value is created in acquisitions. An ecosystem perspective conceives value as inherently relational. More specifically, seen from an ecosystem lens, acquisition outcomes result from episodes of value creation, destruction, or leakage taking place in different areas of the ecosystem, over different time periods and involving different actors. This view does justice to the dynamic and recursive nature of value creation in acquisitions, and it is aligned with a multidimensional view of value in acquisitions (Meglio & Schriber, 2023). In short, acquisitions play out on an arena much wider than traditional notions of industries, and our argument begins to draw attention to the benefits available to acquirers through ecosystem acquisitions.

Relatedly, the ecosystem framework assists in mapping how an acquisition benefits or harms organizations. Early acquisition research was concerned mainly with acquirer performance (e.g., Kitching, 1967) and investors (e.g., Chatterjee, 1986; Kusewitt, 1985). As the scope of attention grew, attention has been paid to customers (Kato & Schoenberg, 2014), competitors (King & Schriber, 2016; Schriber et al., 2022) and rivals (Uhlenbruck et al., 2017). Still, phrased in more general strategic management framework terms, research primarily focuses on actors in the same industry as the acquisition or rivals (i.e., Porter, 1980). Adopting an ecosystem framework to acquisitions offers a structured way to highlight often-neglected actors such as complementors, substitute providers, and regulators.

Conclusion

We contribute to existing research first by showing how ecosystem concepts can integrate and extend what variables are considered when analyzing acquisitions. While extant research is varied and growing, it has only recently begun to consider the external environment surrounding acquisitions. We draw on an ecosystem lens to connect the stakeholder and the competitive dynamic perspectives. While the former offers a wide and fine-grained and varied view of actors inside and outside a focal firm, it assumes stakeholders share a common interest in the survival of the firm. The latter instead largely considers pairs of firms, while assuming relations to a focal acquisition are hostile. Adopting an ecosystem view has allowed us to integrate these perspectives and draw on their strengths, while balancing their relative weaknesses. Specifically, an ecosystem view considers a more varied range of external actors and their relationships, including benevolent, hostile, and coopetitive.

Our second and primary contribution is to broaden acquisition research by highlighting acquisitions tapping into sources of value creation often overlooked by extant research. Acquisitions do not happen in a vacuum, and they shape and are shaped by the external environment and the actors populating it through chains of actions and reactions. We propose the concept of ecosystem acquisitions to denote acquisitions creating gains to the involved firms by involving one or more actors in the ecosystem. Broadly, this complements an embeddedness perspective (Rouzies et al., 2019) to an acquiring firm's external environment. Specifically, it highlights how changing the ecosystem through acquisitions can offer advantages exceeding those considered in traditional acquisition research.

Combined, we offer a step forward in elaborating the notion of an acquisition ecosystem (Schriber & Meglio, 2024) that should stir future research. While conceptual in our development, we call for more empirical research into the relation between ecosystems and acquisitions. First, the acquisition types here are far from exhaustive, and more research is needed both to refine the ones proposed here, and to develop others. Second, an important future line of inquiry is to investigate the architecture of an acquisition ecosystem and how different actors resolve the coordination-autonomy dilemma over time. For example, what types of acquisitions or responses to them work better across different competitive environments? Answers could lead to the development of acquisition ecosystems' typologies that would ultimately enrich and update existing acquisition typologies. A related idea involves analyzing the role different actors play and the degree to which there is an ecosystem orchestrator. In other words, the governance of the ecosystem represents another promising line of inquiry.

Practical Implications

Acquiring managers can benefit from paying attention to the ecosystem in acquisitions. While other involved firms, regulators, and competitors are likely to be included in assessments before acquisitions, our study suggests it is beneficial to also consider opportunities and threats emerging from interaction with actors in the wider ecosystem. Policy makers and regulators likely also can benefit from a broader outlook on the context surrounding acquisitions. In closing, our study suggests that our ecosystem framework offers a structured and improved way to consider acquisitions in their context, along with the playing field in which competition evolves and plays out.

References

Adner, R. (2017). Ecosystem as structure: An actionable construct for strategy. *Journal of Management, 43*(1), 39–58.

Adner, R., & Kapoor, R. (2010). Value creation in innovation ecosystems: How the structure of technological interdependence affects firm performance in new technology generations. *Strategic Management Journal, 31*(3), 306–333.

Ahuja, G., & Katila, R. (2001). Technological acquisitions and the innovation performance of acquiring firms: A longitudinal study. *Strategic Management Journal, 22*(3), 197–220.

Anderson, H., Havila, V., & Salmi, A. (2001). Can you buy a business relationship? On the importance of customer and supplier relationships in acquisitions. *Industrial Marketing Management, 30*(7), 575–586.

Barney, J. (1991). Firm resources and sustained competitive advantage. *Journal of Management, 17*(1), 99–120.

Battisti, E., Nirino, N., Leonidou, E., Thrassou, A., & Vrontis, D. (2024). Mergers and acquisitions and environmental conditions: A systematic literature review to investigate their linkage. *Management Research Review, 47*(2), 226–244.

BBC (2010). https://www.bbc.com/news/10360084, Retrieved January 9, 2025.

Birkinshaw, J., Bresman, H., & Håkanson, L. (2000). Managing the post-acquisition integration process: How the human integration and task integration processes interact to foster value creation. *Journal of Management Studies, 37*(3), 395–425.

Brandenburger, A., & Nalebuff, B. (1996). *Co-opetition*. Doubleday.

Capron, L., & Mitchell, W. (2009). Selection capability: How capability gaps and internal social frictions affect internal and external strategic renewal. *Organization Science, 20*(2), 294–312.

Cassiman, B., & Veugelers, R. (2006). In search of complementarity in innovation strategy: Internal R&D and external knowledge acquisition. *Management Science, 52*(1), 68–82.

Chatterjee, S. (1986). Types of synergy and economic value: The impact of acquisitions on merging and rival firms. *Strategic Management Journal, 7*(2), 119–139.

Chen, M.-J. (1996). Competitor analysis and interfirm rivalry: Toward a theoretical integration. *The Academy of Management Review, 21*(1), 100–134.

Coff, R. (1999). How buyers cope with uncertainty when acquiring firms in knowledge-intensive industries: Caveat emptor. *Organization Science, 10*(2), 144–161.

Cunningham, C., Ederer, F., & Ma, S. (2021). Killer acquisitions. *Journal of Political Economy, 129*(3), 649–702.

Dalziel, M. (2007). The importance of target firm customers in acquisitions of technology-based firms. In *Advances in mergers and acquisitions* (pp. 157–170). Emerald Group Publishing Limited.

DaSilva, C., & Trkman, P. (2014). Business model: What it is and what it is not. *Long Range Planning, 47*(6), 379–389.

Donaldson, T., & Preston, L. (1995). The stakeholder theory of the corporation: Concepts, evidence, and implications. *Academy of Management Review, 20*(1), 65–91.

DW (2022). https://www.dw.com/en/greece-in-the-port-of-piraeus-china-is-the-boss/a-63581221 Retrieved 2 December 2, 2024.

EU (2019). https://eur-lex.europa.eu/legal-content/EN/TXT/?uri=CELEX%3A32019R0631, Point 11. Retrieved 1 October, 2024.

Feldman, E., & Hernandez, E. (2022). Synergy in mergers and acquisitions: Typology, life cycles, and value. *Academy of Management Review, 47*(4), 549–578.

Ferrier, W., & Lee, H. (2002). Strategic aggressiveness, variation, and surprise: How the sequential pattern of competitive rivalry influences stock market returns. *Journal of Managerial Issues*, 162–180.

Freeman, R. (1984). *Strategic management: A stakeholder approach*. Pitman.

Gawer, A. (2021). Digital platforms' boundaries: The interplay of firm scope, platform sides, and digital interfaces. *Long Range Planning, 54*(5), 102045.

Gimeno, J., & Woo, C. Y. (1996). Hypercompetition in a multimarket environment: The role of strategic similarity and multimarket contact in competitive de-escalation. *Organization Science, 7*(3), 322–341.

Graebner, M. (2009). Caveat venditor: Trust asymmetries in acquisitions of entrepreneurial firms. *Academy of Management Journal, 52*(3), 435–472.

Guo, Y., Yang, Y., & Wang, C. (2021). Global energy networks: Geographies of mergers and acquisitions of worldwide oil companies. *Renewable and Sustainable Energy Reviews, 139*, 110698.

Haspeslagh, P., & Jemison, D. (1991). *Managing acquisitions: Creating value through corporate renewal*. Free Press.

Hellgren, B., Löwstedt, J., Puttonen, L., Tienari, J., Vaara, E., & Werr, A. (2002). How issues become (re)constructed in the media: Discursive practices in the AstraZeneca merger. *British Journal of Management, 13*(2), 123–140.

Homburg, C., & Bucerius, M. (2006). Is speed of integration really a success factor of mergers and acquisitions? An analysis of the role of internal and external relatedness. *Strategic Management Journal, 27*(4), 347–367.

Iansiti, M., & Levien, R. (2004). *The keystone advantage: What the new dynamics of business ecosystem mean for strategy, innovation, and sustainability*. Harvard Business School Publishing.

Jacobides, M., Cennamo, C., & Gawer, A. (2018). Towards a theory of ecosystems. *Strategic Management Journal, 39*(8), 2255–2276.

Jemison, D., & Sitkin, S. (1986). Corporate acquisitions: A process perspective. *Academy of Management Review, 11*(1), 145–163.

Kato, J., & Schoenberg, R. (2014). The impact of post-merger integration on the customer–supplier relationship. *Industrial Marketing Management, 43*(2), 335–345.

King, D., Slotegraaf, R., & Kesner, I. (2008). Performance implications of firm resource interactions in the acquisition of R&D-intensive firms. *Organization Science, 19*(2), 327–340.

King, D., Wang, G., Samimi, M., & Cortes, A. (2021). A meta-analytic integration of acquisition performance prediction. *Journal of Management Studies, 58*(5), 1198–1236.

Kusewitt, J., Jr. (1985). An exploratory study of strategic acquisition factors relating to performance. *Strategic Management Journal, 6*(2), 151–169.

Lee, G., & Lieberman, M. (2010). Acquisition vs. internal development as modes of market entry. *Strategic Management Journal, 31*(2), 140–158.

Letina, I., Schmutzler, A., & Seibel, R. (2024). Killer acquisitions and beyond: Policy effects on innovation strategies. *International Economic Review, 65*(2), 591–622.

Lien, L., & Klein, P. (2006). Relatedness and acquirer performance. In C. L. Cooper & S. Finkelstein (Eds.), *Advances in mergers and acquisitions, 5(6)* (pp. 9–23). JAI.

Lisam (2024). https://www.lisam.com/news/10-most-regulated-industries-in-the-us/, retreived March 5, 2025.

Lubatkin, M., Srinivasan, N., & Merchant, H. (1997). Merger strategies and shareholder value during times of relaxed antitrust enforcement: The case of large mergers during the 1980s. *Journal of Management, 23*(1), 59.

Meglio, O., & Schriber, S. (2023). Towards a more inclusive notion of values in acquisition research. *Long Range Planning, 56*(6), 102331.

Meyer, J., & Rowan, B. (1977). Institutionalized organizations: Formal structures as myth and ceremony. *American Journal of Sociology, 83*(2), 340–363.

Moore, J. (1993). Predators and prey: A new ecology of competition. *Harvard Business Review, 71*(3), 75–86.

Öberg, C. (2014). Customer relationship challenges following international acquisitions. *International Marketing Review, 31*(3), 259–282.

Park, C. (2003). Prior performance characteristics of related and unrelated acquirers. *Strategic Management Journal, 24*(5), 471–480.

Porter, M. (1980). *Competitive strategy. Techniques for analyzing industries and competitors*. Free Press.

Puranam, P., & Srikanth, K. (2007). What they know vs. what they do: How acquirers leverage technology acquisitions. *Strategic Management Journal, 28*(8), 805–825.

Reuters (2024). https://www.reuters.com/article/technology/intels-15-billion-purchase-of-mobileye-shakes-up-driverless-car-sector-idUSKBN16K0Z4/ Retrieved 1 October, 2024.

Rouzies, A., Colman, H., & Angwin, D. (2019). Recasting the dynamics of post-acquisition integration: An embeddedness perspective. *Long Range Planning, 52*(2), 271–282.

Ruback, R. (1983). Assessing competition in the market for corporate acquisitions. *Journal of Financial Economics, 11*(1–4), 141–153.

Schriber, S., King, D., & Bauer, F. (2022). Retaliation effectiveness and acquisition performance: The influence of managerial decisions and industry context. *British Journal of Management, 33*(2), 939–957.

Schriber, S., & Löwstedt, J. (2015). Tangible resources and the development of organizational capabilities. *Scandinavian Journal of Management, 31*(1), 54–68.

Schriber, S., & Meglio, O. (2024). An ecosystem perspective of acquisition outcomes: A research agenda. *A Research Agenda for Mergers and Acquisitions*, 199–218.

Scott, R. W. (2003). *Organizations. Rational, natural, and open systems* (5th ed.). Prentice Hall International (UK) Limited.

Sears, J., & Hoetker, G. (2014). Technological overlap, technological capabilities, and resource recombination in technological acquisitions. *Strategic Management Journal, 35*(1), 48–67.

Seatrade Maritime News (2022). https://www.seatrade-maritime.com/ports-logistics/alexandroupolis-port-privatisation-called-off, Retrieved 2 December 2, 2024.

Smit, H., & Moraitis, T. (2010). Serial acquisition options. *Long Range Planning, 43*(1), 85–103.

Smith, K., Ferrier, W., & Ndofor, H. (2001). *Competitive dynamics research: Critique and future directions* (pp. 315–361). The Blackwell Handbook of Strategic Management.

Uhlenbruck, K., Hughes-Morgan, M., Hitt, M., Ferrier, W., & Brymer, R. (2017). Rivals' reactions to mergers and acquisitions. *Strategic Organization, 15*(1), 40–66.

van Marrewijk, A. (2016). Conflicting subcultures in mergers and acquisitions: A longitudinal study of integrating a radical internet firm into a bureaucratic telecoms firm. *British Journal of Management, 27*(2), 338–354.

Stakeholder Performance

David R. King and Anjali Bansal

Introduction

An apparent disconnect between observations that acquisitions do not increase firm value, but managers continue to use them presents an unsolved puzzle (Agrawal & Jaffe, 2000; Capasso & Meglio, 2005). One potential explanation is that research has largely overlooked competitive dynamics surrounding acquisitions (King & Schriber, 2016). A related explanation is that research has not used relevant performance measures for stakeholders impacted by acquisitions. Acquisitions impact more than acquiring firm shareholders, and, while some may be harmed, there are stakeholder groups that benefit from acquisitions.

We thank Kalan Horton for commenting on this section

D. R. King (✉)
Florida State University, Florida, USA
e-mail: drking@fsu.edu

A. Bansal
Indian Institute of Management Lucknow, Lucknow, Uttar Pradesh, India

D. R. King and A. Bansal (eds.), *Navigating Stakeholder Dynamics Surrounding Acquisitions*,
https://doi.org/10.1007/978-3-032-03199-0_11

The primary stakeholder used in acquisition research is acquiring firm shareholders (Meglio & Risberg, 2011). However, as research and the prior chapters outline, acquisitions impact multiple stakeholder groups, and there is less research that considers acquisition outcomes for interested groups other than acquiring firm shareholders. Not considering stakeholder impacts beyond an acquiring firm limits our understanding of acquisition activity and performance. For example, acquiring firm performance can be impacted by responses from competitors, customers and suppliers (Kato & Schoenberg, 2014; Kato and Schoenberg 2014; Rogan, 2014). The purpose of this chapter is to summarize additional impacts of acquisitions.

Evaluating Stakeholders and Performance

Multiple stakeholders have interests following an acquisition, leading both to stakeholder impacts and associated responses to an acquiring firm's value propositions (Bosse et al., 2022). The motives of an acquiring firm shape stakeholder impacts and reactions (Trautwein, 1990), so we summarize potential perspectives of stakeholders covered in the other chapters. Our intent is to facilitate research on additional acquisition performance variables to broaden our understanding of acquisition activity and performance. While prior research advocates for the selection of an acquisition performance measure to be based on theory (e.g., Cording et al., 2010), it may help to consider the perspective of different stakeholder groups. Once a perspective of a given group is known, theoretical development behind construct relationships that influence a relevant performance measure can be developed. Different stakeholders and associated performance measures are shown in Table 1, and each are discussed in the following subsections.

Advisors

Consultants facilitate acquisition completion and integration, and it is worth considering their motivation, as advisors can display opportunistic behavior (Lee, 2013). While some are likely paid for their level of effort, others will only be paid if a deal is completed, or it is important to consider how advisors are paid. Advisors are likely motivated to achieve higher fees (Kesner et al., 1994), and an acquiring firm switching advisors can lower fees (Hunter & Jagtiani, 2003). For example, an acquirer

Table 1 Interests of different acquisition stakeholders

Stakeholder	*Performance Measures*
Advisors	Deal fees Deal completion/abandonment Deal completion speed Repeat business with acquirer
Investment community	Stock returns (short and long-term); changes in
- acquirer's shareholders	profitability; market share; customer retention
- target's shareholders	Stock returns (short-term); target firm premium
- Institutional investors	Combined stock return of acquirer and target (short-term)
- stock analysts	Accuracy of forecasts
Suppliers	Change in prices Acquirer market power Deal premium
Customers	Change in prices (market power) Supply or service disruption Availability of alternate suppliers (industrial base)
Competitors	Market power (industry concentration) Market share Acquisition wave timing Deal premium
Acquiring firm employees	Acquiring firm growth/diversification; firm survival Improved efficiency Layoffs
Target firm employees	Employee resistance Employee turnover
Community/society	Economic growth Corporate social responsibility Changes in pollution
Ecosystem	Growth Sharing of fees Innovation Ecosystem health

repeatedly using the same advisor is associated with negative stock market reactions (Lee, 2013). This reflects conflicting perspectives on the role of advisors.

On one hand, advisors can provide important expertise, and their use is tied to higher acquisition complexity (Kolev & Haleblian, 2018; Saorin-Iborra, 2008). For example, firms can hire advisors to fill shortcomings for in-country experience for cross-border acquisitions (Shimizu et al., 2004; Westbrock et al., 2019) or supplementary human resources staff (Correia et al., 2013). These consultants are likely paid by the project for a certain number of hours of support. For consultants, being retained for additional work or becoming repeat advisors is likely a goal. Lee (2013) examines implications of repeatedly using the same acquisition advisor and finds acquiring firm shareholders often react negatively by acquiring firm shareholders. The implication is that if a relationship between a firm and an advisor becomes embedded, then the value of having an external advisor for a firm is lessened. Yet, information on how advisors can manage relationships and continue to add value has largely been overlooked by research. An exception is that more experienced advisors can help mitigate poor decision-making by an acquiring firm (Kim et al., 2011),

On the other hand, investment bankers, who both pitch target firms and provide financing for deals only are paid when an acquisition they are involved in completes. For example, investment bank lending decisions for acquisitions are likely influenced by the fees associated with advising on an acquisition (Allen et al., 2004). As a result, deal completion becomes a primary goal. Most research only examines deals that complete, but roughly a quarter of announced acquisitions are abandoned (Dikova et al., 2010), making predicting abandoned acquisitions is likely a worthwhile performance metric for advisors, and later acquiring firm managers. Additionally, the speed of deal completion is also relevant (Pavićević & Keil, 2021), and research reports average 120 to 160 days between acquisition announcement and deal completion (Bethel et al., 2009; Boeh, 2011). While advisors can have ulterior motives (Kesner et al., 1994; Lee, 2013), excesses are likely mitigated by reputational effects and the desire for repeat business. Again, how these conflicting motives are managed by advisors is worth additional research attention.

Investor Community

Research already describes multiple performance measures associated with acquiring and target firm shareholders, such as stock market and profitability measures (Cording et al., 2010). For an acquiring firm, shareholders will be interested in short and long-term performance for stock returns and changes in acquiring firm profitability. Acquiring firm shareholders also would be interested in seeing improved market share and customer retention, and these issues contribute to acquisition failure. Additionally, even if acquisitions lower performance, they may help acquiring firms survive by adapting to technology or other environmental changes (King et al., 2018). For example, diversification can lower a firm's risk (Amiri et al., 2022).

For target firm shareholders, the focus is more on short-term stock market returns. For example, target firms typically experience large gains on acquisition announcement, as the premium paid for target firm shares averaged 47 percent with a median of 38 percent between 1997 and 2009 (David, 2021). Deal premium is also relevant to other potential acquirers (i.e., suppliers and competitors), as the premium paid in prior deals anchors the price paid in subsequent acquisitions (Malhotra et al., 2015).

Another group of investors that are impacted are institutional investors that hold many of the shares for most publicly traded firms in the United States. As a result, institutional investors will often own shares in target and acquiring firms, as well as their competitors, and this influences their support for acquisitions. When an institutional investor holds shares of a target and rival firms, they are more likely to vote for acquisitions (Anton et al., 2022). The associated logic is that potential losses by an acquiring firm will be offset by the gains of rivals and/or the premium paid for a target. For example, most acquiring firms lose market share following an acquisition (Harding & Rouse, 2007). The implication is that institutional investors may play a poor governance role for acquisitions.

Another stakeholder from the investor community for acquisitions with limited research involves stock analysts. Analysts are known to be able to influence acquisition completion, as the probability of an announced acquisition completes increases with favorable recommendations from stock analysts (Becher et al., 2015). As a result, advice to acquiring firm managers is to communicate with analysts about an acquisition (Perry & Herd, 2004). While the research is not associated with acquisitions, variation in analyst opinions can provide a measure of risk (Bromiley et al., 2017).

Considering the interests of analysts is worthwhile, as research suggests the value of analysts for external governance is limited (Shi et al., 2017). For example, analysts frequently suggest divestment to managers (Brauer, 2009), but they overestimate the benefits of refocusing firm strategy (Nicolai et al., 2010). The preference appears to stem from diversified firms being harder for analysts to evaluate (Campa & Kedia, 2002) than simpler strategies (Litov et al., 2012). Information asymmetry likely influences analyst reactions to an acquisition announcement, as analysts have more positive views of acquisitions when they cover both a target and acquiring firm (Ali & Hirshleifer, 2020). This likely relates to the primary motivation of analysts is to make their earnings forecasts more accurate (i.e., Beaver et al., 2020).

Suppliers

The suppliers of the combining firms are also impacted by an acquisition (Rogan & Greve, 2015). A combining organization creates value by either gaining access to a new supplier (Hernandez & Menon, 2018), or by increasing bargaining power with existing common suppliers (Devers et al., 2013; Fee & Thomas, 2004). For acquirers, not considering suppliers can also create problems. For example, Alaskan Airlines purchase of Hawaiian Airlines creates a mixed fleet of Boeing and Airbus aircraft (Wint, 2024) that will complicate training, scheduling and maintenance, limiting potential cost savings.

Simply, acquisitions can either strategically weaken or strengthen the position of a supplier. In response, suppliers assess merging firms and how their combined assets will be leveraged, including: 1) the strength of the direct connections (true trading partners), 2) the strength of the nonshared trade linkages (such as an acquisition where the acquired firm has a strong trade relationship with a supplier that the acquirer does not), and 3) the strength of the indirect links (firms that do business with the same supplier or customer; Harford et al., 2019). Following an acquisition, suppliers likely will attempt to counter any increase in market power of an acquirer (King & Schriber, 2016). For example, suppliers can counter market power of their customers by reducing the number of suppliers available to them through consolidation (Ahern & Harford, 2014; Bhattacharyya & Nain, 2011). Another approach is for alliance partners to terminate alliances that provided a source of synergy for an acquisition s (Tandon et al., 2023).

Customers

Traditionally, research has overlooked the impact of acquisitions on customers (Anderson et al., 2001). Unsurprisingly, not considering customers often causes problems for acquiring firms, as combining firms may still compete for customers (Lu, 2014). For example, during the completion period, the price of airfares for both *United* and *Continental* fell over 5 % (Fan, 2020). A reason for the combination was to better compete against lower cost rivals and increase bargaining power, but each firm still competed for customers against themselves until after the announced combination was completed. In a different instance, Schneider Electric (SE), after acquiring Larsen & Toubro Electric and Automation division, SE's largest rival in South Asia, continued to operate them independently with two brands and two sales models, creating duplication and confusion (Bansal et al., 2024). Considering different types of acquisitions are also relevant to the perspective of customers, and we look at horizontal and vertical acquisitions.

Horizontal acquisitions are between firms in the same industry, and they tend to either lead to increased prices or lower quality, or decreased prices or improved quality (Karceski et al., 2005). In the first instance, customers bear a cost to continue with the firm contributing to lower market share, but in the latter case customers benefit, leading to increased market share. Still, while acquisitions can be motivated by serving customers better, they often involve disruptions, such as product adaptations and lapses in customer services that negatively impact customers. As a result, customers may take steps to insulate themselves from a firm that serves them following an acquisition. For example, IBM decreased contracts with combining suppliers that intended to better serve IBM as their primary customer (Marks & Mirvis, 2010).

In a vertical acquisition, a firm acquires a supplier or moves forward to be closer to their customer. As a result, vertical acquisitions can increase competition with suppliers or customers. When an acquisition increases competition with a customer it contributes to a loss of customers (Rogan, 2014). A related potential measure for customers is the strength of a remaining industrial base for each supplying industry. Still, a major outcome of acquisitions is the price of needed products to customers. This has been the traditional focus of antitrust law and limitations on horizontal acquisitions to limit the market power of any given firm in an industry (Shapiro, 2010).

Competitors

While generally assumed to be motivated by improving an acquiring firm's competitive advantage (Feldman & Hernandez, 2022; King et al., 2021), acquisitions often benefit rival firms (Clougherty & Duso, 2009). For example, the rise in concentration within an industry after a horizontal acquisition is associated with higher short-term stock performance for an acquiring firm and its competitors (Shahrur, 2005). Following an acquisition, an acquirer is often focused internally, providing an opportunity for competitive attacks from competitors (King & Schriber, 2016). For example, acquisitions allow rival firms to poach customers and win over the new ones (Meyer, 2008; Papadakis, 2005). As a result, most acquisitions result in a loss of market share and customers (Harding & Rouse, 2007). Additionally, competing firms can use uncertainty surrounding an acquisition for employees to hire away talent (e.g., Brown et al., 2003).

Another consideration is that early acquirers in an acquisition wave tend to perform better (Carow et al., 2004; Haleblian et al., 2012). In prior examples under suppliers and customers from the U.S. airline industry, United and Alaskan Airlines responded to industry consolidation when there was a smaller pool of potential targets, or firms that were "left over" from after other acquirers that were able to pick first. This selection problem is compounded by later acquirers also having to pay higher deal premiums (Martynova & Renneboog, 2008).

Acquiring Firm Employees

The impact of acquisitions on acquiring firm employees likely depends on the level of employee. For senior managers, once a deal is announced, completion may become a goal (Muehlfeld et al., 2012). While roughly one-quarter of acquisitions are abandoned (Dikova et al., 2010), deal abandonment involves reputational losses, and CEOs who abandon announced deals experience increased turnover (Wong & O'Sullivan, 2001). Even for the completed deals, an acquiring firm's senior managers often still face criticism (e.g., purchase price), as well as pressure to reap promised financial and other operational synergies quickly (Fried et al., 1996). For example, right after India's biggest ticketing platform, MakeMyTrip, acquired its close competitor, Goibibo, the top management prioritized integrating operations to realize synergies. This reflects that a one-month delay in realizing $500 million in annual savings can cost one-fifth the value of planned synergies (Chanmugam et al., 2005).

Acquisitions also increase firm size, and larger firm size is significantly correlated with higher CEO pay with firm size explaining more variance than firm performance (Bebchuk & Grinstein, 2005; Tosi et al., 2000). For lower-level employees at an acquiring firm, while an acquisition may offer more opportunities for career advancement by means of an increased product portfolio and expanded market share (Schweizer, 2005), they may feel unease about changes brought about by the acquisition (Zhu et al., 2004).

Acquired Firm Employees

At acquired firms, there is more uncertainty contributing to employee resistance and turnover and causing organizations to struggle following an acquisition (Larsson & Finkelstein, 1999). For example, acquired firm employees report loss of identity and unfair treatment in compensation and performance reviews (Lin & Wei, 2006). Dissatisfied employees can resist changes following an acquisition and/or ultimately decide to leave the combined organization (Horton et al., 2024). For example, senior managers at target firms experience significantly higher turnover (Krug & Shill, 2008). Part of this turnover may be planned, as there is often redundancy in senior level positions. However, turnover is also part of expectations to increase efficiency that impacts all employees (King et al., 2018), and employee turnover is associated with lower acquisition performance due to loss of human capital (Hanncock et al. 2013; Schweizer & Patzelt, 2012). Yet, the negative impacts of turnover may simply reflect that employees stay when acquisitions work and their leaving when they do not (Mayer & Kenney, 2004).

Meanwhile, acquisitions that are more attractive to acquired employees can facilitate acquired employees adapting to new practices and facilitate integration (Nahavandi & Malekzadeh, 1988). Recognition in the value held by acquired employees may be reflected in actual downsizing being lower than initial plans (Graebner, 2004; Schweiger & Denisi, 1991) For acquisitions with a better strategic and organizational fit, post-acquisition changes for acquired employees can be minimized. For example, friendly acquisitions have less turnover than hostile ones (Walsh, 1988).

Society

While negative impacts of acquisitions, including lower acquiring firm performance, employee turnover and disruption, and higher prices, are often highlighted as acquisition outcomes, acquisitions can have broader societal benefits. In general, acquisitions have a positive overall effect from a societal perspective by ensuring resources are put to their most productive use (David, 2021; Healy et al., 1992; Siegel & Simons, 2010). Still, acquisitions improving firm productivity from better asset utilization may depend on an acquiring firm being more productive than a target firm (Maksimovic & Phillips, 2001).

Additionally, there is a need to assess social and environmental impacts of acquisitions, or consider the triple bottom line components of economic, social, and environmental welfare from the perspective of sustainable organization development (Elkington & Rowlands, 1999). Still, most acquirers have not considered environmental management concerns while they are going through a merger or acquisition (Shimell, 1991). This may be changing as increased environmental, social, and governance performance is associated with higher value for an acquirer (Tampakoudis & Anagnostopoulou, 2020). For example, research suggests "green" acquirers that improve perceptions and performance of target firms are associated with higher stock performance (Gordano et al., 2024; Patel & King, 2022).

Ecosystem

An emerging area of acquisition research considers ecosystems, or the web of interdependent relationships that firms belong to create value (Jacobides et al., 2018). Within an ecosystem, acquisitions often impact the organizations involved in materializing an integrated value proposition (Adner, 2017; Teece, 2007). These outcomes can be related to growth (e.g., increase in participants) and/or allocation of fees (e.g., value capture mechanisms) reflecting impacts of an acquisition (Dushnitsky et al., 2022). Additionally, acquisition activity may combine resources to facilitate innovation and create synergy within a combined firm (Cefis & Marsili, 2015; Gay & Dousset, 2005).

However, ecosystems thrive on open innovation (Teece, 2007) and decentralized control (Adner, 2017), and acquisitions may disrupt these benefits. While research on ecosystems has yet to deal directly with the larger impacts of acquisition performance on the ecosystem (Schriber & Meglio, 2024), significant consequences are anticipated. Central actors in ecosystems (e.g., Amazon) often expand into markets of firms providing complementary products or services (Wang & Miller, 2020; Zhu & Liu, 2018). Entry into complementor spaces has led to lower quality product offerings, decreased innovation, product market shakeouts, and an overall decrease in ecosystem health (Iansiti & Levien, 2004; Pierce,

2009; Wang & Miller, 2020). In contrast, acquisitions can be beneficial for maintaining quality control among autonomous organizations or during periods of radical technological shifts (Jones et al., 2021). As a result, examining ecosystem impacts of acquisitions offers a promising research avenue. Interested scholars can investigate: 1) the conditions where ecosystem-related acquisitions enhance or destroy value/growth/innovation at the ecosystem level; and 2) how different types of acquisitions distinctly impact ecosystem health.

Discussion

Prior research has called for managers to consider all stakeholder effects from an acquisition (Chase et al., 1997); however, whether this was heeded has largely been overlooked by research. Even when considered, the perspective has been incomplete, as Dalton and colleagues (1997) maintain that corporate restructuring helps firm shareholders but harms other stakeholders. More specific consideration of stakeholders and related research in our review suggests more complex relationships for both shareholders and other stakeholders. For acquisitions, target firm shareholders generally benefit, but the effect of acquiring firm shareholders is more mixed. Similarly, when separately considered, other stakeholders can either benefit or be harmed. While the focus of this chapter is less on summarizing knowledge and more on identifying varied stakeholder perspectives toward acquisitions to highlight different perspectives of acquisition performance, it can guide future qualitative and quantitative research. For example, exploration of how specific advisor behaviors affect acquisition success, abandonment rates, or the quality of integration is needed. In considering the investment community, while acquisition research has long considered proxy battles for completing hostile takeovers (Manne, 1965), there is less research on potential shareholder activism toward acquiring firms. For example, activist investor *Starboard Value* is considering a proxy battle to hold *Pfizer's* CEO, Albert Bourla, accountable for poor acquisitions (Liu, 2024). In considering supplier and customer impacts, case studies may be useful to provide details of disruptions from acquisitions.

Another limitation of simply reviewing potential performance measures is that there is a lack of practical implications. For instance, "deal premium" is mentioned as of potential interest for several stakeholders. However, research is needed to theoretically develop relationships linking deal premium with stakeholder interests. There is also a need to consider multiple measures of performance (King et al., 2021), providing the benefit of triangulation (Jick, 1979). Using different performance measures in acquisition research (i.e., triangulation) offers the opportunity to identify and evaluate different dimensions of acquisition performance (Cording et al., 2010) that can provide a more comprehensive and reliable assessment of this phenomenon. For example, triangulation of research from multiple perspectives can improve theoretical development that offers the potential to improve decision-making. Additionally, triangulation facilitates understanding of unique impacts of acquisitions to different stakeholders. For instance, measuring acquiring firm market share and customer or employee retention rates can show how each group is affected by acquisitions and underlying relationships linking stakeholder interests.

In closing, research has largely only scratched the surface in considering how acquisitions impact different stakeholder groups' interests. Better understanding stakeholder perspectives should interest acquiring firm managers, as evidence suggests that firms with a stakeholder orientation can improve acquisition performance (Bettinazzi & Zollo, 2017). Additionally, as acquisitions cross-industries and impact economic ecosystems, regulators may want to expand merger approval from a focus on market power.

References

Adner, R. (2017). Ecosystem as structure: An actionable construct for strategy. *Journal of Management, 43*(1), 39–58.

Agrawal, A., & Jaffe, J. (2000). The post-merger performance puzzle. In *Advances in mergers and acquisitions* (Vol. 1, pp. 7–41). Emerald Group Publishing Limited.

Ahern, K., & Harford, J. (2014). The importance of industry links in merger waves. *Journal of Finance, 69*(2), 527–576.

Ali, U., & Hirshleifer, D. (2020). Shared analyst coverage: Unifying momentum spillover effects. *Journal of Financial Economics, 136*(3), 649–675.

Allen, L., Jagtiani, J., Peristiani, S., & Saunders, A. (2004). The role of bank advisors in mergers and acquisitions. *Journal of Money, Credit and Banking, 36*(2), 197–224.

Amiri, S., King, D. R., DeMarie, S., & Brown, J. R. (2022). Predicting the divestment of prior acquisitions. *British Journal of Management, 33*(4), 1803–1819.

Anderson, H., Havila, V., & Salmi, A. (2001). Can you buy a business relationship?: On the importance of customer and supplier relationships in acquisitions. *Industrial Marketing Management, 30*(7), 575–586.
Anton, M., Azar, J., Gine, M., & Lin, L. X. (2022). Beyond the target: M&a decisions and rival ownership. *Journal of Financial Economics, 144*(1), 44–66.
Bansal, A., Dwivedi, N., Mukherjee, R. & Philip, B. (2024). Post-Merger People Integration: Schneider Electric India Pvt. Ltd. Harvard Case Study. W34104-PDF-ENG: https://hbsp.harvard.edu/product/W34104-PDF-ENG?Ntt=post%20merger%20people%20integration
Beaver, W., McNichols, M., & Wang, Z. (2020). Increased market response to earnings announcements in the 21st century: An empirical investigation. *Journal of Accounting and Economics, 69*(1), 101244.
Bebchuk, L., & Grinstein, Y. (2005). The growth of executive pay. *Oxford Review of Economic Policy, 21*(2), 283–303.
Becher, D., Cohn, J., & Juergens, J. (2015). Do stock analysts influence merger completion? An examination of postmerger announcement recommendations. *Management Science, 61*(10), 2430–2448.
Bethel, J., Hu, G., & Wang, Q. (2009). The market for shareholder voting rights around mergers and acquisitions: Evidence from institutional daily trading and voting. *Journal of Corporate Finance, 15*(1), 129–145.
Bettinazzi, E., & Zollo, M. (2017). Stakeholder orientation and acquisition performance. *Strategic Management Journal, 38*(12), 2465–2485.
Bhattacharyya, S., & Nain, A. (2011). Horizontal acquisitions and buying power: A product market analysis. *Journal of Financial Economics, 99*(1), 97–115.
Boeh, K. (2011). Contracting costs and information asymmetry reduction in cross-border M&a. *Journal of Management Studies, 48*(3), 568–590.
Bosse, D., Harrison, J., & Hoskisson, R. (2022). Acquisitions, stakeholder economies of scope, and stakeholder orientation. *Strategic Management Review, 3*(1), 35–65.
Brauer, M. (2009). Corporate and divisional manager involvement in divestitures–a contingent analysis. *British Journal of Management, 20*(3), 341–362.
Bromiley, P., Rau, D., & Zhang, Y. (2017). Is R&D risky? *Strategic Management Journal, 38*(4), 876–891.
Brown, C., Clancy, G., & Scholer, R. (2003). A post-merger IT integration success story: Sallie Mae. *MIS Quarterly Executive, 2*(1), 15–27.
Campa, J., & Kedia, S. (2002). Explaining the diversification discount. *Journal of Finance, 57*(4), 1731–1762.
Capasso, A., & Meglio, O. (2005). Knowledge transfer in mergers and acquisitions: How frequent acquirers learn to manage the integration process. In A. Capasso, G. Dagnino, & A. Lanza (Eds.), *Strategic capabilities and knowledge transfer within and between organizations: New perspectives from acquisitions, networks,learning and evolution* (pp. 199–225).: Edward Elgar Publishing.

Carow, K., Heron, R., & Saxton, T. (2004). Do early birds get the returns? An empirical investigation of early-mover advantages in acquisitions. *Strategic Management Journal, 25*(6), 563–585.

Cefis, E., & Marsili, O. (2015). Crossing the innovation threshold through mergers and acquisitions. *Research Policy, 44*(3), 698–710.

Chanmugam, R., Shill, W., Mann, D., Ficery, K., & Pursche, B. (2005). The intelligent clean room: Ensuring value capture in mergers and acquisitions. *Journal of Business Strategy, 26*(3), 43–49.

Chase, D., Burns, D., & Claypool, G. (1997). A suggested ethical framework for evaluating corporate mergers and acquisitions. *Journal of Business Ethics, 16*, 1753–1763.

Clougherty, J., & Duso, T. (2009). The impact of horizontal mergers on rivals: Gains to being left outside a merger. *Journal of Management Studies, 46*(8), 1365–1395.

Cording, M., Christmann, P., & Weigelt, C. (2010). Measuring theoretically complex constructs: The case of acquisition performance. *Strategic Organization, 8*(1), 11–41.

Correia, M. E., Cunha, R., & Scholten, M. (2013). Impact of M&as on organizational performance: The moderating role of HRM centrality. *European Management Journal, 31*(4), 323–332.

David, J. (2021). The aggregate implications of mergers and acquisitions. *Review of Economic Studies, 88*(4), 1796–1830.

Devers, C., McNamara, G., Haleblian, J., & Yoder, M. (2013). Do they walk the talk? Gauging acquiring CEO and director confidence in the value creation potential of announced acquisitions. *Academy of Management Journal, 56*(6), 1679–1702.

Dikova, D., Sahib, P., & Van Witteloostuijn, A. (2010). Cross-border acquisition abandonment and completion: The effect of institutional differences and organizational learning in the international business service industry, 1981–2001. *Journal of International Business Studies, 41*, 223–245.

Dushnitsky, G., Piva, E., & Rossi-Lamastra, C. (2022). Investigating the mix of strategic choices and performance of transaction platforms: Evidence from the crowdfunding setting. *Strategic Management Journal, 43*(3), 563–598.

Elkington, J., & Rowlands, I. (1999). Cannibals with forks: The triple bottom line of 21st century business. *Alternatives Journal, 25*(4), 42.

Fan, H. (2020). When consumer type matters: Price effects of the united-continental merger in the airline industry. *Economics of Transportation, 21*, 100154.

Fee, C., & Thomas, S. (2004). Sources of gains in horizontal mergers: Evidence from customer, supplier, and rival firms. *Journal of Financial Economics, 74*(3), 423–460.

Feldman, E., & Hernandez, E. (2022). Synergy in mergers and acquisitions: Typology, life cycles, and value. *Academy of Management Review, 47*(4), 549–578.

Fried, Y., Tiegs, R., Naughton, T., & Ashforth, B. (1996). Managers' reactions to a corporate acquisition: A test of an integrative model. *Journal of Organizational Behavior, 17*(5), 401–427.

Gay, B., & Dousset, B. (2005). Innovation and network structural dynamics: Study of the alliance network of a major sector of the biotechnology industry. *Research Policy, 34*(10), 1457–1475.

Gordano, S., Bauer, F., & King, D. (2024). Environmental, social, and governance (ESG) acquisitions: Deal structure and outcome. *Business Strategy and the Environment*. https://doi.org/10.1002/bse.3791

Graebner, M. E. (2004). Momentum and serendipity: How acquired leaders create value in the integration of technology firms. *Strategic Management Journal, 25*(8–9), 751–777.

Haleblian, J., McNamara, G., Kolev, K., & Dykes, B. (2012). Exploring firm characteristics that differentiate leaders from followers in industry merger waves: A competitive dynamics perspective. *Strategic Management Journal, 33*(9), 1037–1052.

Hanncock, J., Allen, D., Bosco, F., McDaniel, K., & Pierce, C. (2013). Meta-analytic review of employee turnover as a predictor of firm performance. *Journal of Management, 39*, 573–603.

Harding, D., & Rouse, T. (2007). Human due diligence. *Harvard Business Review, 85*(4), 124–131.

Harford, J., Schonlau, R., & Stanfield, J. (2019). Trade relationships, indirect economic links, and mergers. *Management Science, 65*(7), 3085–3110.

Healy, P., Palepu, K., & Ruback, R. (1992). Does corporate performance improve after mergers? *Journal of Financial Economics, 31*(2), 135–175.

Hernandez, E., & Menon, A. (2018). Acquisitions, node collapse, and network revolution. *Management Science, 64*(4), 1652–1671.

Horton, K., King, D., Bauer, F., Lamont, B., & Schriber, S. (2024). Integration, employee resistance, and acquisition performance. *European Management Journal*. https://doi.org/10.1016/j.emj.2024.02.003

Hunter, W., & Jagtiani, J. (2003). An analysis of advisor choice, fees, and effort in mergers and acquisitions. *Review of Financial Economics, 12*(1), 65–81.

Iansiti, M., & Levien, R. (2004). Strategy as ecology. *Harvard Business Review, 82*(3), 68–78.

Jacobides, M., Cennamo, C., & Gawer, A. (2018). Towards a theory of ecosystems. *Strategic Management Journal, 39*(8), 2255–2276.

Jick, T. (1979). Mixing qualitative and quantitative methods: Triangulation in action. *Administrative Science Quarterly, 24*(4), 602–611.

Jones, S., Leiponen, A., & Vasudeva, G. (2021). The evolution of cooperation in the face of conflict: Evidence from the innovation ecosystem for mobile telecom standards development. *Strategic Management Journal, 42*(4), 710–740.

Karceski, J., Ongena, S., & Smith, D. (2005). The impact of bank consolidation on commercial borrower welfare. *Journal of Finance, 60*(4), 2043–2082.

Kato, J., & Schoenberg, R. (2014). The impact of post-merger integration on the customer–supplier relationship. *Industrial Marketing Management, 43*(2), 335–345.

Kesner, I., Shapiro, D., & Sharma, A. (1994). Brokering mergers: An agency theory perspective on the role of representatives. *Academy of Management Journal, 37*(3), 703–721.

Kim, J., Haleblian, J., & Finkelstein, S. (2011). When firms are desperate to grow via acquisition: The effect of growth patterns and acquisition experience on acquisition premiums. *Administrative Science Quarterly, 56*(1), 26–60.

King, D., Bauer, F., & Schriber, S. (2018). *Mergers and acquisitions: A research overview*. Routledge.

King, D., & Schriber, S. (2016). Addressing competitive responses to acquisitions. *California Management Review, 58*(3), 109–124.

King, D., Wang, G., Samimi, M., & Cortes, A. (2021). A meta-analytic integration of acquisition performance prediction. *Journal of Management Studies, 58*(5), 1198–1236.

Kolev, K., & Haleblian, J. (2018). When firms learn from prior acquisition experience. *Journal of Organization Design, 7*(1), 8.

Larsson, R., & Finkelstein, S. (1999). Integrating strategic, organizational, and human resource perspectives on mergers and acquisitions: A case survey of synergy realization. *Organization Science, 10*, 1–26.

Lee, J. (2013). Dancing with the enemy? Relational hazards and the contingent value of repeat exchanges in M&a markets. *Organization Science, 24*(4), 1237–1256.

Lin, C., & Wei, Y. (2006). The role of business ethics in merger and acquisition success: An empirical study. *Journal of Business Ethics, 69*, 95–109.

Litov, L., Moreton, P., & Zenger, T. (2012). Corporate strategy, analyst coverage, and the uniqueness paradox. *Management Science, 58*(10), 1797–1815.

Liu, A. (2024). Starboard wants to hold Pfizer leadership 'accountable' for overpaid M&a deals, poor return on R&D investment. *Fierce Pharma*. https://www.fiercepharma.com/pharma/starboard-wants-hold-pfizer-leadership-accountable-overpaid-ma-deals-poor-return-rd

Maksimovic, V., & Phillips, G. (2001). The market for corporate assets: Who engages in mergers and asset sales and are there efficiency gains? *Journal of Finance, 56*(6), 2019–2065.

Malhotra, S., Zhu, P., & Reus, T. (2015). Anchoring on the acquisition premium decisions of others. *Strategic Management Journal, 36*(12), 1866–1876.
Manne, H. (1965). Mergers and the market for corporate control. *Journal of Political Economy, 73*, 110–120.
Marks, M., & Mirvis, P. (2010). *Joining forces: Making one plus one equal three in mergers, acquisitions, and alliances* (2nd ed.). Jossey-Bass.
Martynova, M., & Renneboog, L. (2008). A century of corporate takeovers: What have we learned and where do we stand? *Journal of Banking & Finance, 32*(10), 2148–2177.
Mayer, D., & Kenney, M. (2004). Economic action does not take place in a vacuum: Understanding Cisco's acquisition and development strategy. *Industry and Innovation, 11*(4), 299–325.
Meglio, O., & Risberg, A. (2011). The (mis) measurement of M&a performance—A systematic narrative literature review. *Scandinavian Journal of Management, 27*(4), 418–433.
Meyer, C. (2008). Value leakages in mergers and acquisitions: Why they occur and how they can be addressed. *Long Range Planning, 41*(2), 197–224.
Muehlfeld, K., Rao Sahib, P., & Van Witteloostuijn, A. (2012). A contextual theory of organizational learning from failures and successes: A study of acquisition completion in the global newspaper industry, 1981–2008. *Strategic Management Journal, 33*(8), 938–964.
Nahavandi, A., & Malekzadeh, A. (1988). Acculturation in mergers and acquisitions. *Academy of Management Review, 13*(1), 79–90.
Nicolai, A., Schulz, A., & Thomas, T. (2010). What wall street wants—Exploring the role of security analysts in the evolution and spread of management concepts. *Journal of Management Studies, 47*, 162–189.
Papadakis, V. (2005). The role of broader context and the communication program in merger and acquisition implementation success. *Management Decision, 43*(2), 236–255.
Patel, P., & King, D. (2022). Capability transfer: Improved performance from acquiring polluting targets. In *Acquisitions and corporate strategy* (pp. 128–156). Routledge.
Pavićević, S., & Keil, T. (2021). The role of procedural rationality in debiasing acquisition decisions of overconfident CEOs. *Strategic Management Journal, 42*(9), 1696–1715.
Perry, J., & Herd, T. (2004). Mergers and acquisitions: Reducing M&a risk through improved due diligence. *Strategy & Leadership, 32*(2), 12–19.
Pierce, L. (2009). Big losses in ecosystem niches: How core firm decisions drive complementary product shakeouts. *Strategic Management Journal, 30*, 323–347.

Rogan, M. (2014). Too close for comfort? The effect of embeddedness and competitive overlap on client relationship retention following an acquisition. *Organization Science, 25*(1), 185–203.

Rogan, M., & Greve, H. (2015). Resource dependence dynamics: Partner reactions to mergers. *Organization Science, 26*(1), 239–255.

Saorin-Iborra, M. (2008). Time pressure in acquisition negotiations: Its determinants and effects on parties' negotiation behavior choice. *International Business Review, 17*(3), 285–309.

Schriber, S., & Meglio, O. (2024). An ecosystem perspective of acquisition outcomes: A research agenda. In King, D., & Meglio, O (ed), *a research agenda for mergers and acquisitions*, 199-218.

Schweizer, L. (2005). Organizational integration of acquired biotechnology companies into pharmaceutical companies: The need for a hybrid approach. *Academy of Management Journal, 48*(6), 1051–1074.

Schweiger, D., & Denisi, A. (1991). Communication with employees following a merger: A longitudinal field experiment. *Academy of Management Journal, 34*(1), 110–135.

Schweizer, L., & Patzelt, H. (2012). Employee commitment in the post-acquisition integration process: The effect of integration speed and leadership. *Scandinavian Journal of Management, 28*(4), 298–310.

Shahrur, H. (2005). Industry structure and horizontal takeovers: Analysis of wealth effects on rivals, suppliers, and corporate customers. *Journal of Financial Economics, 76*(1), 61–98.

Shapiro, C. (2010). The 2010 horizontal merger guidelines: From hedgehog to fox in forty years. *Antitrust Law Journal, 77*, 701–759.

Shi, W., Connelly, B., & Hoskisson, R. (2017). External corporate governance and financial fraud: Cognitive evaluation theory insights on agency theory prescriptions. *Strategic Management Journal, 38*(6), 1268–1286.

Shimell, P. (1991). Corporate environmental policy in practice. *Long Range Planning, 24*(3), 10–17.

Siegel, D., & Simons, K. (2010). Assessing the effects of mergers and acquisitions on firm performance, plant productivity, and workers: New evidence from matched employer-employee data. *Strategic Management Journal, 31*(8), 903–916.

Shimizu, K., Hitt, M., Vaidyanath, D., & Pisano, V. (2004). Theoretical foundations of cross-border mergers and acquisitions: A review of current research and recommendations for the future. *Journal of International Management, 10*(3), 307–353.

Tampakoudis, I., & Anagnostopoulou, E. (2020). The effect of mergers and acquisitions on environmental, social and governance performance and market value: Evidence from EU acquirers. *Business Strategy and the Environment, 29*(5), 1865–1875.

Tandon, V., Asgari, N., & Ranganathan, R. (2023). Divestment of relational assets following acquisitions: Evidence from the biopharmaceutical industry. *Strategic Management Journal, 44*(4), 1013–1052.

Teece, D. (2007). Explicating dynamic capabilities: The nature and microfoundations of (sustainable) enterprise performance. *Strategic Management Journal, 28*(13), 1319–1350.

Tosi, H., Werner, S., Katz, J., & Gomez-Mejia, L. (2000). How much does performance matter? A meta-analysis of CEO pay studies. *Journal of Management, 26*(2), 301–333.

Trautwein, F. (1990). Merger motives and merger prescriptions. *Strategic Management Journal, 11*(4), 283–295.

Walsh, J. (1988). Top management turnover following mergers and acquisitions. *Strategic Management Journal, 9*(2), 173–183.

Wang, R., & Miller, C. (2020). Complementors' engagement in an ecosystem: A study of publishers' e-book offerings on Amazon kindle. *Strategic Management Journal, 41*(1), 3–26.

Westbrock, B., Muehlfeld, K., & Weitzel, U. (2019). Selecting legal advisors in M&as: Organizational learning and the role of multiplicity of mental models. *Journal of Management, 45*(5), 2193–2224.

Wint, B. (2024). Alaskan airlines completes acquisition of Hawaiian airlines. GateChecked: https://www.gatechecked.com/alaska-airlines-completes-acquisition-of-hawaiian-airlines-9502

Wong, P., & O'Sullivan, N. (2001). The determinants and consequences of abandoned takeovers. *Journal of Economic Surveys, 15*(2), 145–186.

Zhu, F., & Liu, Q. (2018). Competing with complementors: An empirical look at Amazon. Com. *Strategic Management Journal, 39*(10), 2618–2642.

Zhu, Y., May, S., & Rosenfeld, L. (2004). Information adequacy and job satisfaction during merger and acquisition. *Management Communication Quarterly, 18*(2), 241–270.

Index

D. R. King and A. Bansal (eds.), *Navigating Stakeholder Dynamics Surrounding Acquisitions*,
https://doi.org/10.1007/978-3-032-03199-0

FSC
www.fsc.org
MIX
Papier | Fördert
gute Waldnutzung
FSC® C083411

Kolibri 360 GmbH
Ferdinand-Jühlke-Straße 7
99095 Erfurt, Deutschland
produktsicherheit@kolibri360.de